The Identity and the Life of the Church

Princeton Theological Monograph Series

K. C. Hanson, Charles M. Collier, D. Christopher Spinks,
and Robin Parry—Series Editors

Recent volumes in the series:

Sarah Morice-Brubaker
The Place of the Spirit: Toward a Trinitarian Theology of Location

Brian C. Howell
*In the Eyes of God : A Contextual Approach to
Biblical Anthropomorphic Metaphors*

Brendan Thomas Sammon
*The God Who Is Beauty: Beauty as a Divine Name in
Thomas Aquinas and Dionysius the Areopagite*

Mark R. Lindsay
*Reading Auschwitz with Barth: The Holocaust as Problem
and Promise for Barthian Theology*

Dick O. Eugenio
*Communion with the Triune God:
The Trinitarian Soteriology of T. F. Torrance*

Mara Brecht
*Virtue in Dialogue: Belief, Religious Diversity,
and Women's Interreligious Encounter*

Andrew Shepherd
The Gift of the Other: Levinas, Derrida, and a Theology of Hospitality

The Identity and the Life of the Church

John Calvin's Ecclesiology in the Perspective of His Anthropology

YOSEP KIM

☙PICKWICK Publications • Eugene, Oregon

THE IDENTITY AND THE LIFE OF THE CHURCH
John Calvin's Ecclesiology in the Perspective of His Anthropology

Princeton Theological Monograph Series 203

Copyright © 2014 Yosep Kim. All rights reserved. Except for brief quotations in critical publications or reviews, no part of this book may be reproduced in any manner without prior written permission from the publisher. Write: Permissions, Wipf and Stock Publishers, 199 W. 8th Ave., Suite 3, Eugene, OR 97401.

Pickwick Publications
An Imprint of Wipf and Stock Publishers
199 W. 8th Ave., Suite 3
Eugene, OR 97401

www.wipfandstock.com

ISBN 13: 978-1-62032-494-3

Cataloguing-in-Publication data:

Kim, Yosep.

The identity and the life of the church : John Calvin's ecclesiology in the perspective of his anthropology / Yosep Kim.

xii + 216 pp. ; 23 cm. Includes bibliographical references and index.

Princeton Theological Monograph Series 203

ISBN 13: 978-1-62032-494-3

1. Calvin, Jean, 1509–1564. 2. Church—History of doctrines—16th century. 3. Calvin, Jean, 1509–1564—Anthropology. 4. Calvin, Jean, 1509–1564—Contributions in the doctrine of the church. I. Title. II. Series.

BX9418 .K52 2014

Manufactured in the U.S.A.

To my mother and father, Rev. Chung-soo Kim

Contents

Preface / ix
Abbreviations / xi

Introduction / 1

PART ONE: Calvin's Anthropology

1 The *Imago Dei* in the Divine-Human Relationship / 19

2 The Grace of the Trinity as the Foundation of Christian Identity / 43

3 The Christian Life as the Eschatological Progress / 69

PART TWO: Calvin's Ecclesiology

4 The Church as the Mother of All Believers / 99

5 The Church as the Body of Christ / 126

6 The Church and the Kingdom of Christ / 156

Conclusion / 189

Bibliography / 195
Index / 209

Preface

THE ORIGIN OF THIS BOOK LIES IN MY PhD THESIS AT CAMBRIDGE University, which was the result of my academic journey of exploration of the ideas of a great reformer and of his vision for the Church. This study was initiated by my interest in the theological basis of Calvin's ideas and practical proposals for the Church during my seminary years in Korea. I was able to refine my interest through completing master's degree courses in both the USA and Scotland, leading finally to my doctoral study in Cambridge.

Throughout this journey, a number of people and institutions have supported and enabled me to continue my research. First of all, I would like to appreciate the efforts of my supervisor Dr. Richard Rex, who has offered enormous support and invaluable advice on my work, which has been greatly instructive and encouraging. I am also grateful to Dr. Paul Nimmo, who offered very helpful criticism of the theological aspects of this thesis and whose kindness has not gone unnoticed or unappreciated. I would also express my appreciation to my teachers and mentors of Chongshin Theological Seminary in Korea. I should say thanks to Professors Miroslav Volf, Carlos Eire, and Ronald Rittgers for their unforgettable friendship and academic advices during my time in Yale University. Profound thanks go to the late Professor David Wright of the University of Edinburgh. It has been a great privilege for me to study under his supervision and to continue fellowship with him until his sudden death in 2008, just before I finished my thesis. I would like to thank Professor Anthony Lane of the London School of Theology for giving me useful advice at the early stages of my doctoral research. I also must offer thanks to the staffs of the H. Henry Meeter Center of Calvin Studies at Calvin College and Seminary in Grand Rapids for their help in obtaining and using materials for my thesis. My great debt is to the fellowships of Peterhouse, Cambridge, and Boondang Central Church. I could not complete my research without their help. I hope this book is an expression of my thanks to God and all people who have supported me in many ways.

Preface

Finally and foremost, I express my thanks to my parents who have showed me in person how to serve God and his Church in their ministry for more than thirty years. I appreciate my wife and twin sons who have unceasingly supported me and patiently waited for the completion of my study in foreign countries.

Abbreviations

CO	*Ioannis Calvini opera quae supersunt omnia*. Edited by G. Baum, Edward Cunitz, and Edward Reuss. 59 vols. *Corpus Reformatorum* 29–87 (Brunswick, Germany: Schwetschke & Son, 1863–1900.
OS	*Ioannis Calvini opera selecta*. Edited by Peter Barth, Wilhelm Niesel, and Dora Scheuner. 5 vols. Münich: Kaiser. 1926–1962.
Institutes	*Institutes of the Christian Religion*. Translated by Ford Lewis Battles. Library of Christian Classics 20–21. Philadelphia: Westminster, 1960.
Comm	*Calvin's Commentaries*. 46 vols. Edinburgh: Calvin Translation Society, 1844–1855; reprint, 22 vols. Grand Rapids: Baker, 1979.
Serm	*Calvin's Sermons*
Letters	*Letters of John Calvin*. 4 vols. Edited by Henry Beveridge and Jules Bonnet. Edinburgh: Constable, 1855–1858.
Epistolae	*Ioannis Calvini Epistolae*. Vol. 1, *1530–Sep. 1538*. Edited by Cornelis Augustijn and Frans Pieter Van Stam. Geneva: Droz, 2005.
TT	*Tracts and Treatises*. Translated by Henry Beveridge. 3 vols. London: Oliver & Boyd, 1844–1851.
Ordinances	*Draft Ecclesiastical Ordinances September & October 1541*, OS 2:328–45.
BO	*Martini Buceri Opera Latina*. Vol. 15, *De Regno Christi, Libri Duo 1550*. Edited by François Wendel. Paris: Presses Universitaires de France, 1955.
WA	*Luthers Werke*. Kritische Gesamtausgabe. 65 vols. Weimar: Böhlau, 1883–1993.
LW	*Luther's Works*. 56 vols. Edited by Jaroslav Pelikan and Helmut Lehmann. St Louis: Concordia, 1955–1986.

Introduction

Purpose

THE PRESENT STUDY IS AN EXAMINATION OF JOHN CALVIN'S DOCTRINE OF the Church.[1] It argues that Calvin's idea of the twofold identity of the Church—its spiritual identity as the body of Christ and its functional identity as the mother of all believers—is closely related to his understanding of the Christian identity and Christian life, which are initiated and maintained by the grace of the triune God.

Throughout his writings, Calvin uses the term "Church" in two senses, which represent the twofold identity of the Church. On the one hand, Calvin opens his ecclesiological discussions of the *Institutes* IV with the description of the Church as the institution to which God has entrusted a number of aids for the Christian faith:

> And in order that the preaching of the gospel might flourish, he deposited this treasure in the church. He instituted "pastors and teachers" through whose lips he might teach his own . . . he instituted sacraments, which we who have experienced them feel to be highly useful aids to foster and strengthen faith.[2]

On the other hand, Calvin identifies the Church with the spiritual fellowship of Christians across time and space. In the *Institutes* III, he uses the same terms that he uses for the regeneration of individual Christians in

---

1. As the titles of the recent conferences of the two major research groups for Calvin studies show, Calvin's ecclesiology is still one of the most popular areas for research on Calvin. Foxgrover, *Calvin and the Church*, Selderhuis, *Calvinus Praeceptor Ecclesiae*. Celebrating 500th anniversary of Calvin's birth in 2009, many studies on Calvin's ecclesiology and its influces have been published. We can find useful studies in the following compilatory books. Hirzel and Sallmann, *John Calvin's Impact on Church and Society, 1509–2009*; Beeke, *Calvin for Today*; Thompson, *Engaging with Calvin*; Selderhuis, *The Calvin Handbook*; Billings and Hesselink, *Calvin's Theology and its Reception*.

2. *Institutes*, IV.1.1, OS 5:1.

The Identity and the Life of the Church

his discussion of the restoration of the Church: "God is said to purge his church of all sin, in that through baptism he promises that grace of deliverance, and fulfills it in his elect [Ephesians 5:26–27] . . . God truly carries this out by regenerating his own people, so that the sway of sin is abolished in them."[3] It is correspondingly certain in the *Institutes* IV.1.2, that Calvin conceives two identities of the Church: "The article in the Creed in which we profess to 'believe the church' refers not only to the visible church (our present topic) but also to all God's elect, in whose number are also included the dead."[4] In his ecclesiology, therefore, the Church is understood not only as the institution or the "treasure house" of God's aids for Christians, its functional and visible identity, but also as a spiritual fellowship of believers, its spiritual and invisible identity. What does Calvin think of the theological basis for this twofold identity of the Church? Calvin explains these two identities of the Church in the light of his anthropological ideas: his idea of the Christian's identity as a child of God has significance for the functional identity of the Church; and his trinitarian and eschatological ideas of the Christian life are crucial for the spiritual identity of the Church. In the following pages, I will review the previous studies which have dealt with Calvin's ideas of the Church, and then explain the methodological points of this study, and finally provide an outline of the contents of this study.

Review of Previous Studies

Scholars of Calvin's ecclesiology have generally fallen into two broad groups. On the one hand, those who deal with the theological implications of Calvin's ecclesiological ideas, such as spiritual warfare, Christ's headship and the progress of the Church, tend to focus mainly on the spiritual identity of the Church as the fellowship of Christians. On the other hand, those who examine the practical aspects of the visible Church in Calvin's ecclesiology, such as its government, ministry and discipline, tend to concentrate on the functional identity of the Church as the agent of God's grace for believers.

Before the late 1980s, scholars tended to examine the theological foundations of Calvin's ideas of the Church, usually focusing on its spiritual

---

3. *Institutes*, III.3.11, OS 4:66. Calvin's use of the term "Church" to denote God's people appears frequently in his commentaries on the prophets. For example, he interprets Isaiah 37:26 thus: "I [God] have founded the Church, and therefore the salvation of the Church shall always be my care; because I will not leave unfinished the work which I have begun, but will carry it forward to perfection." *Comm. Isa.* 37:26, CO 36:616.

4. *Institutes*, IV.1.2, OS 5:2.

identity. This group of scholars included Niesel, Wendel, Kroon, Milner and Loeschen. Niesel's study of Calvin's doctrine of the Church represents a tendency in early twentieth-century studies toward a christological understanding of Calvin's theology. He argues that Calvin thinks of the Church as "the sphere of the self-revelation of God and the encounter between Christ and ourselves," and "the means by which the exalted Christ accomplishes His work among men."[5] Niesel does not find any importance attached to the difference between the functional and the spiritual identities of the Church in Calvin's ecclesiology, while he considers Calvin to present his ideas of the Church from a consistent christological perspective. With regard to Calvin's idea of the Church as the mother of believers, Niesel says, "Because the church is placed in the service of Christ, because it has His promise that He desires to meet us there and only there in human earthly guise, Calvin can—nay must—repeat the ancient saying that outside the church there is no salvation."[6] Similarly, considering Calvin's idea of the Church as the body of Christ, Niesel argues, "That very sense of confrontation, in which the ministry of the church is enacted toward us, works itself out in such a way that we become one body with Christ, and by our union with Him are drawn into a fellowship with each other which is distinguished from all earthly and religious fellowship by the fact that it rests, not upon a conviction and a decision of men, but solely upon the saving work of Christ exerted toward us."[7] Although Niesel opens an important theological discussion on Calvin's ideas of the Church, his study fails to take enough account of the two distinct ways in which Calvin speaks about the Church. Niesel does not fully evaluate the significant position of ecclesiology in Calvin's theology by understanding every important topic in Calvin's ecclesiology in terms of christology.

In his study of Calvin's theology in 1950, Wendel warns that "If we want to speak of a 'system' of Calvin, we must do so with certain reservation, owing to the plurality of themes that imposed themselves simultaneously upon its author's thinking."[8] In observing the "plurality" of Calvin's doctrine of the Church, Wendel notes the twofold identity of the Church.

5. Niesel, *Theology of Calvin*, 185.
6. Ibid., 186.
7. Ibid., 188.
8. Wendel, *Calvin*, 357. Against the "Christocentric" interpretation of Calvin's theology, Wendel argues that a dominant preoccupation "to present the divinity of Jesus Christ in the strongest light and guard it against the slightest depreciation" is not "the central idea of his system from which all the rest of it could be deduced." Ibid., 358.

The Identity and the Life of the Church

He argues that for Calvin the Church is of "divine institution, not only inasmuch as it is the body of the faithful, but also in its ministries and the functions assigned to them."[9] Concerning Calvin's functional idea of the Church as the mother of believers, Wendel states, "we depend upon it for the whole of our spiritual life and all our sanctification."[10] He indicates Calvin's idea of "a collective sanctification" of the Church as the body of Christ: "To the sanctification of the individual there corresponds, on the plane of the Church, a collective sanctification. The Church is indubitably the body of Christ, but because of the fact that its members are at present sinners, it must be ever striving to become that body of Christ."[11] Although he developed the understanding of Calvin's ideas of the Church by clearly noting the twofold identity of the Church in his ecclesiology, Wendel does not proceed to explore further either the theological basis of Calvin's ideas of the Church or the connection between the two identities of the Church.[12]

In 1968, the Dutch scholar Marijn de Kroon took Wendel's work further by proposing the divine-human relationship as a theological framework within which Calvin's ideas of the Church can be analysed: "In sum, we are saying that in Calvin's discussion of the church, God and man are sketched as being in a mutual relationship, a relationship expressed in God's election and human salvation."[13] He argues that "it is fascinating to see how Calvin forges the link between the individual believer and the community which is the church."[14] With regard to the functional identity of the Church as mother in Calvin's ecclesiology, Kroon states, "the children whom God chooses are placed under her motherly care. In the church the Father's constant care has its continuation and concretisation." In respect of the spiritual identity of the Church, Kroon says, "in the church of Christ God and man come very near to each other, establishing a profound and intimate bond. God's glory indwells the church: it is clothed with God's

---

9. Ibid., 293.

10. Ibid., 294.

11. Ibid., 301.

12. In 1964, Ganoczy offered a useful study on Calvin's idea of the Church and ministry. Although Ganoczy's study mainly treats Calvin's doctrine of ministry from a dialectical perspective, he provides a valuable analysis of the development of Calvin's ecclesiology throughout the consecutive editions of the *Institutes* and suggests Calvin's christological idea of the unique priesthood of Christ-Mediator as the theological basis of his ideas of the Church and ministry. Ganoczy, *Calvin*, 141ff.

13. Kroon, *Honour of God and Human Salvation*.

14. Ibid., 148.

authority."[15] Kroon tries to understand other ecclesiological issues, such as church discipline and the ministry of the Church, in terms of "the bipolar orientation" between the honour of God and human salvation in Calvin's theology.[16] For Kroon, the dominant anthropological concern in Calvin's ecclesiology is "inexperienced, slothful and vain people" who need "an external support system by which faith can take root and develop in them."[17] One of the significant contributions of Kroon's study is its observation that Calvin's anthropological idea of "human weakness and laxity" forms the theological basis of his ideas of the Church. But Kroon's treatment of Calvin's ideas is too brief to explore sufficiently the relationship between the two identities of the Church in relation to Calvin's anthropological ideas.

While Niesel, Wendel and Kroon deal with Calvin's ecclesiology as part of their interpretations of Calvin's theology as a whole, Milner's monograph of 1970 is fully devoted to a theological analysis of Calvin's doctrine of the Church. In contrast to the previous studies, Milner attempts to interpret the important doctrines of Calvin's theology, such as creation, fall and salvation, from his ecclesiological idea of "the dialectical and absolute correlation between the secret work of the Holy Spirit and the diverse manifestation of the order of the Word (*ordinatione Dei*)." Milner's understanding of the relation between the order of the Word and the secret work of the Spirit in Calvin's dialectical ecclesiology can be summed up thus: "*non separatio* because the Spirit is inseparable from the Word which we have (ordinarily) only in the ordained means: *sed distinctio* because the Spirit is not bound to the means, but exercises a sovereign freedom over them."[18] To prove his dialectical interpretation of Calvin's ideas of the Church, Milner argues that for Calvin the Kingdom of Christ is ruled by God's Word, but that this Kingdom exists only within the elect in whom the Spirit works secretly and dynamically. In a similar vein, Milner argues that in his idea of the Church as the body of Christ Calvin speaks not only of the stability, unity and continuity of the Church on account of Christ's headship over every member, but also of the variety and dynamic of the work of the Spirit from the diversity of spiritual gifts among members to the Spirit's works of daily renewal.[19] Milner's study is significant because it tries to interpret

15. Ibid., 150–51.
16. Ibid., 152, 154.
17. Ibid., 149.
18. Milner, *Calvin's Doctrine of the Church*, 191.
19. Ibid., 173–83.

The Identity and the Life of the Church

Calvin's ideas of the Church from a perspective coherent with the rest of Calvin's theology. Furthermore, this study shows that Calvin regards the Church not as a static institution, but as a sphere of the dynamic work of the Holy Spirit in the world. However, while he tries to prove his hypothesis of the dialectical relation between the order of the Word and the secret work of the Holy Spirit in the Church, Milner's study does not sufficiently treat the functional identity of the Church as the means through which grace is given to believers. He thus ignores the important identification of the Church as the mother of believers and its anthropological basis in Calvin's ecclesiology.

After Milner, Loeschen's study *The Divine Community* (1981), which compares the theologies of Luther, Menno Simons and Calvin, suggests a variety of useful perspectives from which we can understand Calvin's idea of the Church in the *Institutes* (1559), including trinitarian, eschatological and ethical perspectives. However, Loeschen does not fully deal with the functional identity of the Church and its relationship with the Church's spiritual identity in Calvin's ecclesiology. He focuses mainly on the ethical implications of the spiritual identity of the Church, considered in the *Institutes* III. In Loeschen's study, accordingly, the term "Church" can generally be interpreted as "Christians."[20]

While studies of Calvin's ecclesiology before the late 1980s generally attempted to interpret the theological implications of his ideas of the Church, studies since then have predominantly engaged with their historical and practical aspects. Bouwsma's study on Calvin's life and theology in 1988 signals this shift. Since Bouwsma's study, there have been few theological analyses of Calvin's doctrine of the Church.[21] As Selderhuis points out, recent research on Calvin's ecclesiology has laid much stress on "the more organizational aspects of the church, such as church discipline, church offices, the church-state relation and the unity of the church."[22]

---

20. Loeschen, *Divine Community*. Similar use of the term "Church," which is identical to (the fellowship of) Christians, had already appeared in Wallace's study of Calvin's idea of the two ministries of the Church. Wallace, *Calvin's Doctrine of the Word and Sacrament*.

21. Before Bouwsma, Schümmer produced theological studies of Calvin's ideas of the Church, which focused on the mystical identity of the Church as the "mother" in Calvin's thought. Schümmer, *L'Ecclesiologie de Calvin à la lumière de l'Ecclesia Mater*. Wiley also analysed the development and maintenance of the idea of the invisible Church as the elect throughout the editions of the *Institutes*. Wiley, "Church as the Elect," 96–117.

22. Selderhuis, "Church on Stage," 46. Significantly, with the exception of Selderhuis's paper, all the articles in *Calvin and the Church* deal with the historical, ethical, and institutional aspects of Calvin's ecclesiology.

Bouwsma argues that "chiefly concerned with its effectiveness in the world, he [Calvin] gave little attention to the church as a subject of theological reflection; his program for the church was again thoroughly practical."[23] To advance his argument, Bouwsma points to Calvin's emphasis on the particularity of the local: "When Calvin laid down regulation for 'the church,' then, he had in mind chiefly a church based on a town such as Geneva."[24] He therefore argues that Calvin is mainly concerned with the establishment of the visible and institutional Church, the effective means by which the Christians' spiritual needs are provided. He identifies two tendencies in Calvin's proposals for church government which support his argument: "clericalism" in his stress on the congregation's obligation of obedience to their pastor; and flexibility in allowing each local Christian community to choose a suitable government according to its circumstances.[25] Bouwsma seems to offer the best understanding of the anthropological basis of Calvin's ecclesiology. According to him, Calvin's idea of the Church as a "school," his emphasis on "zeal" in the teaching role of the Church, and his concept of "the mixture of the wicked and the faithful" in the Church reflect his concern for the spiritual needs of individual Christians.[26] However, Bouwsma focuses too exclusively on the functional identity of the Church. His claim that Calvin does not consider the Church as a subject of theology overlooks Calvin's identification of the Church with the body of Christ.

In 1990s, there have been a number of studies which dealt with the practical and historical aspects of Calvin's ecclesiology. Kingdon and his colleagues have painstakingly produced editions, translations and studies of the registers of the Consistory of Geneva, which shed light on Calvin's

---

23. Bouwsma, *John Calvin*, 214.

24. Ibid., 216

25. "Still another tension in his program for the church arose from his awareness, along with the needs of community, of the individuality of Christian experience. Even when Christians sit together as a body to hear the Gospel, he declared, God 'speaks to individuals,' each of whom is 'to apply to himself whatever God promises to his church collectively.'" Ibid., p. 227.

26. "As 'God's school,' Calvin's church was more like a humanist academy than a school of theology, and he imagined God now looking over the shoulders of his pupils watching 'their gestures, walking, words, and everything else.' . . . He gave much attention to what makes teaching effective in the church. It must be practical . . . It must also be presented with fervor." Ibid., 227. "But Calvin could also be less grudging. He knew well enough that the problem of 'mixture' was deeper than the mingling of reprobate and elect in the church, that every Christian, even among the elect, is also a mixture of good and evil." Ibid., 229.

The Identity and the Life of the Church

ideas and practices of church discipline in Geneva.[27] Historical investigations of Calvin's Geneva church have uncovered not only the historical background of his theological ideas of the Church but also on their application in practice.[28] Scholars who approach Calvin's ecclesiology from the viewpoint of political science have offered fresh insights into his ideas of church government, the church-state relationship, and other political and social issues concerned with his ecclesiology.[29] Those who have examined the hermeneutical and historical contexts of his ecclesiology have illustrated the significance of Calvin's doctrine of the Church in the history of Christian theology.[30] Calvin's doctrine of the sacraments is still one of the most popular areas of research and we can find material on his ideas of the Church in studies of this.[31]

In his study of Calvin's ecclesiology, Selderhuis raises again the question of the identities of the Church in Calvin's ecclesiology. Analysing the dynamic understanding of the Church in Calvin's commentary on Psalms, Selderhuis posits five identities of the Church in Calvin's ecclesiology: the church as the community of the covenant, as *corpus mixtum*, as the body of Christ, as *ecclesia militans*, and as *ecclesia ministrans*. Selderhuis believes that firstly, Calvin thinks of the Church as the community of the covenant which is always the "church-in-action" because "God has entrusted the covenant of eternal life to the church; hence the heavenly splendor shines most clearly in the church."[32] Secondly, with regard to the identity of the Church as *corpus mixtum*, in Calvin's ecclesiology "a church can even be decayed in large part, but when there are some sincere believers—even when they are

---

27. For further details on the Geneva Consistory, see Kingdon, "Geneva Consistory in the time of Calvin," 21–34. See also Kingdon, *Registers of the Consistory of Geneva in the Time of Calvin*.

28. Wallace, *Calvin, Geneva and Reformation*; Naphy, *Calvin and the Consolidation of the Genevan Reformation*.

29. Höpfl, *Christian Polity of John Calvin*; Hancock, *Calvin and the Foundations of the Modern Politics*; Stevenson, *Sovereign Grace*; Pattison, *Poverty in the Theology of John Calvin*.

30. McKee, *John Calvin on the Diaconate and Liturgical Almsgiving*; McKee, *Elders and the Plural Ministry*.

31. Gerrish, *Grace and Gratitude*; Elwood, *Body Broken*; Riggs, *Baptism in the Reformed Tradition*; Wandel, *Eucharist in the Reformation: Incarnation and Liturgy*.

32. Selderhuis, "Church on Stage," 50. He argues that "the church for Calvin is not just an orgnization but a demonstration; it is not something passive, just standing there. It is dynamic, it is a show on the road, it is a show in progress—yet, even a 'travelling salvation show.'" Ibid., 46.

only a small group—you may not withhold from them the name 'people of God.'"[33] Thirdly, from the identity of the Church as the body of Christ, Calvin finds the theological basis of the unity, existence, and richness of the church in the bond between Christ and the church. At this point, Selderhuis argues that the communion between Christ and the church "is invisible, but that it does not result in an invisible church. Just as Christ's body was visible and tangible, so is the church."[34] Fourthly, from Calvin's idea of the *ecclesia militans* illustrates his understanding of the suffering of the Church in history as "the sign of progress in the Kingdom of Christ." According to Selderhuis, Calvin tries to comfort the struggling church by recalling its relationship with Christ, because in this relationship "God acts in protection."[35] Fifthly, Selderhuis argues that in the idea of *ecclesia ministrans* Calvin stresses the benevolence of God in inviting believers to salvation by the testimony of the preacher, and "ascribes great value to the official proclamation of the Word, but without making the office the 'owner' of Word and Spirit."[36] Selderhuis reminds us of the importance of the issue of Calvin's identifications of the Church. In elaborating his own fivefold model of Calvin's ideas of the Church, however, he does not examine clearly how these five identities are distinguished and related to each other in Calvin's ecclesiology. Among the five identities of the Church that Selderhuis indicates, the community of the covenant, we may say that the body of Christ, and the *ecclesia militans* belong to the spiritual or invisible Church, and the *corpus mixtum* and the *ecclesia ministrans* pertain to the functional and visible Church. Without a proper understanding of the theological perspectives that connect these two identities, how can Calvin write of the Church as "a travelling show" of God's glory and at the same time write of the Church that is *corpus mixtum*? How can Calvin hold the view that "the spiritual unity of believers," which belongs to the identity of the church as the communion of the covenant, cannot exist without the visible unity of the church, in which hypocrites surely exist? How can Calvin assure believers of God's protection by positing that "God does not always protect the church in a visible way," and at the same time state that "the church is sure of God's continuous protection" without contradiction?

33. Ibid., 54.
34. Ibid., 55. "For Calvin the spiritual unity of believers cannot exist without the visible unity of the church. But unity for Calvin is not static, since it is always a 'unity under construction' or better put 'the church on the road of unity.'" Ibid., 57.
35. Ibid., 60.
36. Ibid., 63.

The Identity and the Life of the Church

Although the various studies surveying the theological, historical and practical aspects of Calvin's ecclesiology have contributed much to our knowledge, the questions about the theological basis of Calvin's idea of the Church seems not to have been sufficiently answered. The theological task of finding an answer to these crucial questions in Calvin's ecclesiology should be carried out because without a proper understanding of the theological foundations of Calvin's practical ideas of the Church, it is difficult for us either to understand precisely or to evaluate effectually those practical ideas. Calvin's proposals for the government, ministry, and discipline of the Church are not merely responses to historical situations and to the practical needs of his Church, but rather the results of efforts to realise his vision of the godly community in Scripture in the institutional Church. Therefore, in the opening chapter of the *Institutes* IV (1559), he makes it clear that the major subjects of the ecclesiological discussions in this book are to be the practical aspects of the institutional and visible Church: "Accordingly, our plan of instruction now requires us to discuss the church, its government, orders, and power; then the sacraments; and lastly, the civil order."[37] Yet, as a theologian and an exegete who made a great effort to embody his biblical vision of the Church in practice, Calvin always tries to discuss his idea of the Church from a theological perspective. Therefore, the need for a theological investigation of Calvin's idea of the Church remains, and is crucial for evaluating the success or failure of the reformation of the Church in Geneva according to Calvin's vision of the Church.

Methodological Points

Three methodological points will be used to investigate Calvin's doctrine of the Church in this study: a focus on Calvin's anthropological ideas; an analysis of the *Institutes* and related passages in Calvin's other writings; and an examination of his theological use of metaphors.

As the first methodological point, in investigating Calvin's idea of the Church, I will examine Calvin's theological anthropology among the various *loci* in his theology which may open a useful perspective on the relationship between the two identities of the Church in his ecclesiology. This choice arises simply from the view that it is necessary for anyone who tries to analyse a theologian's ecclesiology to pay attention to his or her

---

37. *Institutes*, IV.1.1, OS 5:1. Cf. "[I]t is now our intention to discuss the visible church." *Institutes*, IV.1.4, CO 5:7.

understanding of the Christian identity and the Christian life because the Church can be regarded as the divinely appointed community of and for Christians. It means that a theologian who discusses both the theoretical and the practical aspects of the Church should deal with the nature and the needs of Christians in the Church.

Calvin is no exception. Just before outlining his plan in the *Institutes* IV, he describes the condition of Christians on account of which the outward aids of the Church are required: "Since, however, in our ignorance and sloth (to which I add fickleness of disposition) we need outward helps to beget and increase faith within us, and advance it to its goal, God has added these aids that he may provide for our weakness."[38] The significance of the anthropological ideas in Calvin's doctrine of the Church is obvious in his definition of the Church: "By the term 'church' it means that which is actually in God's presence, into which no persons are received but those who are children of God by grace of adoption and true members of Christ by sanctification of the Holy Spirit."[39] In this statement, Calvin tries to explain the Church from his idea of who Christians are in the grace of the Triune God. Who is the Christian? A more elaborate way of asking this is: what happens in the Christian self and life by the grace of God? The attempt to find an answer to this question is key to understanding Calvin's idea of the Church. The examination of Calvin's anthropology occupies the first half part of this study because there are many important issues to be discussed in his anthropology with regard to the ecclesiological themes in the second part. Futhermore, we can observe the close connection between Calvin's anthropology and his ecclesiology if it becomes clear that he presents his discussion in both doctrines from the common and penetrating perspectives, such as teleological, trinitarian and eschatological perspectives. Among the many controversial and significant issues in Calvin's anthropology, however, I will focus mainly on the matters of the identity and the life of Christians after a preliminary examination of Calvin's idea of the *imago Dei*, the key concept to his anthropology, in the first chapter.

As the second methodological point, I will investigate Calvin's anthropology by focusing on the *Institutes* III, and his ecclesiology in the *Institutes* IV. This is not because I agree with Wendel's claim that Calvin's theology is completely presented in the *Institutes*,[40] but because the fourth book of

---

38. *Institutes*, IV.1.1, OS 5:1.
39. *Institutes*, IV.1.7, OS 5:12.
40. Wendel, *John Calvin*, 111.

The Identity and the Life of the Church

the *Institutes* is the most mature and organised presentation of Calvin's ecclesiology, and his writing here is closely related to the anthropological (soteriological) discussion of the previous book. Although the development through successive editions of the *Institutes* will not be ignored, it should be noted that there is no drastic change or revision in the *Institutes* IV. I will additionally refer in this study to diverse passages in Calvin's commentaries, sermons, treatises and letters, but I will try to restrict these references to passages in which Calvin explicitly handles material relevant to his anthropology and ecclesiology. These references are chiefly to be found in Calvin's New Testament Commentaries, because his explanation of the Church by means of metaphors is chiefly based on his interpretation of New Testament passages.[41]

As the third methodological point, in investigating Calvin's anthropology and ecclesiology, I will focus on certain core metaphors used by Calvin in the presentation of his explanations. In the first part of this study, I will focus on three biblical concepts significant for Calvin's anthropology: the image of God; Christians as children of God; and the Christian life as pilgrimage and warfare. For the investigation of Calvin's ecclesiology, I will examine Calvin's use of the following metaphors of the Church: the mother of all believers, the body of Christ, and the Kingdom of Christ. I have chosen these metaphors because these are the ones Calvin predominantly and effectively appeals to in his presentation of the Christian and the Church. Calvin's use of these metaphors reflects the underpinning theological focus of his ecclesiology. Of course, he uses these metaphors in part for rhetorical effect. However, this does not imply that his metaphorical understanding of the Church is empty rhetoric without any coherent theological foundation. Instead, for Calvin, the metaphors are effective tools with which to deliver his theological ideas.[42] As we shall see, it is his consistent theological

---

41. I shall quote the *Institutes* from Battles's English translation, *Institutes of the Christian Religion* [1559]. The quotations from Calvin's commentaries come from *Calvin's Commentaries*, which was originally published in Edinburgh, 1844–1855. I will refer to the original Latin texts of Calvin's writings in CO in the footnotes when I think that English translation are not clear and it is useful for us to see the original Latin terms and expressions for some important concepts.

42. Noting a possible influence of the rhetorical tradition of the Renaissance on Calvin, Willis suggests the rhetorical characteristics of Calvin's thought can be summarised in three points: Calvin's view of faith as persuasion, of knowledge as efficacious truth, and of revelation as God's persuasive accommodation. Willis, "Rhetoric and Responsibility in Calvin's Theology," 45, 50–51. There have been studies that shed light on the rhetorical characteristics of Calvin's thought. Girardin, *Rhétorique et théologique*; Millet, *Calvin*

Introduction

perspective and concern that determine his use of these metaphors, including their rhetorical usage. Thus I will focus on Calvin's theological idea of the Church, as explained through these metaphors, rather than investigate the intellectual background or the rhetorical style of his ecclesiological discussions.

Contents and Arguments

The first part of this study analyses Calvin's anthropology, and in particular his ideas of the identity and the life of the Christian. Although plausible ways to understand or resolve certain controversial issues in Calvin's anthropology are suggested, more detailed discussion about these issues is dealt with relatively briefly because this initial anthropological investigation aims principally to find and expound the three focal points of Calvin's anthropology: the restoration of the image of God in humanity in the course of regeneration; the grace of the triune God for Christian regeneration; and the consolation and hope of Christians in God's promise of protection and their future perfection. Each point shows that Calvin presents his anthropology from a relational, trinitarian and eschatological perspective.

As a preliminary examination of Calvin's anthropology, chapter 1 will review the previous studies of Calvin's idea of the image of God to outline the problems and the recent bias in the research of Calvin's anthropology. In this chapter, I will argue that Calvin's anthropology is an explanation of the restoration of the *imago Dei* in humanity in its relationship with God. This means that although Calvin deals with the "structural" aspects of the image of God, such as the immortality of the soul and the rational dignity of humanity, the essential focus of his anthropology is the restoration of the "relational" aspects of the image, which have been totally destroyed by sin.

In chapter 2, Calvin's idea of the identity of Christians as children of God will be examined. For Calvin, Christians cannot be assured of this

---

et la dynamique de la parole; Jones, *Calvin and the Rhetoric of Piety*. Concerning the rhetorical characteristics of Calvin's thought, Higman argues that "it is the subject which determined the choice of words and rhythms; they have not been selected in order to convey a certain effect so much as because they are only fitting ones." Higman, *Style of John Calvin in his French Polemical Treatises*, 121. Similarly, after analyzing and evaluating the interest of current studies in the rhetorical characteristics of Calvin's through, Wright argues that Calvin was "so acutely sensitive to the biblical style of plain simplicity and to the implications he drew from it that we should be very surprised to detect him, as we may from time to time, getting so carried away in flights of rhetoric as to lose sight of coherence and truth." Wright, "Was John Calvin a 'Rhetorical Theologian'?," 68-69.

The Identity and the Life of the Church

identity through anything they do themselves because they are imperfect: they experience a struggle between the two conflicting parts of their "divided self" in the course of regeneration. Calvin insists that Christians nonetheless can be assured of their identity only from their union with Christ in which they are justified and regenerated by the grace of the triune God.

Chapter 3 will attempt to show that Calvin explains the present life of Christians from an eschatological perspective: in describing the Christian life as "warfare" and "pilgrimage," Calvin concentrates not only on the present imperfection of the Christian, but also on the certainty of God's promise of the future perfection of the Christian at death and in the final resurrection. It will be argued that Calvin's discussion of the last things is directed by his concern to provide Christians with consolation in their present life. To show how Calvin's pastoral concern is applied to his explanation of the Christian life, I will deal with his consideration of three spiritual exercises, which affect the personal dimensions of the Christian life, and the duty of love toward neighbours, which concerns its communal dimensions.

The second part of this study will examine Calvin's ecclesiology to show how his anthropological idea of the Christian identity and the Christian life direct his idea of the Church. To do so, I will investigate Calvin's idea of the twofold identity of the Church: its functional and the spiritual identities. I will also investigate his idea of the three important practical aspects of the Church: its ministry, its government, and its discipline.

The main purpose of chapter 4 is to argue that Calvin calls the Church "the mother of all believers" and uses this idea to support his arguments for the necessity, the unity and the authenticity of the Church in order to emphasise the teaching and caring functions of the Church. This investigation aims to show that Calvin's functional understanding of the Church as "mother" is based on his anthropological idea that Christians are God's children and need therefore the motherly care of the Church. I will also investigate three foci of Calvin's idea of the ministry of the Church: God's grace of accommodation, the imperfection of human instruments, and the dynamic between the effectuating work of the Holy Spirit and the human response to grace. This investigation will show that it is not the nature or authority of the Church but God's grace of regeneration that occupies the centre of Calvin's ecclesiology, and is especially central to his ideas of the two main ministries of the Church—preaching and the sacraments.

In chapter 5, I will examine Calvin's use of the biblical metaphor of the body of Christ to argue that in Calvin's theology the spiritual identity of the Church as the body of Christ is nothing but an extension of the identity of the individual Christian to the communal level: as the identity of individual Christians is established and maintained in their union with Christ, so too the spiritual identity of the Church is established and maintained in the relationship of Christians with Christ and with each other. Christ is the Head of this body and Christians are the members. As a result of this concept of the spiritual identity of the Church, Calvin stresses that it is the grace of the triune God which distinctively but harmoniously operates in the relationship between Christ and members, just as it is this grace which allows the identity of the individual Christian, in union with Christ, to be defined. Calvin finds three spiritual dimensions of this understanding of the body of Christ in Ephesians 4:16, which he tries to apply to his outline of church government in the *Institutes* IV and the *Draft Ecclesiastical Ordinances* (1541): the headship of Christ, the communication of the diverse gifts, and the necessity of mutual love. This chapter will show that Calvin's idea of the Church as the body of Christ is the theological principle upon which he bases his directions for church government.

The final chapter will examine Calvin's eschatological understanding of the Church as the Kingdom of Christ, and argue that from this eschatological perspective, Calvin's two identities of the Church, as "the mother of all believers" and as "the body of Christ," are finally brought together. To show this, it will be argued that Calvin pays attention to the present imperfection and future perfection not only of the individual Christian but also of the Church, and from the same eschatological perspective. It will be seen that Calvin's eschatological understanding of the Church is offered with the underlying concern of providing believers with consolation in their Christian life. Next, I will examine the special relationship between the Church and the Kingdom of Christ in Calvin's ecclesiology in order to show that Calvin connects the Church with Christ's Kingdom because he thinks that the eschatological manifestation of the Kingdom of Christ, namely, the rule of Christ by means of the Word, happens not only in the invisible Church but also in the visible Church. Finally, I will examine Calvin's view of church discipline and try to prove that Calvin's idea of the eschatological relationship between the Church and Christ's Kingdom directs the important points of Calvin's idea of church discipline, such as the necessity of discipline, the omission of discipline from the marks of the true church and the emphasis on moderation in the administration of discipline.

The ultimately aim of this study is to show that Calvin's ecclesiology is presented in a close connection with his anthropological ideas of Christian

The Identity and the Life of the Church

identity and of the Christian life in the eschatological course of regeneration through the grace of the triune God. In his ecclesiology, Calvin associates the spiritual identity of the Church as the body of Christ with its functional identity as the mother of believers in order to highlight the grace of the triune God who regenerates His children in an eschatological way through the ministries of the Church. It will also be demonstrated that the common purpose of Calvin's anthropology and ecclesiology is his pastoral concern of providing Christians with consolation and hope in God's promises of protection and perfection.

PART ONE

Calvin's Anthropology

The *Imago Dei* in the Divine-Human Relationship

Introduction: Calvin's Theological Anthropology

CALVIN'S ANTHROPOLOGY CAN BE CALLED A THEOLOGICAL ANTHROPOLogy in the sense that he maintains that the knowledge of humanity is possible only through piety. In the opening chapter of the final Latin edition of the *Institutes*, Calvin states the importance of the knowledge of humanity in his theology by arguing that knowledge of humanity and knowledge of God are inseparably "joined by many bonds." He then argues, "true and sound wisdom consists of the knowledge of God and of ourselves."[1] In the following section in the *Institutes*, Calvin emphasises that "piety" is a prerequisite for the knowledge of God. He thinks that any discussion about God would be meaningless if it did not consider His grace towards human race: "Man never achieves a clear knowledge of himself unless he has first looked upon God's face."[2] Calvin defines piety as "reverence joined with love of God which the knowledge of his benefits induces," and it depends on men's recognition that "they owe everything to God, that they are nourished by his fatherly care, that he is the Author of their every good."[3] Therefore, an investigation of Calvin's idea of the image of God is useful to understand his idea of humanity in the divine-human relationship. He states the image

---

1. *Institutes*, I.1.1; *Tota fere sapientiae nostrae summa, quae vera demum ac solida sapientia censeri debeat, duabus partibus constat, Dei cognitione et nostri.* OS 3:31. Dowey argues that in Calvin's theology "man is always described in terms of his relation to this known God . . . Thus every theological statement has an anthropological correlate, and every anthropological statement, a theological correlate." Dowey, *Knowledge of God in Calvin's Theology*, 20.

2. *Institutes*, I.1.2, OS 3:32.

3. *Institutes*, I.2.1, OS 3:34.

PART ONE—Calvin's Anthropology

of God as the key to his theological anthropology at the beginning of the first edition of the *Institutes*: "In order for us to come to a sure knowledge of ourselves, we must first grasp the fact that Adam, parent of all, was created in the image and likeness of God."[4]

With regard to the concept of the image of God in Calvin's anthropology, I will use Grenz's framework of the "structural" and "relational" aspects of the image of God in humanity: the "structural" aspects apply to "the very structure of human nature," such as reason and the immortal soul, and the "relational" aspects refer to "a relationship between Creator and creature" and "what occurs as a consequence of the relationship."[5] This chapter investigates the theological focus of Calvin's theological anthropology by examining Calvin's discussion of the image of God according to the three stages which are implicitly supposed in his anthropology in the *Institutes*, namely creation, the fall, and restoration. That is because Calvin's anthropological discussions appear in this order in the *Institutes* (1559): the original condition of humanity in creation is discussed in the *Institutes*, I.15; the human condition after the fall in the *Institutes* II.1–3; and the human condition in the course of regeneration in the *Institutes* III, 3–10. This investigation will show that although Calvin deals with the "structural" aspects of the image of God in some specific contexts, he focuses mainly on its "relational" aspects, in particular, the restoration of the image of God in humanity by grace from this teleological perspective.

The Image of God in Creation

The Two Aspects of the Imago Dei

Calvin's idea of the image of God has been one of the most controversial topics among scholars.[6] The controversy arises basically from the absence of any firm definition of this concept within Calvin's writings themselves. According to Schreiner's summary, two groups of studies have emerged:

---

4. *Institutes* [1536] 1.1; *Quo in certam nostri notitiam veniamus, hoc prius habendum est: parentem omnium nostrum Adam esse creatum ad imaginem et similitudinem Dei.* OS 1:37. He makes almost the same statement in the *Institutes* [1559]: "Knowledge of ourselves lies first in considering what we were given at creation . . . In the beginning God fashioned us after his image that he might arouse our mind both to zeal for virtue and to meditation upon eternal life." *Institutes*, II.1.1, OS 3:228.

5. Grenz, *Social God and the Relational Self*, 142, 162.

6. Stauffer, *Dieu, la création et providence dans la prédication de Calvin*, 201.

The Imago Dei in the Divine-Human Relationship

while some have commented on Calvin's relational understanding of the *imago Dei*, such as "the right spiritual attitude," "gratitude," the role of either "reflecting God's glory" and "mirroring God's image," others have pointed out his structural understanding of the image of God as found in "reason," "immortality of the soul" and "human dignity."[7]

The former group of studies has tended to argue that Calvin's discussion of the image of God focuses mainly on the relationship between Christ and a Christian. Both Torrance and Niesel argue that Calvin discussed the image of God in order to explain Christ's benefits for the salvation of humanity, who has been alienated from God and lost his original "orientation towards his Creator."[8] Likewise, Prins claims that the theological emphasis, concerning the relationship between the restored image of God and the original image of God in Adam, is more essential to Calvin's thought than analysis of its nature from a mere anthropological perspective.[9] This group has a tendency to systematise Calvin's idea of the *imago Dei* from christological perspective.

The latter group of studies have complained that a systematic approach of the former group to Calvin's idea of the *imago Dei*, focusing on the relationship between Christ and a Christian, tends to ignore the other dimensions of Calvin's anthropology. Cairns argues that the relational and existential interpretation of Calvin's understanding of the image of God "is not exhaustive."[10] Likewise, Stauffer states that practical and ethical concerns, which is based on the structural aspects, are also important in Calvin's understanding of the image of God, and thus the systematic interpretations have not taken sufficient account of the diverse aspects of the "image of God" to be found in Calvin's writings.[11] Faber criticises the systematic approach to Calvin's anthropology and then tries to show that Calvin understands the image of God in other contexts than just the christological one.[12] In contrast to those studies of the first group, which concentrate on

---

7. Schreiner, *Theater of His Glory*, 51.

8. Torrance, *Calvin's Doctrine of Man*; Niesel, *Theology of John Calvin*.

9. Prins, "Image of God in Adam and the Restoration of Man in Jesus Christ," 32–44.

10. Cairns argues, "The image is, indeed, something very complex, which from one point of view, as God's gift to man, has certainly not been obliterated by man's sin, while from another viewpoint, regarded as the integrity of man's response of heart and will, it certainly is obliterated.... the complexity and the paradoxical nature of the reality Calvin is trying to describe become very evident." Cairns, *Image of God in Man*, 134.

11. Stauffer, *Dieu, la création et providence dans la prédication de Calvin*, 201.

12. Faber, *Essays in Reformed Doctrine*, 227–81. Faber argues that Calvin was far

PART ONE—Calvin's Anthropology

God's grace in Calvin's understanding of the *imago Dei*, Cairns, Stauffer and Faber tried to manifest the ethical implications of Calvin's understanding of the image of God.[13]

More recently, another kind of studies has emerged which moves the centre of attention from Calvin's definition of the *imago Dei* to the context in which he employs this concept. They suggest that the inconsistency between the relational and structural aspects of Calvin's idea of the *imago Dei* is the result of an intentional choice of different forms of expression which varied according to the particular contexts in which Calvin deals with this concept. But there have been various arguments concerning the reason for this inconsistency. According to Bouwsma, this inconsistency results from Calvin's rhetorical devotion to the thoroughly practical goal of convincing his contemporaries of their sinfulness.[14] Higman, however, criticises an entirely rhetorical approach to the context of Calvin's understanding of the image of God. For Higman, the apparent inconsistency in Calvin's discussion results from a twofold theological "context" in which Calvin treats the *imago Dei*: while Calvin maintains that God's image still remains within humanity with regard to earthly things, he also thinks that the image has been "totally destroyed" with regard to celestial things.[15] Higman's suggestion of a twofold theological context is similar to Engel's idea of a twofold perspective in Calvin's understanding of the image of God. Engel argues that Calvin regards the image of God as still remaining from the "relative-human" perspective, but as having been totally destroyed from the "absolute-divine" perspective.[16] Schreiner sees two levels of human existence—spiritual and natural—within Calvin's understanding of the image of God; her idea does not differ significantly from the viewpoints of either Engel or Higman. However, while Higman focuses more on Calvin's idea of the destruction of the image where heavenly things are concerned, Sch-

---

different from the modern Barthians' understanding of the image of God. As proof, Faber asserts that his polemical confrontation with Osiander's view of the image of God kept Calvin from directly associating the biblical idea of the image of God with christological issues.

13. Schreiner, *Theater of His Glory*, 51.
14. Bouwsma, *John Calvin*, 141–42.
15. Higman, "Calvin et l'imago Dei," 139–48.
16. Engel, *John Calvin's Perspectival Anthropology*, 37–72. There are other works treating the image of God in Calvin's theology which relate this topic to gender issues: Douglass, "The Image of God in Humanity: A Comparison of Calvin's Teaching in 1536 and 1559," 175–203; Thompson, "*Creata ad Imaginem Dei, Licet secundo Gradu*," 125–43.

The Imago Dei in the Divine-Human Relationship

reiner focuses more on "Calvin's fascination with the remnant" of the image of God with regard to natural law and the continuation of human society.[17]

As those recent studies have suggested, it would be a difficult to derive a systematic and determinate definition of the "image of God" from Calvin's anthropological discussion because he provides no such definition. We face this difficulty not only in examining his idea of the image of God, but also in the other related issues to this idea in his anthropology.[18] Yet an examination of the contexts of those apparent inconsistent notions in Calvin's anthropology, in particular his notion of "the image of God," is still productive because it is the key concept in Calvin's theological anthropology that helps us to find the essential focus and perspective of his anthropology.

The Dignity of Humankind in Creation

Calvin's most thorough discussions of the *imago Dei* in creation appear in the *Institutes* (1559), II, 15 and his *Commentary on Genesis* 1:26–27. In each, he mentions both the structural and relational aspects of the *imago Dei*. Between these two aspects, his main concern is not to anatomise the structural aspects of the divine image in humanity, but to explain its relational aspects such as God's grace and purpose in creating humankind according to His image.

In Calvin's anthropology, structural aspects of the *imago Dei* closely relate to the human nature which makes humankind superior to other creatures. In his *Commentary on Genesis*, Calvin understands the image of God to be an indication of the uniqueness and blessedness of humankind, who is superior to other creatures. Interpreting Genesis 1:26, "let us make man," Calvin argues, "God certainly might here command by his bare word what he wished to be done but he chose to give tribute to the excellency of humankind, that he would, in a manner, enter into consultation concerning his creation."[19] Stauffer, noting Calvin's view that the *imago Dei* marks humankind's superiority over other creatures, argues that this is evidence

---

17. Schreiner, *Theater of His Glory*, 72.

18. Engel deals with five points out four controversial issues in Calvin's anthropology: the image of God, heavenly wisdom and earthly wisdom, divine providence and human freedom, immortality and resurrection. I will engage with the first and the fourth issues in this study. Engel, *John Calvin's Perspectival Anthropology*, ix–xv.

19. *Comm. Gen.* 1:26, CO 23:25.

PART ONE—Calvin's Anthropology

of the importance of the structural dimension of the *imago Dei* in Calvin's anthropology.[20] Stauffer then argues that Torrance's systematic study of Calvin's anthropology largely ignores this evidence while he concentrates too much on Calvin's soteriological ideas of the relational aspects of the *imago Dei*.[21] However, Stauffer himself seems to concentrates too much on the structural aspects and thus fails to observe that the exegetical focus of Calvin's interpretation of the *imago Dei* in Genesis 1:26 is the grace of God.[22] In fact, in his commentary on Genesis 1:26, Calvin immediately turns to admiration of the wonderful wisdom of God in creating humankind, without any further discussion of the superiority of human beings or other "structural aspects":

> The dignity of our nature, he, in taking counsel concerning the creation of man, testifies that he is about to undertake something great and wonderful . . . if you rightly weigh all circumstances, man is, among other creatures, a certain pre-eminent specimen of Divine wisdom, justice, and goodness, so that he is deservedly called by the ancients *micricosmos,* "a world in miniature."[23]

As Schreiner points out, Calvin's omission of any articulated discussion of the special status of human nature in his commentary on Genesis 1:26 is in marked contrast to other major theologians, such as Augustine, Chrysostom and Aquinas, who developed a fuller anthropology on the basis of this passage.[24] Instead of following his predecessors, Calvin criticises Augustine and Chrysostom for speculating too much about the *imago Dei* in Genesis 1:26. Considering Augustine's idea of the *imago Dei* as a trinitarian structure within the human being, Calvin says, "Augustine, beyond all others, speculates with excessive refinement, for the purpose of fabricating a Trinity in man . . . but a definition of the image of God ought to rest on a firmer basis than such subtleties."[25] He also rejects Chrysostom's idea of the

---

20. Stauffer, *Dieu, la création et la providence dans la prédication de Calvin*, 201-2.

21. Ibid., 202-4.

22. Stauffer refers to some passages of Calvin's sermons on Job but he briefly mentions Calvin's rejections of the distinction between the image and the likeness in his commentary and sermons on Genesis 1:26. Ibid., 202.

23. *Comm. Gen.* 1:26, CO 23:25.

24. Schreiner offers a useful summary of the idea of the image of God as discussed by the major theologians before Calvin, such as Irenaeus, Augustine, and Aquinas. Schreiner, *Theater of His Glory*, 55–57.

25. *Comm. Gen.* 1:26, CO 23:26.

image representing the dominion of humankind over other creatures: "The exposition of Chrysostom is not more correct, who refers to the dominion which was given to humankind in order that he might, in a certain sense, act as God's vice regent in the government of the world."[26]

In the *Institutes* I.15, Calvin speaks of the superiority of humankind as created according to the *imago Dei*: "From this we may gather that when his image is placed in humanity a tacit antithesis is introduced which raises humankind above all other creatures and, as it were, separates him from the common mass."[27] Here again, however, he does not present any further sophisticated treatment about human nature, but, instead, highlights God's grace in creating humanity: "But by this particular title [the image of God] Moses rightly commends God's grace toward us, especially, when he compares only the visible creatures with man."[28] In these two key places, therefore, the main point of Calvin's discussion of the image of God is not the dignity of humanity itself, but rather the wisdom and grace of the God who created humankind. And he focuses on the fact that these divine wisdom and grace were reflected in the image of God in main.

The Soul and the Body

Calvin relates the image of God more closely to the soul than to the body. The close relation between the soul and the image of God in Calvin's thought seems to be evidence of his focus on the structural aspects of the *imago Dei* because he deals with the structural aspects such as the immortality of the soul and the significance of reason in his anthropology. Yet it should be noted that the relational aspect of the *imago Dei* and its original purpose still form the central point of Calvin's anthropological discussion of the soul and the body even though he associates the *imago Dei* with the soul more than the body.

Calvin calls the soul "an immortal yet created essence" and the "nobler part" of humanity, and then says that "the many pre-eminent gifts with which the human mind is endowed proclaim that something divine has been engraved upon it; all are testimonies of an immortal essence." Furthermore, Calvin thinks that immortality was given to the human soul when God engraved His image upon it:

26. *Comm. Gen.* 1:26, CO 23:26.
27. *Institutes*, I.15.3, OS 3:178.
28. *Institutes*, I.15.3, OS 3:178.

PART ONE—Calvin's Anthropology

> Three gradations, indeed, are to be noted in the creation of man; that his dead body was formed out of the dust of the earth; that it was endued with a soul, whence it should receive vital motion; and that on this soul God engraved his own image, to which immortality is annexed.[29]

Still more specifically, Calvin identifies reason as the faculty of the soul which distinguishes human beings from other creatures: "He [Adam] was endued with understanding and reason, that being distinguished from brute animals he might meditate on a better life, and might even tend directly towards God, whose image he bore engraven on his own person."[30]

Calvin argues that humankind is superior to the other animals, whose perception "does not go beyond the body, or at least extends no farther than to material things presented to it."[31] Stressing that the character of the soul is nobler than the body, Calvin rejects the view of the "Anthropomorphites" who regard the *imago Dei* as the bodily form of humanity.[32] For Calvin, the *imago Dei* is "the inner good" of the soul: "Whereas, God's image is properly to be sought within him, not outside him, indeed, it is an inner good of the soul."[33] For the same reason, he rejects Osiander's doctrine that the image of God resides in the whole human being, equally in body and soul. Arguing against Osiander, Calvin declares, "although God's glory shines forth in the outer man, yet there is no doubt that the proper seat of His image is in the soul."[34] Calvin even argues, "Although the soul is not man, it is not absurd for man, in respect of his soul, to be called God's image."[35]

---

29. *Comm. Gen.* 2:7, CO 23:47.
30. *Comm. Gen. Argument*, CO 23:12.
31. *Institutes*, I.15.2, OS 3:174.
32. "The Anthropomorphites were too gross in seeking this resemblance in the human body; let that reverie therefore remain entombed . . . Others proceed with a little more subtlety, who, though they do not imagine God to be corporeal, yet maintain that the image of God is in the body of man, because his admirable workmanship there shines brightly; but this opinion, as we shall see, is by no means consonant with Scripture." *Comm. Gen.* 1:26, CO 23:26.
33. *Institutes*, I.15.4, OS 3:179.
34. *Quamvis enim in homine externo refulgeat Dei Gloria, propriam tamen imaginis sedem in anima esse dubium non est. Institutes*, I.15.3; OS 3:178.
35. *Quamvis ergo anima non sit homo, absurdum tamen non est, eum animae respectu vocari Dei imaginem. Institutes*, I.15.3, OS 3:178.

It is true that in awarding such a high evaluation of the soul in relation to the *imago Dei* Calvin holds a structural understanding of the *imago Dei*.[36]

However, it is not the comparison between the soul and the body but the glory of God that takes the centre of Calvin's discussion of the image of God with regard to the two parts of human beings. To understand this, we need to find the reason for Calvin's identification of the soul with the *imago Dei* in the *Institutes* I.15.3. In this section, Calvin tries to refute Osiander's doctrine that the image of God was found in both the soul and body of Adam. He argues that Adam's body was formed according to Christ's body before Christ's incarnation. In Calvin's view, accordingly, Osiander's doctrine of the *imago Dei* confuses the image of God in Adam with the perfect image of God in Christ. According to Calvin, Osiander argues that "not a part of humanity—say, the soul with its endowments—is called God's image, but the whole Adam, whose name was given him from the earth whence he was taken." For Calvin, if this opinion is accepted, "man was formed only after the type and exemplar of Christ as man; and thus the pattern from which Adam was taken was Christ in so far as he was to be clothed with flesh."[37] In the *Institutes* I.15.3, Calvin feels the need to argue against Osiander concerning the relationship between the soul and the image of God from a christological rather than an anthropological point of view: "He says that the Father, Son, and the Holy Spirit place their image in man, because however upright Adam might have remained, yet Christ would have to become man."[38] For Calvin, Osiander's idea that Adam was created according to the image of God has a totally different implication to the notion that Christ is the perfect image of God. In his commentary on Genesis, Calvin argues thus: "It is also truly said that Christ is the only image of the Father, but yet the words of Moses do not bear the interpretation that 'in the image' means 'in Christ.'"[39]

---

36. At this point, Torrance's argument seems too strong to be a precise understanding of Calvin's own idea of the *imago Dei*: "There is no doubt that Calvin always thinks of the *imago* in terms of a mirror ... He does use such expressions as *engrave* and *sculptured*, but only in a metaphorical sense and never dissociated from the idea of the mirror." Torrance, *Calvin's Doctrine of Man*, 36.

37. *Institutes*, I.15.3; OS 3:177. Calvin senses danger in Osiander's teaching that Adam was created according to Christ who is the living image of God, and, therefore, believers are justified by "a substantial infusion" of Christ's righteousness. *Institutes*, II.11.10–12, OS 3:432–35.

38. *Institutes*, I.15.3, OS 3:177.

39. *Comm. Gen.* 1:26, CO 23:26.

PART ONE—Calvin's Anthropology

If we consider the polemical context of Calvin's discussion in the *Institutes*, it is certain that he places greater emphasis on the soul not to highlight the superiority of the soul to the body,[40] but to underline the original role of the soul in the relationship between God and humanity. Human reason should contemplate and reflect his Creator's image. Calvin argues in this sense that, "to begin with, God's image was visible in the light of the mind, in the uprightness of the heart, and in the soundness of all the parts."[41] Focusing on this relational aspects, he includes the human body in the sphere of the *imago Dei* which reflects God's glory in humanity: "although the primary seat of the divine image was in the mind and heart, or in the soul and its power, yet there was no part of humanity, not even the body itself, in which some sparks did not glow."[42]

The Original Purpose of Creation

As shown above, Calvin's discussion of the image of God is consistently presented with his focus on the role of the *imago Dei* in humanity, that is, to reflect God's glory. Especially, his idea of the *imago Dei* as "the integrity of the first human being" shows this teleological perspective:

> Accordingly, *the integrity* with which Adam was endowed is expressed by this word [*imago Dei*], when he had full possession of right understanding, when he had his affections kept within the bounds of reason, all his senses tempered in right order, and he truly referred his excellence to *exceptional gifts* bestowed upon him by his Maker.[43]

---

40. Faber argues that this polemical context is evidence of the Barthians' misunderstanding of Calvin's idea of the *imago Dei*. Faber, *Essays in Reformed Doctrine*, 234–39. However, Faber's argument is not applicable to interpretation of Calvin's discussion in the *Commentary on Genesis* because there is no polemical argument against Osiander in this commentary. This is because this commentary was published in 1554 before Calvin's debates against Osiander's doctrine took place (between 1554 and 1559). Thus it is difficult to conclude with Faber that Calvin's debate against Osiander is the most important context for Calvin's discussion of the image of God in general.

41. *Institutes*, I.15.4; *unde colligimus imaginem Die initio in luce mentis, in cordis rectitudine, partiumque omnium sanitate conspicuam fuisse Die imaginem*. OS 3:179.

42. *Institutes*, I.15.3; *Ac quamvis primaria sedes Divinae imaginis fuerit in mente et corde, vel in anima eiusque potentiis: nulla tamen pars fuit etiam usque ad corpus, in qua non scintillae aliquae micarent*. OS 3:178.

43. *Institutes*, I.15.3, OS 3:178. As this statement shows, this integrity means the perfect order in Adam's humanity. In his commentary on Genesis 1:26, Calvin offers

The Imago Dei in the Divine-Human Relationship

For Calvin, this original integrity means a perfect order in humanity, including the order between the soul and body: "In the mind perfect intelligence flourished and reigned, uprightness attended as its companion, and all the senses were prepared and moulded for due obedience to reason: and in the body there was a suitable correspondence with this internal order."[44] This statement seems to show that Calvin indicates the structural aspects of the *imago Dei*, such as the desirable relationship between the soul and the body. In his discussion of creation, however, Calvin does not offer an analysis of the soul and reason separately from their purpose in reflecting God's glory. With regard to this, it should be noted that in his idea of original integrity, Calvin indicates the higher divine purpose of creating the first man to reflect His glory rather than the order inside the first human being: "Nevertheless, it seems that we do not have a full definition of 'image' if we do not see more plainly those faculties in which man excels, and in which he ought to be thought the reflection of God's glory."[45] For Calvin, the superiority of human beings over other creatures should be understood in the context of God's purpose in creating Adam according to His image.

Similarly, Calvin focuses more on the purpose of reason than on the excellence of reason in itself. He clarifies the central concerns of his concept of reason in his commentary on John 1:4 thus:

> He [John] separates man from the rank of other creatures; because we perceive more readily the power of God by feeling it in us than by beholding it at a distance . . . namely, that they [men] were not created like the beasts, but having been endued with reason, they had obtained a higher rank . . . it follows that the purpose for which they were created was, that they might acknowledge Him who is the Author of so excellent a blessing.[46]

Calvin's teleological perspective is also evident in his criticism of the philosophers' views about human reason. He grants that Plato had some genuine, though very limited, knowledge about the soul insofar as he

---

a similar statement about human integrity: "Therefore by this word the perfection [*integritas*] of our whole nature is designated, as it appeared when Adam was endued with a right judgment, had affections in harmony with reason, had all his senses sound and well-regulated, and truly excelled in everything good." *Comm. Gen.* 1:26, CO 23:26.

44. *Comm. Gen.* 1:26, CO 23:26.
45. *Institutes*, I.15.4, OS 3:179.
46. *Comm. John* 1:4; CO 47:5.

PART ONE—Calvin's Anthropology

acknowledged its immortality.[47] Yet, in the same section, the uselessness of philosophical speculation about the soul is pointed out: "It would be foolish to seek a definition of 'soul' from the philosophers."[48] In Calvin's view, philosophers inevitably misunderstand humanity because they do not understand Scriptural teaching about the wretched condition of the soul after the Fall: "ignorant of the corruption of nature that originated from the penalty for man's defection, [they] mistakenly confuse two very diverse states of man."[49] Criticising such philosophical speculation, Calvin feels it quite sufficient to underline the "upbuilding of godliness" as the reason for the knowledge that humanity was made in God's image: "But I leave it to the philosophers to discuss these faculties in their subtle way. For the upbuilding of godliness a simple definition will be enough for it."[50]

Calvin's negative attitude to the purely philosophical approach to the soul confirms his teleological perspective that the creation of humankind was in accordance with the *imago Dei*. For Calvin, the most important anthropological implication of Genesis 1:26 is that "in our image, after our likeness" is on "that glory of God which peculiarly shines forth in human nature, where the mind, the will, and all the senses, represent the Divine order."[51] From Calvin's teleological perspective, it therefore becomes more evident that the focal point of his anthropological discussion is on the relational rather than the structural aspects of the image of God.

The Image of God after the Fall

As is shown by the famous debate between Barth and Brunner concerning the possibility of natural theology, one of the most controversial issues in Calvin's anthropology is whether he thinks that the image of God was totally eliminated by the fall or that it partially survived.[52] This controversy is

47. "Hence Plato's opinion is correct, because he considers the image of God to be in the soul." *Institutes*, I.15.6, OS 3:182.

48. *Institutes*, I.15.6, OS 3:182. About Calvin's idea of the soul, Partee argues that Calvin tries to present his anthropology through the "spectacles of Scripture" rather than through the framework of Platonism. Partee, *Calvin and Classical Philosophy*, 65.

49. *Institutes*, I.15.7, OS 3:185.

50. *Institutes*, I.15.6, OS 3:183.

51. *Comm. Gen.* 1:26, CO 23:26.

52. This debate was precipitated by Brunner's *Natur und Gnade* and Barth's response *Nein!* Both books were translated into English in Frankel, *Natural Theology*. Also see Dowey's discussion in "The Barth-Brunner Controversy on Calvin," in Dowey, *Knowledge*

also related to Calvin's recognition of the two aspects of the image of God: those who emphasise Calvin's idea of the partial survival of the *imago Dei* tend to concentrate on Calvin's references to its structural aspects, while those who emphasise its total destruction tend to refer to Calvin's attention to its relational aspects.

This problem has not yet been solved because Calvin speaks of both "the total destruction" and "the partial survival" of the image of God. According to Faber, Calvin's statements about the condition of the image of God after the fall can be divided into three categories: the total destruction of the image by the verb *delere* and *extinguere*; the survival of the image after the fall in texts such as the *Institutes* III.7.6; the partial destruction of the image.[53] Faber argues that Calvin himself never saw a contradiction in his inconsistent statements about the condition of the *imago Dei* after the fall. According to Faber, when Calvin makes these statements each has a specific focal point with respect to context, and he is always aware of the specific contexts of those statements. However, Faber's argument still leaves the impression that Calvin's anthropology floats between two incompatible foci without any attempt to make them coherent. In his discussion of creation, as examined in the following pages, it can be argued that Calvin's focus in discussing the fall is more on the relational aspects than the structural aspects of the *imago Dei* as far as he maintains his teleological perspective. As a result, it can be argued that in his anthropology the "partial survival" is not as important as the "total destruction."

"Partial Survival" of the Imago Dei

The following statement from Calvin's commentary on Genesis is one of his most noticeable observations of the extent of the damage done to the *imago Dei* in humanity by the fall:

> But now, although some obscure lineaments of that image are found remaining in us: yet are they so vitiated and maimed, that they may truly be said to be destroyed. For besides the deformity which everywhere appears unsightly, this evil also is added, that no part is free from the infection of sin.[54]

---

of God in Calvin's Theology, 247–49.

53. Faber, *Essays in Reformed Doctrine*, 253–57.

54. *Comm. Gen.* 1:26; *Nunc etsi obscura quaedam imaginis illius lineamenta in nobis residua manent: sunt tamen adeo vitiata et mutila, ut vere dicere liceat esse deleta. Nam*

PART ONE—Calvin's Anthropology

In this statement, Calvin affirms the partial survival of the image of God, "some obscure lineaments," after the fall. Yet he claims at the same time that the image of God "may truly be said to be destroyed." This guarded clause suggests that Calvin's use of the expression "destruction" of the image of God is rhetorical with a particular theological intention. What might his intention in making such a claim be?

Throughout his theology, Calvin highlights the drastic downfall of the human condition after the fall. In doing so, he concentrates more on what happened to the relational aspects than to the structural aspects of the *imago Dei*. He thinks that the structural aspects of the *imago*, such as reason and the immortal soul, still remain in humankind after the fall, but that the relational aspects of the *imago*, such as its original purpose and the relationship with God, are totally destroyed. Here we should note that Calvin distinguishes between two kinds of gifts given by God to Adam through creation: natural and supernatural gifts. When he discusses free will in the *Institutes*, Calvin speaks of the patristic distinction between these two gifts in fallen men: "And, indeed, that common opinion which they have taken from Augustine pleases me: that the natural gifts were corrupted in man through sin, but that his supernatural gifts were stripped from him."[55] Calvin then acknowledges that reason remains in humankind after the fall even albeit severely damaged:

> Since reason, therefore, by which man distinguishes between good and evil, and by which he understands and judges, is a natural gift, it could not be completely wiped out; but it was partly weakened and partly corrupted, so that its misshapen ruins appear.[56]

Although reason lost its capacity for "heavenly things" through the fall, it still works for "earthly things" and enables human beings to manage life in this world.[57] The survival of reason in humanity after the fall is proved not only by common sense but also by God's Word: "When we so condemn hu-

---

praeter deformitatem quae ubique foeda apparet, hoc quoque malum accedit, quod nulla pars est peccati labe non infecta. CO 23:27.

55. *Institutes*, II.2.12, OS 3:254.

56. *Institutes*, II.2.12, OS 3:255.

57. Calvin defines earthly things as "those which do not pertain to God or his Kingdom, to true justice, or to the blessedness of the future life; but which have their significance and relationship with regard to the present life and are, in a sense, confined within its bounds." He argues that the effectiveness of human reason for such things "clearly testifies to a universal apprehension of reason and understanding by nature implanted in men." *Institutes*, II.2.14, OS 3:257.

man understanding for its perpetual blindness as to leave it no perception of any object whatever, we not only go against God's Word, but also run counter to the experience of common sense."[58]

Moreover, as Stauffer emphasises, Calvin argues that the survival of the natural gifts in humanity after the fall is the first reason for our ethical responsibility to acknowledge the dignity of the rest of humankind. In his commentary on Genesis 9:6, Calvin argues thus: "First, there yet exists some remnants of it [the image of God], so that man is possessed of no small dignity."[59] In his explanation of the sixth of the Ten Commandments that "You shall not kill," Calvin maintains that the dignity of men due to the remaining image of God in them is preserved even after the fall:

> Scripture notes that this commandment rests upon a twofold basis: man is both the image of God, and our flesh. Now, if we do not wish to violate the image of God, we ought to hold our neighbor sacred. And if we do not wish to renounce all humanity, we ought to cherish his as our own flesh.[60]

Recognition of the survival of the *imago Dei* in humanity not only reminds believers of the commandment of "You shall not kill," but also exhorts them to love their neighbours: "here [Heb. 13:16] Scripture helps in the best way when it teaches that we are not to consider that men merit of themselves, but to look upon the image of God in all men, to which we owe honour and love."[61]

"Total Destruction" of the Imago Dei

Despite Calvin's belief that same part of the *imago Dei* has survived the fall, his descriptions of the condition of humankind after the fall are strongly worded. In the *Institutes* II.1.8, for example, he declares, "Whatever is in man, from the understanding to the will, from the soul even to the flesh, has been defiled and crammed with this concupiscence. Or to put it more

---

58. *Institutes*, II.2.12, OS 3:255.

59. *Comm. Gen.* 9:6; *Si quis obiiciat imaginem illam deletam esse: solutio facilis est, manere adhuc aliquid residuum, ut praestet non parva dignitate homo.* CO 23:147. For Stauffer, this is the evidence that Calvin is discussing the image of God within the contexts of creation and providence of God, and not within the soteriological context alone. Stauffer, *Dieu, la création et providence dans la prédication de Calvin*, 202.

60. *Institutes*, II.8.40, OS 4:380.

61. *Institutes*, III.7.6, OS 4:157.

PART ONE—Calvin's Anthropology

briefly, the whole man is of himself nothing but concupiscence."[62] But if Calvin admits the "partial survival" of the *imago Dei*, how is it that he uses such expressions as the "total destruction" of the image after the fall? Cairns argues that this inconsistent expression results from "the complexity and the paradoxical nature of the reality" that Calvin is trying to describe.[63] As mentioned above, Engel's suggestion of the twofold perspective in Calvin's treatment of the *imago Dei* would be one possible way of solving this matter.[64] Yet both suggestions do not answer the question about the theological reasons for Calvin's strong and apparently contradictory expressions for his description of the condition of the *imago Dei* in humanity after the fall.

To answer this question, we should note again that Calvin maintains a teleological perspective throughout his discussion of the image of God after the fall. He constantly concentrates on the purpose of both natural and supernatural gifts, that is, that they should reflect God's glory. At this point, Cairns correctly observes Calvin's view of humankind after the fall thus: "those passages where the darkest picture of man is painted, all deal less with the gifts God has bestowed on human nature than with the use to which they are put by man."[65] This teleological perspective is evident in the *Institutes* II.2.4 where Calvin mentions the patristic division between the natural and supernatural gifts within humanity:

> For my part, if I wanted clearly to teach what the corruption of nature is like, I would readily be content with these words. But it is more important to weigh carefully what man can do, vitiated as he is in every part of his nature and shorn of supernatural gifts.[66]

---

62. *Institutes*, II.1.8, OS 3:238.

63. Cairns states, "The image is, indeed, something very complex, which from one point of view, as God's gift to man, has certainly not been obliterated by man's sin, while from another viewpoint, regarded as the integrity of man's response of heart and will, it certainly is obliterated." Cairns argues then that Calvin painted the darkest picture of man because he dealt "less with the gifts God has bestowed on human nature than with the use to which they are put by man." In Cairns' view, Calvin's "apparent contradictions" on the subject of the image of God are "at least in part due to two aspect of the reality": the nature of the image of God in man as the gift and its proper use. Cairns, *Image of God in Man*, 134, 144.

64. Engel argues that Calvin can say that "humankind became nothingness and the image was completely destroyed" from the absolute perspective of God, but that he can also say that the image still remains after the fall from the relative perspective of humankind. Engel, *Calvin's Perspectival Anthropology*, 54–61.

65. Cairns, *Image of God in Man*, 138.

66. *Institutes*, II.2.4, OS 3:245.

The Imago Dei *in the Divine-Human Relationship*

As this statement shows, Calvin emphasises that after the fall humankind is now totally incapable of glorifying God. He even claims that without the aid of revelation the reason of fallen humanity should form a false picture of God and then it "robs" God of His glory:

> He then who has a right notion of God ought to give him the praise due to his eternity, wisdom, goodness, and justice. Since men have not recognized these attributes in God, but have dreamt of him as though he were an empty phantom, they are justly said to have impiously robbed him of his own glory.[67]

As we have seen, Calvin acknowledges that the vestiges of the image of God after the fall still function for "earthly things."[68] But it is more significant to him that reason is so corrupted that it can no longer serve its original and ultimate purpose, that is, to perceive and reflect God's glory.[69] He maintains thus that these vestiges do not work for "heavenly things" because human reason after the fall is totally "blind" to God.[70] The vestiges of the image are not only incapable of this, but are also despicable, producing nothing but sin: "Here I only want to suggest briefly that the whole man is overwhelmed—as by a deluge—from head to foot, so that no part is immune from sin and all that proceeds from him is to be imputed to sin."[71] Therefore, the vestiges of the image of God make human sinfulness inexcusable before God's judgment:

---

67. *Comm. Rom.* 1:21; *Ergo qui conceptam Dei notitiam habet, iam illi laudem debet aeternitatis, sapientiae, bonitatis, iustitiae. Eiusmodi virtutes quum non recognoverint homines in Deo, sed somniarint tanquam inane phantasma: merito dicuntur illum sua gloria improbe spoliasse.* CO 49:24.

68. For Calvin's terms *aliquid residuum, ruina, aliquas superstites* to describe the survival of the *imago Dei* in the fallen humanity, Torrance argues, "When Calvin uses quantitative terms such as portion or remnants it is clear that his mind is for the moment running on psychological rather than on theological lines, and he is thinking of our natural gifts which, though they have been corrupted, still remain in man, for they are part of the groundwork of his creation." Torrance, *Calvin's Doctrine of Man*, 95.

69. "Indeed, Paul shows us in every part of life how empty reason is in the Lord's sight when he denies, 'that we are sufficient of ourselves to claim something as coming from us as if it really did' [II Cor. 3:5]. He is not speaking of the will or the emotions; but he even takes from us the ability to think how the right doing of anything can enter our minds." *Institutes*. II.2.25, OS 3:267.

70. "Because man's keenness of mind is mere blindness as far as the knowledge of God is concerned. For when the Spirit calls men 'darkness' he at once denies them any ability of spiritual understanding." *Institutes*, II.2.19, OS 3:261.

71. *Institutes*, II.1.9, OS 3:239.

PART ONE—Calvin's Anthropology

> Some sparks of intelligence remain, but so far from leading any man into the way, they do not enable him to see it. Hence whatever reason and intelligence there is in us, it does not bring us into the path of obedience to God, and much less leads by continual perseverance to the gospel. What then? These very sparks shine in the darkness to render men without excuse.[72]

It is the broken relationship between God and humankind that Calvin believes to be the chief effect of the fall: "As it was the spiritual life of Adam to remain united and bound to his Maker, so estrangement from him was the death of his soul."[73] After defining Adam's fall as the result of his ingratitude to the grace of God, which endowed him with the honourable and excellent gift of His image, Calvin asserts in his commentary on Genesis 3:6 that the result of the fall is alienation from God and loss of all rectitude:

> Afterwards followed the fall of Adam, whereby he alienated himself from God; whence it came to pass that he was deprived of all rectitude. Thus Moses represents man as devoid of all good, blinded in understanding, perverse in heart, vitiated in every part, and under sentence of eternal death.[74]

The result of Adam's fall is a serious contamination of both the soul and reason of the whole human race.[75] In the same commentary, he explains the reasons for God's punishment on the human race in terms of the divine-human relationship:

> For apostasy is no light offence, but a detestable wickedness, by which man withdraws himself from the authority of his Creator, yea, even rejects and denies him. Besides, it was not a simple

---

72. *Comm. Ezek.* 11:19–20. CO 40:245.

73. *Institutes*, II.1.5; *Sicut spiritualis Adae vita erat, manere opifici suo coniunctum et devinctum; ita alienatio ab eo fuit animae interitus.* OS 3:232. Cf. *Comm. Gen.* 3:6, CO 23:47.

74. *Comm. Gen. Argument*, CO 23:12. "For truly they did exalt themselves against God, when, honour having been divinely conferred upon them, they, not contented with such excellence, desired to know more than was lawful, in order that they might become equal with God. Here also monstrous ingratitude betrays itself. They had been made in the likeness of God; but this seems a small thing unless equality be added." *Comm. Gen.* 3:6, CO 23:47.

75. "[T]hat we are also lost and condemned, and subjected to death, is both our hereditary condition, and, at the same time, a just punishment, which God, in the person of Adam, has inflicted on the human race." *Comm. Gen.* 3:6, CO 23:47.

apostasy, but combined with atrocious contumelies and reproaches against God himself.[76]

When he affirms the partial survival of the image of God with respect to ethical responsibility, Calvin does not forget to highlight the "unworthiness" of humanity for God's benevolence after the fall: "Men are indeed unworthy of God's care, if respect be had only to themselves; but since they bear the image of God engraven on them, He deems himself violated in their person."[77] Commenting on Genesis 9:6, immediately after mentioning that the survival of the *imago Dei* in humanity forms the basis of dignity of humankind, Calvin argues thus:

> Secondly, the Celestial Creator himself, however corrupted man may be, still keeps in view the end of his original creation; and according to his example, we ought to consider for what end he created men, and what excellence he has bestowed upon them above the rest of living beings.[78]

Calvin understands sin in terms of the broken relationship between God and humanity. For him, the incapacity of men to fulfil their original purpose of glorifying God is the most serious outcome of sin. This is the reason for Calvin's use of such forceful language to describe the destruction of the image of God: "Now God's image is the perfect excellence of human nature which shone in Adam before his defection, but was subsequently so vitiated and almost blotted out that nothing remains after the ruin except what is confused, mutilated, and disease-ridden."[79] Therefore, Calvin's idea of the total destruction of the image of God in men after the fall is presented in line with his focus on those relational aspects of the *imago Dei*, and he presents this focus from the teleological perspective.

---

76. *Comm. Gen.* 3:6, CO 23:47.

77. *Comm. Gen.* 9:6, CO 23:147.

78. *Comm. Gen.* 9:6, CO 23:147.

79. *Institutes*, I.15.4; *Ergo quum Dei imago sit integra naturae humanae praestantia, quae refulsit in Adam ante defectionem, postea sic vitiata et prope deleta, ut nihil ex ruina nisi confusum, mutilum, labeque infectum supersit.* OS 3:180.

Image of God in Regeneration

The Restoration of the Imago Dei

In his discussion of regeneration, just as in his discussion of the initial condition of that image in creation and its impairment in the fall, Calvin is concerned primarily with the relational rather than the structural aspects of the image.

Calvin declares, "The end of regeneration is that Christ should reform us to God's image,"[80] which "has been disfigured and all but obliterated through Adam's transgression."[81] It means that regeneration is not the ontological change of a human being into an entirely different being from his old sinful self. It is rather God's work of "reformation" of His damaged image in a sinner. Although the image of God is "all but" destroyed in humanity, his human identity does not change in regeneration. The structural aspects of the image of God, such as reason and other important faculties of the soul, remain as they had been after the fall. Hence, when Calvin defines regeneration as the restoration of the damaged *imago Dei* in humanity, he is concerned mainly with the relational aspects of the image. It is Calvin's preoccupation with the relational aspects of the *imago Dei* that enables him to call regeneration the "second creation" even though he does not consider regeneration in terms of the creation of another human self within a humanity: "There is, no doubt, a far more rich and powerful manifestation of Divine grace in this second creation than in the first."[82] Calvin prefers this biblical notion of a "second creation" because he can use it to emphasise the awesome nature of the restoration of the *imago Dei* in humanity. For Calvin, these are the two highly remarkable aspects of the image of God which are wonderfully restored by God's grace of regeneration: God's original purpose in the creation of humankind; and the divine-human relationship.

To begin with, Calvin thinks of the restoration of the image of God in terms of the recovery of God's original purpose in creating human beings, that is, to reflect the glory of God. This is clearly stated in his interpretations of the concept of "the new man" in the Pauline epistles. For example,

---

80. *Institutes*, I.15.4, OS 3:179. "The regeneration of the godly is indeed—as we have formerly explained—nothing else that the formation anew (*reformatio*) of the image of God in them." *Comm. Eph.* 4:24, CO 51:208.

81. *Institutes*, III.3.9, *imago Dei quae per Adae transgressionem foedata, et tantum non obliterata fuerat, in nobis reformetur.* OS 4:63.

82. *Comm. Eph.* 4:24, CO 51:208.

Calvin interprets "put on the new man" in Ephesians 4:24 as pointing to the recovery of the original purpose of humankind:

> Adam was at first created after the image of God, and reflected [in order to reflect], as in a mirror, the Divine righteousness; but that image, having been defaced [deleted] by sin, must now be restored in Christ . . . The design contemplated by regeneration is to recall us from our wandering to that end for which we were created.[83]

Calvin also mentions this original purpose in his interpretation of "new creation of our knowledge" in Colossians 3:10:

> Hence, too, we learn, on the one hand, what is the end of our regeneration, that is, that we may be made like God, and that his glory may shine forth in us; and, on the other hand, what is the image of God, of which mention is made by Moses in *Genesis* 9:6, the rectitude and integrity of the whole soul, so that man reflects, like a mirror, the wisdom, righteousness, and goodness of God.[84]

In the *Institutes*, III, in which we find Calvin's fullest discussion of regeneration, there is no discussion about the newly restored capability of human reason by regeneration. Instead, Calvin stresses the ongoing necessity for the Spirit to illuminate Christian faith and knowledge due to human dullness:

> Indeed, the Word of God is like the sun, shining upon all those to whom it is proclaimed, but with no effect among the blind. Now, all of us are blind by nature in this respect. Accordingly, it cannot penetrate into our minds unless the Spirit, as the inner teacher, through his illumination makes entry for it.[85]

Throughout his discussion of regeneration in the *Institutes*, Calvin shows little interest in the upgraded moral capability of the human self. Instead, concerning the holiness obtained by believers in the course of regeneration, he speaks consistently of the Spirit leading the Christian life and of the Christian obligations of humility and repentance: "But even while by the leading of the Holy Spirit we walk in the ways of the Lord; to keep us

---

83. *Comm. Eph.* 4:24; *Nam et initio creatus fuit Adam ad imaginem Dei, ut iustitiam Dei quasi in speculo repraesentaret. Sed quoniam imago illa deleta est per peccatum, ideo nunc in Christo instaurari oportet . . . Quare huc spectare docet regenerationem, ut ex errore reducamur ad eum finem ad quem sumus conditi.* CO 51:208-9.

84. *Comm. Col.* 3:10, CO 52:121.

85. *Institutes*, III.2.34, OS 4:45.

PART ONE—Calvin's Anthropology

from forgetting ourselves and becoming puffed up, traces of our imperfection remain to give us occasion for humility."[86] This all provides evidence of the consistency of Calvin's teleological perspective in his discussion of the *imago Dei* in the stage of regeneration: Calvin concentrates more on the restoration of the original purpose, part of the relational aspects by grace, than on any enhanced quality of the structural aspects of the *imago Dei* that might appear during the course of regeneration. In the *Institutes*, Calvin declares conclusively that "the object of regeneration" is "to manifest in the life of believers a harmony and agreement between God's righteousness and their obedience, and thus to confirm the adoption that they have received as sons."[87]

The Importance of Regeneration for the Knowledge of Man

In Calvin's anthropology, knowledge of ourselves relies on the knowledge of the original condition of humanity in creation and his impaired condition after the fall: "But knowledge of ourselves lies first in considering what we were given at creation and how generously God continues his favor toward us . . . Secondly, to call to mind our miserable condition after Adam's fall."[88] Calvin then argues that knowledge of the condition of the image in creation and after the fall becomes nothing unless humanity grasps the knowledge of the restoration of the image of God: "this principle cannot be overthrown, that what was primary in the renewing of God's image also held the highest place in the creation itself."[89] Calvin notes Paul's idea that the *imago Dei* in the stage of creation consists of "sound knowledge" and "pure righteousness and holiness."[90] However, he also notes that Scripture relates these virtues to the *imago Dei* in creation because they are the most

---

86. *Institutes*, III.14.9, OS 4:49. For commentary on the Spirit and the necessity of repentance, see, *Institutes*, III.2.39, OS 4:49; III.3.15, OS 4:71; III.6.2, OS 4:147. For commentary on commentary on good works and the power of the Spirit, see, *Institutes*, III.11.5, OS 4:180; III.11.15, OS 4:199.

87. *Institutes*, III.6.1; *Scopum regenerationis esse diximus ut in vita fidelium appareat inter Dei iustitiam et eorum obsequium symmetria et consensus: atque ita adoptionem confirment qua recepti sunt in filios.* OS 4:146. "It is, however, made perfect when, resembling their Heavenly Father in righteousness and holiness, they prove themselves sons true to their nature." *Institutes*, III.18.1, OS 4:271.

88. *Institutes*, II.1.1, OS 3:228.

89. *Institutes*, I.15.4, OS 3:179.

90. *Comm. Gen.* 1:26, CO 23:26. *Institutes*, I.15.4, OS 3:180; III.3.9, OS 4:63.

significant things to be restored by God's grace of regeneration. He argues that, because "the image of God has been destroyed in us by the fall, we may judge from its restoration what it originally has been."[91] Thus, humanity can have knowledge of the image of God after the fall only through Scripture's teaching about its restoration:

> The whole third chapter of Romans is nothing but a description of original sin. From the "renewal" that fact appears more clearly. For the Spirit, who is opposed to the old man and to the flesh, not only marks the grace whereby the lower or sensual part of the soul is corrected, but embraces the full reformation of all the parts.[92]

Calvin concentrates on the relational aspects, those things that are restored by God's grace of regeneration and states:

> Therefore, even though we grant that God's image was not totally annihilated and destroyed in him, yet it was so corrupted that whatever remains is frightful deformity. Consequently, the beginning of our recovery of salvation is in that restoration which we obtain through Christ, who also is called the Second Adam for the reason that he restores us to true and complete integrity.[93]

He pays attention to those relational aspects of the *imago Dei*, using forceful language, to describe the effect of the fall on the image of God in order, ultimately, to highlight God's grace shown through regeneration. In his anthropology, although some vestiges of the image of God remain after the fall—enough to secure human dignity and to provide the basis for ethical responsibility—the significance of this partial survival is secondary and minor point when compared to his primary and focal point of God's grace of regeneration.

---

91. *Comm. Gen.* 1:26, CO 23:26. However, Calvin does not explicitly follow Luther's argument that the knowledge of the original condition of the *imago Dei* became impossible after the destruction of the image by the fall because this destruction implies the total loss of the knowledge before the fall. Luther, *Lectures on Genesis* 1:26, WA 42:41ff. For Luther's understanding of the *imago Dei*, see Cairn, *Imago Dei*, 115–27.

92. *Institutes*, II.1.9, OS 3:239.

93. *Institutes*, I.15.4, OS 3:180.

Conclusion: Focus on Regeneration in Calvin's Anthropology

Through examination of Calvin's idea of the image of God in the *Institutes* and the *Commentary on Genesis*, two particular points emerge. Firstly, although the structural aspects of the image of God have a place in his anthropology, Calvin concentrates more on the relational aspects from his teleological perspective. For him, the original purpose of the image of God, to shine forth His glory, is the most important theme to be treated in his discussion of the image of God. Secondly, Calvin presents his anthropology within the context of salvation history and considers that God's grace of regeneration provides the proper perspective through which one can properly understand the condition of humanity in creation and after the fall.

It is not only Calvin's discussion of the image of God, but also his entire anthropology, that focuses on the regenerative grace of God, which restores the relationship between God and humanity. Calvin's comment on Genesis 1:27 summarises this focus thus:

> The reiterated mention of the image of God is not a vain repetition. For it is a remarkable instance of the Divine goodness which can never be sufficiently proclaimed. And, at the same time, he [Moses] admonishes us from what excellence *we have fallen*, that he may excite in us the desire of its *recovery*.[94]

Calvin's teleological perspective and his focus on the restoration of the image of God should enable us to see his anthropology neither as static analysis nor as philosophical speculation about human beings but as theological anthropology that tries to offer an explanation of the dynamics of the Christian self in a redeeming relationship with God.[95]

---

94. *Comm. Gen.* 1:27, CO 23:28.

95. Suggesting the inter-relational operation between the absolute perspective of God and the relative perspective of humankind in Calvin's thought, Engel argues that the "dynamic" character of Calvin's anthropology is a result of the perspective of God as creator: "From the absolute perspective of God as *creator*, the *imago Dei* appears as a dynamic relation with the Source of all being; it is nothing unless it receives the gift of being every moment in this relationship." Engel, *Calvin's Perspectival Anthropology*, 54. Grenz also finds the "dynamic" character of Calvin's anthropology in his idea of the image of God as "the mirror" of God: "In drawing out his central metaphor, Calvin emphasizes the dynamic aspect of the *imago Dei*, the divine image consists of the actual act of mirroring God." Grenz, *Social God and the Relational Self*, 166–70.

2

The Grace of the Trinity as the Foundation of Christian Identity

Introduction: Christian Identity in Calvin's Anthropology

THIS CHAPTER WILL EXAMINE CALVIN'S ATTEMPT TO HIGHLIGHT THE RE-lationship between Christians and Christ as the foundation of Christian identity. Who are Christians? Calvin's answer to this simple but important anthropological question is that Christians are "the children of God" who can call God their father: "It is the most necessary to fix in our minds this doctrine of Paul, that no man is a Christian who has not learned, by the teaching of the Holy Spirit, to call God his Father."[1] Calvin thinks that Christians obtain this filial identity through the grace of God alone:

> God designates as his children those whom he has chosen, and appoints himself their Father. Further, by calling, he receives them into his family and unites them to him so that they may together be one. But when the call is coupled with election, in this way Scripture sufficiently suggests that in it nothing but God's free mercy is to be sought.[2]

The definition of Christians as "children" or "youth" is significant for Calvin's anthropology because he highlights both Christians' present imperfection and continuous progress in the life of regeneration by this definition:

---

1. *Comm. Gal.* 4:6, CO 50:228. In the *Institutes* [1559], Calvin frequently identifies Christians with "the children of God." *Institutes*, I.9.1, 9.3, 14.18, 14.19; II.6.1, 7.8, 7.9, 7.10, 8.59, 9.3, 10.11, 10.14, 10.22, 12.2, 12.7, 13.2; III.1.4, 2.11, 2.12, 2.13, 2.30, 2.39, 3.20, 3.11, 3.14, 4.27, 4.34, 4.34, 9.5, 13.4, 17.6, 20.10, 20.36, 20.39, 20.43, 20.44, 24.9, 25.5, 25.9, 25.11; IV.1.7, 1.15, 2.3, 13.6, 15.6, 15.22, 16.30.

2. *Institutes*, III.24.1, OS 4:411.

PART ONE—Calvin's Anthropology

"the life of believers, marked by a constant desire and progress towards those attainments which they shall ultimately reach, bears a resemblance to youth."[3] However, Calvin's identification of Christians with the children of God has not received the attention it deserves in studies of his anthropology.[4] To shed light on the significance of this topic which has received insufficient treatment, I will first investigate Calvin's idea of the Christian's "divided self" in regeneration by examining his interpretation of Romans 7:14–25. This investigation will show that Calvin lays particular emphasis on the spiritual struggle in Christian's divided self, and tries to show that Christians cannot find the foundation of their identity as children of God in themselves. Following this will be an investigation of Calvin's idea of union with Christ in his soteriology in order to show that he seeks the foundation of the identity of Christians in the relationship between Christ and Christians, instead of Christian's humanity. Finally, I will examine the trinitarian perspective in Calvin's idea of union with Christ to argue that Calvin understands Christian identity in the light of the grace of the triune God. This examination will provide us with a proper view to understand Calvin's anthropology. Moreover, an observation of Calvin's trinitarian perspective enables us to find theological connection between Calvin's anthropology and his ecclesiology, which will be discussed in the next part of this study.

Christian Identity and the Divided Self

The Christian Struggle

Calvin maintains that the inner struggle between two divided parts of the Christian heart tends to make it difficult for believers to remain confident of their identity as children of God:

---

3. *Comm. Eph.* 4:14; *Ita fidelium vita, quae assiduo profectu ad statum suum gradum adspirat, adulescentiae similis est.* CO 51:201.

4. In their studies of Calvin's anthropology both Torrance and Engel barely deal with the topic of Christians' identity as children of God or with the grace of adoption. Niesel, Wendel and Leith also ignore this fundamental anthropological topic in their classic studies of Calvin's theology. Only Gerrish's monograph deals briefly with Calvin's idea of the identity of Christians as the adopted sons of God. Gerrish, *Grace and Gratitude*. However, there are some article-length studies on this topic, which deal mainly with Calvin's doctrine of adoption. Ferguson, "The Reformed Doctrine of Sonship," 81–88; Westhead, "Adoption in the Thought of John Calvin," 102–15; Griffith, "The First Title of the Spirit," 135–53.

> Therefore the godly heart feels in itself a division because it is partly imbued with sweetness from its recognition of the divine goodness, partly grieves in bitterness from an awareness of its calamity; partly rests upon the promise of the gospel, partly trembles at the evidence of its own iniquity; partly rejoices at the expectation of life, partly shudders at death. This variation arises from imperfection of faith, since in the course of the present life it never goes so well with us that we are wholly cured of the disease of unbelief and entirely filled and possessed by faith.[5]

According to Calvin, however, this struggle is itself a characteristic of Christian identity because it "does not exist in man before he is renewed by the Spirit of God." This means that no Christian is free from this struggle.[6] Accordingly, he adopts Augustine's term "the Christian struggle" to explain this: "Here we see what sort of division there is in the pious soul, from which arises that contest between the spirit and the flesh, which Augustine in some place calls the Christian struggle."[7] Unbelievers are also "tormented by the stings of conscience" and have "some taste of bitterness" in their vices. Yet, this torment proceeds "from the opposition in the judgment, rather than from any contrary inclination in the will." In contrast, a regenerate man struggles with a "feeling of genuine repugnance," which does not arise from human nature but from the Spirit.[8]

In presenting this idea of "Christian struggle," Calvin appeals largely to the concept of the two conflicting laws in Romans 7:14–25, in which he sees a biblical account of the believer's condition in regeneration:

> We may hence learn the truth of what we have stated—that Paul speaks here of the faithful, in whom the grace of the Spirit exists, which brings an agreement between the mind and the righteousness of the law; for no hatred of sin is to be found in the flesh.[9]

---

5. *Institutes*, III.3.18, OS 4:75.

6. "Though the will of a faithful man is led to good by the Spirit of God, yet in him the corruption of nature appears conspicuously; for it obstinately resists and leads to what is contrary." *Comm. Rom.* 7:15, CO 49:129.

7. *Comm. Rom.* 7:22, CO 49:133. Cf. *Institutes*, II.2.27, OS 3:270.

8. *Comm. Rom.* 7:15, CO 49:130. "This [spiritual struggle] refers, unquestionably, to the regenerate. Carnal men have no battle with depraved lusts, no proper desire to attain to the righteousness of God. Paul is addressing believers." *Comm. Gal.* 5:17; CO 50:253.

9. *Comm. Rom.* 7:15; *Hinc vero colligere licet quod diximus, Paulum hic de fidelibus disserere, in quibus viget aliqua spiritus gratia, quae illustret sanae mentis consensum cum iustitia legis: quia in carnem non cadit peccati odium.* CO 49:131. Calvin argues that, for a time, Augustine misunderstood this passage as the description of the human condition

PART ONE—Calvin's Anthropology

The Christian struggle, Calvin argues, comes about because of the division between the spirit and the flesh in the Christian self:

> The godly . . . in whom the regeneration of God is begun, are so divided, that with the chief desire of the heart they aspire to God, seek celestial righteousness, hate sin, and yet they are drawn down to the earth by the relics of their flesh: and thus while pulled in two ways they fight against their own nature, and nature fights against them. And they condemn their sins, not only as being constrained by the judgement of reason, but because they really in their hearts abominate them, and on their account loathe themselves. This is the Christian conflict between the flesh and the spirit, of which Paul speaks in Galatians 5:17.[10]

Calvin's observation of the Christian struggle in Romans 7:14–25 is not original. Prior to Calvin, other reformers and Roman Catholic exegetes had interpreted it as the description of the believer's condition, and Calvin himself was well aware of this. Stephens argues that Bucer, especially, observes within this passage the notion of the reality of sin remaining in Christians after justification.[11] Bucer's focus on the reality of sin in Christians probably influenced Calvin's interpretation of Romans 7:14–25. But Calvin takes a somewhat different position in interpreting Romans 7 to the other leading reformers. In the first place, this passage is one of his best occasions to present a discussion about Christian identity. As Steinmetz demonstrates, while Luther finds "an opportunity to talk about justification" in Romans 7,

---

before grace. Holder suggests that Calvin's interpretation of this passage is one of the cases of his "transformation" of the Augustinian interpretation of *Romans*. Holder, *John Calvin and the Grounding of Interpretation*, 228–29.

10. *Comm. Rom.* 7:15; *Pii contra, in quibus coepta est Dei regeneratio, sic divisi sunt, ut praecipuo cordis desiderio ad Deum suspirent, coelestem iustitiam expetant, peccatum oderint: sed rursum carnis suae reliquiis in terram retrahantur. Itaque, dum sic distrahuntur, vim ipsi naturae suae faciunt, et sibi fieri ab ipsa sentiunt. Neque iudicio rationis tantum coacti peccata sua damnant: sed quia serio cordis affectu ea abominantur, et in iis sibi displicent. Haec est lucta christiana, de qua Paulus ad Galatias (5, 17) loquitur, inter carnem et spiritum.* CO 49:129–30.

11. Stephens argues that, "if the reality of sin is less strong for Bucer than for Luther, he is, nevertheless, aware that the saints on earth are never without sin." Stephens, quoting Bucer's commentary on Romans, also argues that, "Bucer's use of the word flesh is ambiguous, as indeed the biblical use is. Sometimes it is used in the sense of man's living in the flesh or in the body, sometimes of man's being sinful, of his living according to his flesh. The opposition of flesh and Spirit is primarily the opposition of man's sinful nature to the Holy Spirit." Stephens, *Holy Spirit in the Theology of Martin Bucer*, 81–82.

The Grace of the Trinity as the Foundation of Christian Identity

Calvin uses this passage as "an occasion to discuss anthropology."[12] Calvin also has a different focus to Melanchthon.[13] Both reformers basically agree in understanding that Romans 7:14-25 is the teaching about the Law and that this teaching is based on the apostle's personal experience. But it is more important to Calvin than it is to Melanchthon to find "an example in a regenerate man" within this passage.[14] In Muller's terms, while Melanchthon focuses on "the personal fervour of the apostolic rhetoric," Calvin finds "a general portrait of the already-regenerate person" within this passage.[15] That Calvin finds an occasion to discuss an anthropological matter in this passage is also obviously different from the interpretations of Bullinger and Oecolampadius who deal mainly with the matter of the Law here.[16]

12. Steinmetz, *Calvin in Context*, 118. Although he does not develop as full an anthropological discussion as Calvin does, Luther notes in his commentary that Romans 7:14-25 shows the identity of the Christian to be "at the same time a sinner and a righteous man": *Ideo simul peccator et iustus, quia facio malum et odio malum, quod facio.* WA 56:70.

13. In the dedicatory letter to Simon Grynaeus, Calvin mentions his predecessors, Melanchthon, Bullinger and Bucer as having produced the most outstanding interpretations of this epistle. CO 10:402. Two significant editions of Melanchthon's commentary on *Romans*, which might have influenced Calvin's commentary, are edited as *Commentarii in Epistolam Pauli ad Romanos* (1540) in CR 15:493-796, and as *Enarratio Epistolae Pauli ad Romanos* (1556) in CR 15:779-1052. For information about Melanchthon's commentary on *Romans*, see Wengert, "The Biblical Commentaries of Philip Melanchthon," 133-39. For further information on the textual history of Calvin's commentary on *Romans*, see Girardin, *Rhétorique et théologique*; Parker, *Commentaries on the Epistle to the Romans 1532-1542*; and Parker, *Calvin's New Testament Commentaries*, 6-35.

14. However, the difference between Melanchthon and Calvin is not about the contents of this passage, which is about the inward struggle of the Christian with regard to the Law of God, but about the particular emphases within it. Calvin's comment on Romans 7:8 argues, "It is general truth, which he [Paul] presently applies to his own case. I hence wonder what could have come into the minds of interpreters to render the passage in the preterimperfect (*praeterito imperfecto*) tense, as though Paul was speaking of himself; for it is easy to see that his purpose was to begin with a general proposition, and then to explain the subject by his own example." *Comm. Rom.* 7:8, CO 49:125.

15. Muller, "'*Scimus enim quod lex spiritualis est*,'" 231-32. For an English translation of Melanchthon's commentary on *Romans*, see Melanchthon, *Commentary on Romans*.

16. Kok compares Bullinger's commentary on *Romans* with that of Calvin and argues that "it is too much to say that Bullinger is Calvin's model" because of the theological difference between the two reformers' interpretations, especially their different attitudes to the philosophers." Kok, "Heinrich Bullinger's Exegetical Method," 252-53. Akira Demura, in his comparative study of Oecolampadius's commentary on *Romans* and Calvin's, notes the similarity between the two reformers' interpretations concerning the use of the Law and the identification of the "ego" as the apostle himself. Demura, "Two Commentaries on the Epistle to the Romans," 175-80.

PART ONE—Calvin's Anthropology

Calvin summarises the general anthropological theme of his interpretation of Romans 7:14–25 as follows: "Man, thus impelled by contrary desires, is now in a manner a twofold being."[17] For him, "the divided self" described in the Pauline epistles is the Christian self during the course of regeneration: "The spiritual life will not be maintained without a struggle. We are here informed of the nature of the difficulty, which arises from our natural inclinations being opposed to the Spirit."[18] Therefore, it is inevitable that Christians will be continuously challenged with respect to their assurance of faith and the certainty of their identity because of the spiritual struggle in their divided self.

The "Old Man" in the Christian

In analysing the Christian identity in regeneration, Calvin often uses the Pauline concept of a spiritual battle between the old man and the "inner man" or the "new man," which appears in Ephesians 4:22. He defines the "old man" as the sinful human nature which remains in the Christian, and the "new man" as the new spiritual nature bestowed on the Christian by God's regenerative grace:

> In two persons, Adam and Christ, he [Paul] describes to us what may be called two natures. As we are first born of Adam, the depravity of nature which we derive from him is called the old man; and as we are born again in Christ, the amendment of this sinful nature is called the new man.[19]

In Paul's description of the old and the new man, Calvin perceives the reality of the spiritual struggle in the Christian self, which is not merely a conflict between two temperamental inclinations. When interpreting the contrast between the desire of "the inner man or mind" and "the law of the members" in Romans 7:14–25, Calvin identifies these two conflicting sides with "the spirit" and "the flesh": "The inner man then is not simply the soul, but that spiritual part which has been regenerated by God; and the members signify the other remaining part."[20]

17. *Comm. Rom.* 7:22, *Homo ita variis voluntatibus distractus iam quodammodo duplex est.* CO 49:133.

18. *Comm. Gal.* 5:17, CO 50:253.

19. *Comm. Eph.* 4:22, CO 51:207.

20. *Comm. Rom.* 7:22; *Interior igitur homo non anima simpliciter dicitur, sed spiritualis eius pars quae a Deo regenerata est: membrorum vocabulum residuam alteram partem*

The Grace of the Trinity as the Foundation of Christian Identity

Calvin's turn of phrase can sometimes cause confusion among scholars about his understanding of this division. Above all, his description of the body as the "prison house" has been regarded to imply a Platonic dualism. Calvin, however, argues thus:

> Accordingly, so long as we dwell in the prison house of our body we must continually contend with the defects of our corrupt nature, indeed with our own natural soul. Plato sometimes says that the life of a philosopher is a meditation upon death.[21]

Despite his Platonic turn of phrase, however, Calvin is consistent in his view that "the flesh" does not mean the bodily form alone prior to regeneration, but the whole human being, both body and soul: "I have already reminded you that the word *body* is not to be taken for flesh, and skin, and bones, but, so to speak, for the whole of what man is."[22] As we have seen in the previous chapter, Calvin speaks of the soul as the nobler side of humanity than the body. But in regarding the dignity of humanity created after the *imago Dei*, he does not denigrate the body: "Although the primary seat of the divine image was in the mind and heart, or in the soul and its power, yet there was no part of man, not even the body itself, in which some sparks did not glow."[23] Calvin finds the cause of original sin, and thus the condition of humanity after the fall, not in appetite or desire but in disobedience. And disobedience can be included in the sphere of the will, one of the major faculties of the soul:

> Since the woman through unfaithfulness was led away from God's Word by the serpent's deceit, it is already clear that disobedience was the beginning of the Fall. This Paul also confirms, teaching

---

significat. CO 49:133–34. For Calvin, the term "the external man" denotes the same thing as the terms "the flesh," "the body" and "the members": "But the word 'body' means the same as the external man and members; for Paul points out this as the origin of evil, that man has departed from the law of his creation, and has become thus carnal and earthly." *Comm. Rom.* 7:24, CO 49:135.

21. *Institutes*, III.3.20, OS 4:77. In the *Institutes* alone, the Platonic metaphor of "prison" for the body occurs eleven times: *Institutes*, I.15.2, II.7.13, 13.4, III.3.20, 6.5, 9.4, 25.1, IV.1.1, 15.11, 16.19, 17.30.

22. *Comm. Rom.* 6:12, CO 49:111. For discussion of the difference between Platonic dualism and Calvin's understanding of the soul and the body, see Torrance, *Calvin's Doctrine of Man*, 116–27, Partee, *Calvin and the Classical Philosophy*, 51–65, and Engel, *John Calvin's Perspectival Anthropology*, 161–75.

23. *Institutes*, I.15.3, OS 3:178. Cf. *Institutes*, I.15.1, OS 3:173.

PART ONE—Calvin's Anthropology

that all were lost through the disobedience of one man (Rom. 5:19).[24]

Calvin believes that after the fall, sin defiles not only the body but also the whole of human nature: "whatever in man, from the understanding to the will, from the soul even to the flesh, has been defiled and crammed with this concupiscence."[25] Consequently, as the whole human being, both body and soul, is damaged by sin, so both parts need to be reformed in the course of regeneration: "Hence it follows that there is nothing in us that is not sinful; for if reformation is necessary in the whole and in each part, corruption must have been spread throughout."[26] Moreover, Calvin's view of the body differs from Plato's in its emphasis on the resurrection: "It is difficult to believe that bodies, when consumed with rottenness, will at length be raised up in their season. Therefore, although many of philosophers declared souls immortal, few approved the resurrection of the flesh."[27] Therefore, it is apparent that Calvin does not think of the "old man" or the "flesh" as merely the bodily substance of human beings like Platonic ideas.

For Calvin, the "old man" is the sinfulness which remains in Christians: "By the body of death he [Paul] means the whole mass of sin, or those ingredients of which the whole man is composed."[28] Calvin claims that the "old man" in Romans 6:6, which equates to the "members" and "body of death" of Romans 7, indicates corrupt human nature, "which we bring from the womb, and which is so incapable of the kingdom of God that it must so far die as we are renewed to new life."[29] He declares that everything that comes from corrupt human nature is sin: "we teach that all human desires are evil, and charge them with sin not in that they are

---

24. *Institutes*, II.1.4, OS 3:231.

25. *Institutes*, II.1.8, OS 3:237.

26. *Comm. John* 3:3, CO 47:63.

27. *Institutes*, III.25.3, OS 4:434. Partee notes the three convictions of Calvin, which distinguish his anthropology from that of Platonism: the immortality of the body before sin, the dependence of the immortality of the soul on God's grace and the resurrection of the body. Partee, *Calvin and the Classical Philosophy*, 62–65.

28. *Comm. Rom.* 7:24; *Corpus mortis vocat massam peccati, vel congeriem, ex qua totus homo conflates est.* CO 49:134. "Under the term flesh is included whatever men bring from the womb; and flesh is what men are called, as they are born, and as long as they retain their natural character; for as they are corrupt, so they neither taste nor desire anything but what is gross and earthly." *Comm. Rom.* 7:14, CO 49:128.

29. *Comm. Rom.* 6:6, CO 49:107. "The old man means the natural disposition which we bring with us from our mother's womb." *Comm. Eph.* 4:22, CO 51:207.

natural, but because they are inordinate. Moreover, we hold that they are inordinate because nothing pure or sincere can come forth from a corrupt and polluted nature."[30] For Calvin, although sin loses its ruling power over Christians after justification, some vestiges of sin, which is called "the old man," still dwell within them and trouble their consciousness:

> But sin ceases only to reign; it does not also cease to dwell in them. Accordingly, we say that the old man was so crucified (Romans 6:6), and the law of sin so abolished in the children of God, that some vestiges remain; not to rule over them, but to humble them by the consciousness of their own weakness.[31]

Calvin's idea of the "old man," therefore, implies that for as long as children of God stay in this world—before putting off the prison of the body—they have to confront the reality of sin remaining within them.

The "New Man" in the Christian

In Calvin's anthropology, while the "old man" represents the sin that remains within Christians, "the heart and the secret feeling" of the "new man," which is interchangeably used with the "inner man" or the "spirit" in his writings, indicate the newly regenerated part of the Christian self through God's regenerative grace.[32] In his commentary on Romans 7:22, Calvin argues that "the inner man" is superior to the "members" or the "old man" because of its excellent qualities: "it is called the inner man by way of excellency, for it possesses the heart and the secret feelings, while the desires of the flesh are vagrant, and are, as it were, on the outside of man."[33] However, the superiority of the "inner man" to the "members" does not mean the platonic view that the soul is superior to the body by nature. Calvin argues that in Scripture the "spirit" does not refer to the soul itself, but to the regenerated part of the Christian self: "Spirit, on the contrary, is the

---

30. *Institutes*, III.3.12; *Aut omnes hominum cupiditates malas esse docemus, et peccati reas peragimus: non quatenus sunt naturales, sed quia inordinatae: inordinatas autem esse, quia ex natura corrupta et polluta nihil puri et synceri prodire potest*. OS 4:68.

31. *Institutes*, III.3.11; *sed regnare tantum, non etiam habitare desinit. Proinde sic dicimus veterem hominem crucifixum esse, legem peccati sic abolitam esse in filiis Dei, ut reliquiae tamen supersint [Rom. 6 a. 6]: non ut dominentur, sed ut eos suae infirmitatis conscientia humilient.* OS 4:66.

32. *Comm. Eph.* 4:22, CO 51:207. See note 20 above.

33. *Comm. Rom.* 7:22, CO 49:134.

renewal of the nature, when God forms us anew after his own image."[34] In the Christian self, no part of "the spirit" is out of regeneration, it is only "the flesh" which needs regeneration: "The Spirit is so contrasted with flesh that no intermediate thing is left. Accordingly, whatever is not spiritual in man is by this reckoning called "carnal." We have nothing of the Spirit, however, except through regeneration."[35] Therefore, in his commentary on the will of the "spirit" in Romans 7:18, Calvin argues, "This [the will of the 'spirit'] . . . is the readiness of faith, when the Holy Spirit so prepares the godly that they are ready and strive to render obedience to God."[36]

The creation and sustenance of the "new man" within a Christian is impossible without regeneration through God's grace. Calvin's interpretation of the Pauline concept of the "new man," which appears in Ephesians 4:24 and Colossians 3:10, is argued thus: "we are restored by this regeneration through the benefit of Christ into the righteousness of God; from which we had fallen through Adam. In this way it pleases the Lord fully to restore whomsoever he adopts into the inheritance of life."[37] Because inner renewal depends on God's regenerative grace, the entire identity of the Christian is shown to be similarly dependent. It implies that Christians cannot overcome their sinful nature by their natural capabilities. Without the grace of God, not even faith (or what might look like faith) can assure the Christian of his identity as a child of God:

> We seek a faith that distinguishes the children of God from the wicked, and believers from unbelievers. If someone believes that God both justly commands all that he commands and truly threatens, shall he therefore be called a believer? By no means! Therefore, there can be no firm condition of faith unless it rests upon God's mercy.[38]

Christian Identity and Union with Christ

In pointing out the dependent nature of the identity of Christians as children of God, Calvin seeks a secure foundation for this identity by looking

---

34. *Comm. Rom.* 7:14; *Spiritus contra corruptae naturae instauratio vocatur, dum nos Deus ad imaginem suam reformat.* CO 49:128.

35. *Institutes*, II.3.1, OS 3:272.

36. *Comm. Rom.* 7:18, CO 49:132.

37. *Institutes*, III.3.9, OS 4:63.

38. *Institutes*, III.2.30, OS 4:40.

The Grace of the Trinity as the Foundation of Christian Identity

at the divine-human relationship in which God regenerates Christians through Christ's redemptive grace. As many scholars have pointed out, "union with Christ" is the key to understanding Calvin's idea of this divine-human relationship.[39] Calvin defines union with Christ as follows:

> That joining together of Head and members, that indwelling of Christ in our hearts—in short, that mystical union– are accorded by us the highest degree of importance, so that Christ, having been made ours, makes us sharers with him in the gifts with which he has been endowed.[40]

The importance of the concept of "union with Christ" in Calvin's theology is evident if we consider the frequency of the appearance of this idea in his writings. The terms "union" and "communion," used interchangeably in Calvin's writings, occur more than forty times in the *Institutes* (1559), more than any other terms used to describe the divine-human relationship.[41] Furthermore, this concept plays an important role in Calvin's attempt to base Christian identity upon the secure foundation of God's grace, given to them through the distinct, but inseparable relationship between the two dimensions of their salvation: justification and regeneration.

---

39. Partee suggests "union with Christ" as "a useful and comprehensive way of introducing and surveying Calvin's theology." Partee, "Calvin's Central Dogma Again," 191–99. Tamburello presents a useful study on this theme by comparing Calvin's idea of union with Christ with that of St. Bernard. Tamburello, *Union with Christ*, 84–101.

40. *Institutes*, III.11.10, OS 4:191.

41. The term "communion" is used with the same meaning as "union": *Institutes*, IV.1.10; III.6.2, 14.4, 15.1, 17.8, 20.24, 25.6; IV.1.3, 1.5, 1.20, 1.22, 15.15, 20.2. The second most frequent expression concerning the divine-human relationship in his writings is "engrafting"(*inserere*), which will be dealt with in chapter 5 of this study: *Institutes*, III.2.24, 2.35, 3.20, 6.3, 14.6, 17.10, 22.7, 24.5; IV.15.5, 15.6. Calvin uses the term "partaking"(*participes*) to relate Christians to the benefits of Christ in *Institutes*, III.2.24, 11.23, 15.5; IV.15.6; 16.17, 17.5, 17.8. The term "fellowship" is used to describe the relationship mainly when dealing with sacraments and unity of the church: *Institutes*, I.14.14; II.8.33; III.8.1, 11.20; IV.6.2, 6.7, 15.6. The other important terms used by Calvin to explain the relationship between the believer and Christ are "putting on"(*induere*), "indwelling"(*habitatio*) and "spiritual marriage"(*spiritum coniugium*): *Institutes*, II.12.7; III.1.1, 2.24; IV.17.5, 19.35. Also see Tamburello's list in Tamburello, *Union with Christ*, 111–13.

PART ONE—Calvin's Anthropology

The Distinction between Justification and Regeneration

According to Calvin, the grace of God, which sustains Christian identity, is conferred only through the mystical union between Christ and Christians: "we are taught by Scripture to perceive that apart from Christ, God is, so to speak, hostile to us, and his hand is armed for our destruction; to embrace his benevolence and fatherly love in Christ alone."[42] When discussing the benefits of the relationship between Christians and Christ, Calvin draws attention to the two dimensions of salvation: reconciliation, the principal result of justification; and sanctification or regeneration:

> By partaking of him [Christ], we principally receive a double grace: namely, that being reconciled to God through Christ's blamelessness, we may have in heaven instead of a Judge a gracious Father; and secondly, that sanctified by Christ's spirit we may cultivate blamelessness and purity of life.[43]

Richard aptly comments on the distinction between justification and regeneration, saying that for Calvin justification "is the imputation of righteousness" and regeneration "is the process of continual struggle on the part of man with the assistance of the Holy Spirit toward the restoration of the image of God."[44]

Besides referring to the distinct nature and purposes of justification and regeneration, Calvin notes the different manners by which grace is conferred for these two dimensions in order to find a secure foundation for the filial identity of Christians, through their relationship with Christ. On the one hand, the grace of justification is given in an instantaneous

---

42. *Institutes*, II.16.2, OS 3:483.

43. *Institutes*, III.11.1, OS 4:182. Cf. "Christ lives in us in two ways. The one life consists in governing us by his Spirit and directing all our actions; the other, in making us partakers of his righteousness; so that, while we can do nothing of ourselves, we are accepted in the sight of God. The first relates to regeneration, the second to justification by free grace." *Comm. Gal.* 2:20, CO 50:199; *Comm. Rom.* 8:13, CO 47:147; *Comm. 1 Cor.* 1:30, CO 50:331. There is no sharp distinction between "regeneration" and "sanctification" in Calvin's theology. But I will use the term "regeneration" in this study because it shows more efficiently Calvin's idea of salvation as being the restoration of the original purpose of the *imago Dei* in man.

44. Richard, *Spirituality of John Calvin*, 106–8. For the relationship between justification and regeneration or sanctification in Calvin's theology, see Boisset, "Justification et sanctification chez Calvin"; McGrath, *Iustitia Dei*, 253–58; and Lane, *Justification by Faith in Catholic-Protestant Dialogue*, 17–43. Torrance's study succinctly points out this contrast in Calvin's anthropology. Torrance, *Calvin's Doctrine of Man*, 75–82.

way when God freely reckons a sinner to be righteous. Following Luther's forensic idea of justification, Calvin defines justification as "the acceptance with which God receives us into his favor as righteous men. And we say that it consists in the remission of sins and the imputation of Christ's righteousness."[45] The grace of regeneration, on the other hand, is conferred gradually throughout life in order to work towards the perfect restoration of the *imago Dei*: "The closer any man comes to the likeness of God, the more the image of God shines in him. In order that believers may reach this goal, God assigns to them a race of repentance, which they are to run throughout their lives."[46]

Justification should be distinguished from regeneration for the assurance of Christian identity in the course of regeneration. Throughout the course of regeneration, as we saw in section 2.1, Christians can find it difficult to be assured of their identity when they consider their vulnerability in the unceasing inner struggle between "the flesh" and "the spirit":

> Thus, then, are the children of God freed through regeneration from bondage to sin. Yet they do not obtain full possession of freedom so as to feel no more annoyance from their flesh, but there still remains in them a continuing occasion for struggle whereby they may be exercised; and not only be exercised, but also better learn their own weakness.[47]

Calvin, however, states that their identity as children of God can be confirmed despite this difficulty by remembering that God has already adopted them through the freely given grace of justification:

> For Paul surely refers to justification by the word "acceptance" when in Ephesians 1:5–6 he says: "We are destined for adoption through Christ according to God's good pleasure, to the praise of his glorious grace by which he has accounted us acceptable and

---

45. *Institutes*, III.11.2, OS 4:183. Observing the consistent forensic definition of justification in Calvin's *Institutes* from 1536 to 1559, McGrath argues that this definition shows the influence of Luther rather than Bucer on Calvin's doctrine of justification. McGrath, *Iustitia Dei*, 254.

46. *Institutes*, III.3.9, OS 4:65.

47. *Institutes*, III.3.10; *Sic ergo a peccati servitute liberantur filii Dei per regenerationem, non ut quasi plenam libertatis possessionem iam adepti, nihil amplius molestiae a carne sua sentient: sed ut illis maneat perpetua certaminis materia, unde exerceantur: neque exerceantur modo, sed infirmitatem quoque suam melius discant*. OS 4:65.

PART ONE—Calvin's Anthropology

beloved," that means the very thing that he commonly says elsewhere, that "God justifies us freely" (Romans 3:24).[48]

As Griffith argues, Calvin holds a forensic idea of instantaneous adoption through the grace of justification. Calvin holds this idea in opposition to those who argue that Christ "deserved for us the first grace" (or "the occasion of deserving"), but believes that it still remains for Christians "not to fail the occasion offered." In Calvin's view, Christians became God's children not because they obtained "the opportunity to gain merit, but [because] all the merits of Christ . . . are communicated" to them.[49] After justification, God's adoptive grace is also steadfast and irrevocable:

> Therefore if one seeks the first cause that opens for the saints the door to God's Kingdom, and hence gives them a permanent standing ground in it, at once we answer: Because the Lord by his own mercy has adopted them once for all, and keeps them continually.[50]

In explaining the distinction between the two dimensions of salvation, Calvin asserts that Christians can be assured of their identity as the adopted children of God in the course of regeneration from their relationship with Christ. And this relationship reminds them of the fact that they are freely accounted righteous through the benefit of justification by grace:

> [Boldness and confidence] surely does not take place through the gift of regeneration, which, as it is always imperfect in this flesh, so contains in itself manifold ground for doubt. Therefore, we must come to this remedy: that believers should be convinced that their only ground of hope for the inheritance of the Heavenly Kingdom lies in the fact that, being engrafted in the body of Christ, they are freely accounted righteous.[51]

---

48. *Institutes*, III.11.4, OS 4:184.
49. *Institutes*, III.15.6, OS 4:245. Griffith, "'First Title of the Spirit,'" 147.
50. *Institutes*, III.17.6, OS 4:259.
51. *Institutes*, III.13.5; OS 4:220. "For God so begins this second point in his elect, and progresses in it gradually, and sometimes slowly, throughout life, that they are always liable to the judgment of death before his tribunal. But he does not justify in part but liberally, so that they may appear in heaven as if endowed with the purity of Christ. No portion of righteousness sets our consciences at peace until it has been determined that we are pleasing to God, because we are entirely righteous before him." *Institutes*, III.11.11; OS 4:193.

The Inseparability of Justification and Regeneration

Calvin argues that these two dimensions of salvation, justification and regeneration, are inseparable because the grace for both justification and regeneration comes from Christ, just as the heat of the sun is inseparable from its light.[52] He maintains that Christians should be united with Christ to attain his blessings of salvation: "as long as Christ remains outside of us, and we are separated from him, all that he has suffered and done for the salvation of the human race remains useless and of no value for us."[53] When referring to justification, Calvin argues that Christians are justified by the attribution of Christ's righteousness in union with him:

> The sinner, received into communion with Christ, is reconciled to God by his grace, while, cleansed by Christ's blood, he obtains forgiveness of sins, and clothed with Christ's righteousness as if it were his own, he stands confidently before the heavenly judgment seat.[54]

This is the beginning of the life of Christians as children of God: "Therefore, as soon as you become engrafted into Christ through faith, you are made a son of God, an heir of heaven, a partaker in righteousness, a possessor of life."[55] Therefore, union with Christ is a prerequisite of the Christian's filial identity.

Calvin relates regeneration, on the other hand, to repentance, and argues that "we must strive toward repentance itself, devote ourselves to it throughout life, and pursue it to the very end if we would abide in Christ."[56]

---

52. "The sun, by its heat, quickens and fructifies the earth, by its beams brightens and illumines it. Here is a mutual and indivisible connection." *Institutes*, III.3.7, OS 4:61. With respect to Calvin's focus on Christ, Lane says, "Faith unites us with Christ and it is only in him that we have justification and sanctification. They are held together by the fact that we have them only in and through Christ." Lane, *Justification by Faith*, 18.

53. *Institutes*, III.1.1, OS 4:1.

54. *Institutes*, III.17.8; *Eam porro iustitiam definimus, quod in Christi communionem receptus peccator, eius gratia Deo reconciliatur : dum illius sanguine purgatus, peccatorum remissionem obtinet : et iustitia non secus ac propria vestitus, coram caelesti tribunali securus subsistit*. OS 4:259.

55. *Institutes*, III.15.6; *Proinde simulatque per fidem insertus es Christo, iam filius Dei factus es, caelorum haeres, iustitiae particeps, vitae possessor*. OS 4:245. Concerning this point, Tamburello argues that Calvin's inclusive scope of union with Christ, which embraces all the elect, is different from St. Bernard's selective scope of mystical union applying only to a few believers at the end of life. Tamburello, *Union with Christ*, 93-96.

56. *Institutes*, III.3.1, OS 4:55; III.3.20; *ita in poenitentiam ipsam eniti, tota vita in*

PART ONE—Calvin's Anthropology

In his explanation of Christ's merits of regeneration in the *Institutes*, Calvin draws attention to the biblical notion of Christ as the living image of God: "Scripture shows that God the Father, as he has reconciled us to himself in his Christ, has in him stamped for us the likeness to which he would have us conform."[57] When Calvin discusses the notion of Christ as "the perfect image of God," his principal concern is not to investigate the inner life of the Godhead, but to indicate that it is through Christ's merit that the *imago Dei* is restored in Christians. In his commentary on Hebrew 1:3, Calvin thus argues, "It ought to be observed that frivolous speculations are not here taught, but an important doctrine of faith. We ought therefore to apply these high titles given to Christ for our own benefit, for they bear relation to us."[58] To conform to Christ's image is not to share "the essence" of Christ, but to participate in Christ's death and resurrection:

> If we truly partake in his [Christ's] death, "our old man is crucified by his power, and the body of sin perishes," that the corruption of original nature may no longer thrive. If we share in his resurrection, through it we are raised up into newness of life to correspond with the righteousness of God.[59]

---

eam incumbere, eam ad ultimum prosequi nos oportet, si in Christo consistere volumus. OS 4:77.

57. *Institutes*, III.6.3; *ostendit Deum Patrem quemadmodum nos sibi in Christo suo conciliavit, ita in eo nobis imaginem signasse ad quam nos conformari velit.* OS 4:148. The idea that Christ is the living image of God to which Christians should conform is discussed more than any other topic in Calvin's understanding of the image of God in the *Institutes* (1559) and his *Commentaries on New Testament*. *Institutes*, I.15.4; II.2.20, 6.2, 6.4, 12.7; III.2.1, 6.3, 24.1; *Comm. Matt* 11:27, 13:16, 16:24, 20:23; *Comm. John* 1:18, 2:16, 5:22, 6:27, 6:47, 8:19, 8:44, 12:13, 14:1, 14:7; *Comm. Rom.* 1:3, 6:8, 13:4; *Comm. 2 Cor.* 3:18, 4:4; *Comm. Phil.* 2:7, 2:9; *Comm. Col.* 1:15; *Comm. Heb.* 1:3, 11:26; *Comm. 1 Pet.* 1:21, 2:21; *Comm. 1 John* 2:22, 3:23, 5:20. Also see Zachman, *The Assurance of Faith*, 173.

58. *Comm. Heb.* 1:3, CO 55:12. Calvin discusses the deity of the Son with the biblical notion of Christ as the image of God, for example, in the *Institutes*, I.13.2. Yet, he usually connects this notion with the revelation of God in Christ. "The term 'image' is not made use of in reference to essence, but has a reference to us; for Christ is called the "image of God" on this ground that he makes God in a manner visible to us." *Comm. Col.* 1:15, CO 52:84. Also see, *Institutes*, I.16.4, II.2.20, 9.1, 16.14, III.2.1, 6.3.

59. *Institutes*, III.3.9, OS 4:63. Calvin argues that Osiander's doctrine of justification by the infusion of Christ's "essential righteousness" misleads believers to think that they are righteous not by the Attribution of Christ's reconciling benefit but by the infusion of essential righteousness from Christ's divinity: "For since God, for the preservation of righteousness, renews those whom he freely reckons as righteous, Osiander mixes that gift of regeneration with this free acceptance and contends that they are one and the same. Yet Scripture, even though it joins them, still lists them separately in order that

The Grace of the Trinity as the Foundation of Christian Identity

In this sense, union with Christ is essential for Christians to secure their identity through the course of regeneration. They can be assured of their identity by depending on the benefit of justification in Christ which applies despite their infirmities and remaining sinfulness:

> We experience such participation in him that, although we are still foolish in ourselves, he is our wisdom before God; while we are sinners, he is our righteousness; while we are unclean, he is our purity; while we are weak, while we are unarmed and exposed to Satan, yet ours is that power which has been given him in heaven and on earth, by which to crush Satan for us and shatter the gates of hell; while we still bear about with us the body of death, he is yet our life. In brief, because all his things are ours and we have all things in him, in us there is nothing. Upon this foundation, I say, we must be built if we would grow into a holy temple to the Lord.[60]

The identity of Christians as the children of God, therefore, depends entirely on their relationship with Christ in which they are justified and regenerated by grace.

The Identity of Christians and the Grace of the Trinity

Calvin's Trinitarian Perspective

While highlighting the benefits given by Christ in his attempt to find a secure foundation for Christian's filial identity as seen in their relationship with God, Calvin discusses this matter from a trinitarian perspective. Wendel argues that the trinitarian perspective is not "an element" but "the essential part" of Calvin's theology.[61] We can find this trinitarian perspective throughout Calvin's discussions of salvation. Calvin consistently states that each person of the Trinity works distinctively but harmoniously: "to the Father is attributed the beginning of activity, and the fountain and wellspring of all things; to the Son, wisdom, counsel, and the ordered disposition of all things; but to the Spirit is assigned the power and efficacy

---

God's manifold grace may better appear to us." *Institutes*, III.11.6, OS 4:187.

60. *Institutes*, III.15.5, OS 4:244.

61. Wendel, *Calvin*, 168–69. Regrettably, however, Wendel does not provide a full treatment of the theological and anthropological implications of Calvin's doctrine of the Trinity. He simply points out that believers can recognise "the presence of God indubitably from the unity of the divine essence in Christ."

PART ONE—Calvin's Anthropology

of the activity."[62] Calvin's definition of faith in the *Institutes* also shows his trinitarian perspective:

> Now we shall possess a right definition of faith if we call it a firm and certain knowledge of God's benevolence toward us, founded upon the truth of the freely given promise in Christ, both revealed to our minds and sealed upon our heart through the Holy Spirit.[63]

Since Wendel's observation, however, the trinitarian perspective in Calvin's discussion of union with Christ has not been properly appreciated. Niesel declares that there is no theological anthropology for Calvin "apart from Christology" and argues that the important topics in Calvin's idea of union with Christ all indicate the main concern of Calvin's theology being "to exalt the Mediator Jesus Christ."[64] While criticising Niesel's christological emphasis for ignoring the obvious twofold perspective in Calvin's anthropology, Engel herself ignores the trinitarian perspective evident in Calvin's theological anthropology.[65] More recently, Tamburello has observed a trinitarian perspective in Calvin's idea of union with Christ, but he presents no further discussion; he merely remarks that "it is appropriate to say that Calvin's notion of *unio* contains a trinitarian element" when he "speaks frequently enough of union with the Father, and quite frequently of union being in the power of the Spirit."[66] It is not wrong to say that Calvin's discussion of union with Christ focuses primarily on the "benefits of Christ" for salvation. However, it is not correct to view all the important issues of Calvin's idea of union with Christ from an exclusively christological perspective because, as we shall see, his discussion of "union with Christ" attempts to highlight not only the benefits of Christ but also the works of all three persons of the Trinity with regard to the Christian identity.[67]

---

62. *Institutes*, I.13.18; *Ea autem est, quod Patri principium agendi, rerumque omnium fons et scaturigo attribuitur: Filio sapientia, consilium, ipsaque in rebus agendis dispensatio: at Spiritui virtus et efficacia assignatur actionis.* OS 3:132.

63. *Institutes*, III.2.7; *Nunc iusta fidei definitio nobis constabit si dicamus esse divinae erga nos benevolentiae firmam certamque cognitionem, quae gratuitae in Christo promissionis veritate fundata, per Spiritum sanctum et revelatur mentibus nostris et cordibus obsignatur.* OS 4:16.

64. Niesel, *Theology of Calvin*, 70, 120–39.

65. Engel, *John Calvin's Perspectival Anthropology*, 62. Engel includes Torrance's study under the category of an "exclusive Christological" interpretation.

66. Tamburello, *Union with Christ*, 93.

67. Westhead's study is a significant exception of this general negligence because he observes and investigates a trinitarian perspective in Calvin's doctrine of adoption: "For

The Grace of the Trinity as the Foundation of Christian Identity

Useful investigations of the trinitarian perspective in Calvin's theology can be found in the studies of Loeschen and Butin.[68] They demonstrate that Calvin's doctrine of the Trinity was developed during the course of his disputes with other thinkers. In 1537, Pierre Caroli charged Calvin with Arianism, mainly because of the lack of a full treatment of the doctrine of the Trinity in the first edition of the *Institutes*. Caroli's charge forced Calvin to engage more with doctrine of the Trinity in later editions of the *Institutes*. During the development of his doctrine, Calvin had to defend the traditional Nicene doctrines of the Trinity against the anti-trinitarian opinions expressed by Servetus in his *Christianismi Restitutio* (1531). In the 1550s, Calvin faced another anti-trinitarian movement led by Italians such as Valenti Gentile.[69] In this polemical context, Calvin paid more and more attention to the unity of the three hypostases and, in particular, to the eternal deity of the Son.[70] Yet while Butin's study succinctly notes the historical context of the development of Calvin's doctrine of the Trinity and points out its soteriological implication, he does not deal with the way in which Calvin's trinitarian perspective shapes his anthropological theme of the Christian identity.[71]

Calvin, adoption is very much a privilege for which all three Persons of the Trinity are responsible, albeit in diverse ways in accordance with their respective functions in the Godhead." Westhead, "Adoption in the Thought of John Calvin," 102–7. However, Westhead does not mention Calvin's idea of union with Christ at all.

68. For examples Loeschen, *Divine Community*; and Butin, *Revelation, Redemption, and Response*.

69. Loeschen, *Divine Community*, 129. About Calvin's debates with Michael Servetus, and the figures of the Italian anti-Nicene movement such as Matthias Gribaldi, Giorgio Blandrata, Gianpaulo Alciati, and Giovanni Valenti Gentile, see Butin, *Revelation, Redemption, and Response*, 32–38.

70. Torrance insists that Gregory Nazianzen's doctrine of the Trinity must have influenced Calvin's arguments for the eternal deity of the Son. Torrance, "Calvin's Doctrine of the Trinity," 63–64. Yet, Torrance's insistence linking Calvin's doctrine of the Trinity with that of Gregory Nazianzen is difficult to justify from the textual evidence. Lane claims, "His citations of Gregory point strongly to the conclusion that Calvin knew a little of him prior to 1550 and did not thereafter study either of the new editions of his works." Lane, *John Calvin*, 83–85.

71. Butin points out that the trinitarian perspective in Calvin's theology is presented with a soteriological focus: "Calvin's commitment to the orthodox trinitarian doctrine of the Nicene period was increasingly motivated by his sense that it was the immediate theological implication of the New Testament teaching of God's gracious redemption of believers in Christ." Butin, *Revelation, Redemption, and Response*, 29–38.

PART ONE—Calvin's Anthropology

However, Calvin's anthropological concern with the foundation of Christian identity is one of the essential features of his doctrine of the Trinity. Calvin endeavours to contrast the works of each person of the Trinity with the incapacity of the human person. Firstly, Calvin thinks that it is the Father who plans and begins human salvation by adopting sinners as His children: "we have been adopted unto him as sons and heirs by our Heavenly Father."[72] Concerning this point, Calvin distinguishes the Father's initiating grace from the Son's mediating grace: "The Father has given all power to the Son that he may by the Son's hand govern, nourish, and sustain us, keep us in his care, and help us."[73]

In the *Institutes* III.13.8 Calvin calls the Son "wisdom" and "counsel" in the sense that Christ works distinctly from the other persons of the Trinity as the source of Christian justification and regeneration: "The origin of (eternal) life is, indeed, the Father; but the fountain from which we are to draw it is Christ."[74] Calvin also emphasises that believers are united with Christ by his death and that they partake of the spiritual benefits of Christ in this union: "The love of Christ led him to unite himself to us, and he completes the union by his death. By giving himself for us, he suffered in our own person; as, on the other hand, faith makes us partakers of everything which it finds in Christ."[75]

The Holy Spirit is defined as the bond "by which Christ effectually unites us to himself."[76] Calvin clearly distinguishes the works of the second and the third persons of the Trinity in his argument that Christ unites us to himself not by himself but by the Spirit: "Christ, then, is the source of all blessing to us: from him we obtain all things; but Christ himself, with all his blessings, is communicated to us by the Spirit."[77] The Spirit's work is

72. *Institutes*, III.15.5, OS 4:244.

73. *Institutes*, II.15.5; *Dedit enim Pater omnem potestatem Filio ut per eius manum nos gubernat, foveat, sustentet, sub eius tutela nos protegat, nobisque auxilietur*. OS 3:478.

74. *Comm. 1 John* 5:20; *Vitae quidem origo est pater: sed fons, ex quo haurire licet, Christus est*. CO 55:376.

75. *Comm. Gal.* 2:20, CO 50:199.

76. *Institutes*, III.1.1; *Huc summa redit, Spiritum sanctum vinculum esse, quo nos sibi efficaciter devincit Christus*. OS 4:1. "He [Christ] unites himself to us by the Spirit alone. By the grace and power of the same Spirit we are made his members, to keep us under himself and in turn to possess him." *Institutes*, III.1.3, OS 4:5. *Comm. Eph.* 5:32: CO 51:227.

77. *Comm. 1 Cor.* 6:11; *Christus ergo nobis omnium bonorum fons est, ab ipso omnia obtinemus: sed Christus ipse cum omnibus suis bonis per spiritum nobis communicatur*. CO 49:395.

The Grace of the Trinity as the Foundation of Christian Identity

necessary, not only to start the new life of Christians by justification, but also to confirm their identity through regeneration: "This unique life which the Son of God inspires in his own so that they become one with him, Paul here contrasts with that natural life which is common also to the wicked."[78] Calvin also notes the intrinsic harmony within the Trinity's work of salvation. For example, in his commentary on John 15:1–2:

> The Father is the first Author of all blessings, who plants us with his hand; but the commencement of life is in Christ, since we begin to take root in him . . . In order to prove that he did not begin the work of our salvation for the purpose of leaving it imperfect in the middle of the course, he promises that his Spirit will always be efficacious in us, if we do not prevent him.[79]

Therefore, when Calvin calls the Father "the first Author," the Son "the fountain," and the Holy Spirit "the bond" in his writings, he assigns those metaphorical titles to each person to explain their distinctive but harmonious works for human salvation, brought about by the union of Christians with Christ.

The Grace of the Trinity and the Incapacity of Humanity

The ultimate aim of Calvin's discussion of union with Christ from his trinitarian perspective is to base Christian identity in the grace of the triune God. In his discussion of justification, Calvin repeatedly speaks of the inability of human nature to obtain or secure salvation in order to emphasise that "the efficient cause of our obtaining eternal life is the mercy of the Heavenly Father and his freely given love toward us."[80] Calvin condemns as sacrilege any suggestion that human action can achieve merit:

> We never truly glory in him unless we have utterly put off our own glory. On the other hand, we must hold this as a universal principle: whoever glories in himself, glories against God . . . To sum

---

78. *Institutes*, III.1.2, OS 4:3.

79. *Comm. John* 15:1–2, CO 47:339–40. Also see *Comm. Eph.* 3:17, CO 51:186. Butin links the harmonious work between the persons of the Trinity with the "perichoretic ideas about the Trinity of the Greek fathers." As with Torrance's suggestion that Gregory Nazianzen influenced Calvin's argument of Christ's deity, however, Butin offers no sufficient textual evidence from Calvin's writings, with the exception of one passage in the *Institutes*, which mentions Gregory Nazianzen. Butin, *Revelation, Redemption, and Response*, 42–43.

80. *Institutes*, III.14.17, OS 4:235.

PART ONE—Calvin's Anthropology

up, man cannot without sacrilege claim for himself even a crumb of righteousness, for just so much is plucked and taken from the glory of God's righteousness.[81]

The contrast between the necessity of the Father's grace and the incapacity of humanity is also obvious in his notion of "union with God."[82] In the *Institutes*, for example, Calvin says, "while for the short time we wander away from God, Christ stands in our midst, to lead us little by little to a firm union with God."[83] In Calvin's terminology, the term "God" in the expression of "union with God" usually refers to the Father: "Because the peculiar qualities in the persons carry an order within them . . . so often as mention is made of the Father and the Son together, or the Spirit, the name of God is peculiarly applied to the Father."[84] Tamburello argues that there is no difference in Calvin's terminology between union with Christ and union with God.[85] But we need to note a slight but significant difference between the terms "union with Christ" and "union with God" used in the *Institutes*. In the places where he mentions "union with God," Calvin is usually concerned with the ultimate condition of man after the whole course of regeneration.[86] The following statement is one such example where he uses "union with God" in this sense:

> When we hear mention of our union with God, let us remember that holiness must be its bond; not because we come into communion with him by virtue of our holiness! Rather, we ought to cleave unto him so that, infused (*perfusi*) with his holiness; we may follow whither he calls.[87]

81. *Institutes*, III.13.2; OS 4:216.

82. "The ancient philosophers anxiously discussed the sovereign good, and even contended among themselves over it. Yet, none but Plato recognised man's highest good as union with God, and he could not even dimly sense its nature. And no wonder, for he had learned nothing of the sacred bond of that union." *Institutes*, III.25.3, OS 4:434. Also see, George, "Calvin's *Psychopannychia*: Another Look," 313–15, and Partee, *Calvin and the Classical Philosophy*, 64–65.

83. *Institutes*, II.15.5, OS 3:478.

84. *Institutes*, I.13.20, OS 3:134. Cf. *Institutes*, II.16.3, III.6.2.

85. Tamburello, *Union with Christ*, 93, 113.

86. For the term "union with God" in Calvin's writings, see, *Institutes*, II.16.3; III.6.2, 25.3; *Comm. 1 Cor.* 3:23; *Comm. 1 John* 4:15, 5:20.

87. *Institutes*, III.6.2; *Quum nostrae cum Deo coniunctionis mentionem audimus, meminerimus sanctitatem oportere eius esse copulam: non quia sanctitatis merito veniamus in eius communionem: (quum potius adhaerere primo illi oporteat ut eius sanctitate perfusi sequamur quo vocat).* OS 4:147. Battles's translation of "infused" for *perfusi* does

The Grace of the Trinity as the Foundation of Christian Identity

This is different from the focus of Calvin's use of "union with Christ," which is usually related to the beginning and maintenance of the Christian life through Christ's mediating grace.

In his notion of "union with God," however, Calvin does not speak of any sort of ontological change to human beings either during or at the end of the course of regeneration.[88] Calvin argues that in the eschaton "we shall be partakers of divine and blessed immortality and glory, so as to be as it were one with God as far as our capacities will allow."[89] Regeneration is not a process by which the divine essence is shared, but the restoration of the image of God, that is, of the original relationship with God by grace: "When Paul discusses the restoration of the image, it is clear that we should infer from his words that man is made to conform to God, not by an inflowing of substance, but by the grace and power of the Spirit."[90] Therefore, even when it reaches a perfect state of union with God, Christians still remain as creatures. Hence, Christians cannot claim any dignity of their own apart from the grace of, and union with, God.

When he interprets the metaphor "the vine" for Christ in John 15, Calvin contrasts the incapacity of the Christian self with the benefits which believers have from Christ: "The general meaning of this comparison is, that we are, by nature, barren and dry, except in so far as we have been ingrafted into Christ, and draw from him a power which is new, and which does

---

not look appropriate because Calvin sharply distinguishes "infusion" from "imputation" of Christ's merits for our salvation, especially against Osiander's concept of "essential righteousness." I think that either "imbued" or "inspired" would be a better translation of *perfusi* at this point.

88. For the element of deification in Calvin's theology, Carl Moser argues that "One should not overstate the significance of deification's presence in Calvin," because "it would be wrong to say that deification per se is a major element of Calvin's theology or that is presence warrants a radical reinterpretation of Calvin's theology." Moser, "The Greatest Possible Blessing," 36–57. Billings also argues that there is a distinctive but clear doctrine of deification in Calvin's theology. Billings especially connects Calvin's idea of believers' union with God with his notion of "participation." Billings, "United to God through Christ," 315–34. Slater, however, offers a useful analysis of the possibility of the doctrine of deification in Calvin's theology against Moser's arguments. Slater argues, "Rather than understanding salvation as a communication of properties from Christ's divine nature to his human nature so that through Christ's human nature we may come to share in the divine nature, Calvin's position is that believers share in what is Christ's according to his human nature." Slater, "Salvation as participation in the humanity of the Mediator in Calvin's *Institutes of the Christian Religion*," 39–58.

89. *Comm. 2 Pet.* 1:4, CO 55:446.

90. *Institutes*, I.15.5, OS 3:479.

PART ONE—Calvin's Anthropology

not proceed from ourselves."[91] In the *Institutes*, he repeatedly highlights Christ's benefits of justification by contrasting them with human works: "But Scripture, when it speaks of faith righteousness, leads us to something far different: namely, to turn aside from the contemplation of our own works and look solely upon God's mercy and Christ's perfection."[92] Calvin maintains that 'there is no sanctification apart from union with Christ.'[93]

When discussing the part played by the Holy Spirit as the bond of union with Christ, Calvin says: "Hence, too, we infer that we are one with the Son of God; not because he conveys his substance to us, but because, by the power of his Spirit, he imparts to us his life and all the blessings which he has received from the Father."[94] Because of the distinctive role of the Spirit as providing the bond of union with Christ, Calvin refutes Osiander's idea of "essential righteousness": "For the fact that it comes about through the power of the Holy Spirit that we grow together with Christ, and he becomes our Head and we his members, he reckons of almost no importance unless Christ's essence be mingled with ours."[95]

The very humanity of Christians means that they are incapable of earning their own redemption, for only the twofold work of the Holy Spirit—illumination and provision of the divine power of regeneration—can communicate the benefits of Christ to them. On the one hand, Calvin insists that it is necessary to regeneration for the Holy Spirit's illumination to strengthen the faith of Christians because they still remain dull in understanding the Word of God: "Indeed, man's mind, because of its dullness, cannot hold to the right path, but wanders through various errors and stumbles repeatedly, as if it were groping in darkness, until it strays away and finally disappears."[96] On the other hand, another essential task of the

---

91. *Comm. John* 15:1, CO 47:339.

92. *Institutes*, III.11.16, OS 4:200. "[H]e who, excluded from the righteousness of works, grasps the righteousness of Christ through faith, and clothed in it, appears in God's sight not as a sinner but as a righteous man." *Institutes*, III.11.2, OS 4:182. As Lane points out, Calvin adheres to the reformation doctrine of "justification by faith alone" to speak the uniqueness of Christ's merit for our salvation rather than contrast faith with works. Lane, *Justification by Faith*, 26–29.

93. *Institutes*, III.14.4, OS 4:223.

94. *Comm. John* 17:21, CO 47:387.

95. *Institutes*, III.11.5, OS 4:186.

96. *Institutes*, II.2.12, OS 3:255. Calvin calls the Holy Spirit "the inner teacher" (*internus doctor, interior magister*), "the Spirit of discernment"(*Spiritus intelligentiae*) and "key" (*claves*) with regard to the Holy Spirit's role of illumination in the regeneration of believers. *Institutes*, III.1.4, OS 4:5.

Holy Spirit is the provision of divine power to vivify the spirit within God's children. It is the Holy Spirit who provides the power "to nourish believers to bring forth the buds of righteousness, to enflame their hearts toward regeneration and to flow all heavenly riches forth to them."[97] This secret power vivifies "the new man" day by day in order to mortify "the old man" in Christians during the course of regeneration:

> We confess that while through the intercession of Christ's righteousness God reconciles us to himself, and by free remission of sins accounts us righteous, his beneficence is at the same time joined with such a mercy that through his Holy Spirit he dwells in us and by his power the lusts of our flesh are each day more and more mortified.[98]

In his discussion of the distinct tasks of each person of the Trinity, therefore, Calvin tries to highlight the freely given grace of the triune God by indicating the inability of human nature to maintain the Christian identity. Furthermore, this ultimate concern of Calvin's trinitarian perspective appears not only in his anthropological discussions, but throughout his other theological discussions, including his ecclesiological discussions.

Conclusion: Christian Identity in Union with Christ

In his anthropology, Calvin tries to explicate Christian identity as children of God in the relationship of them with Christ. This is primarily because no one can fully assure himself of the promise of God for his identity by relying upon his own merits or works:

> These promises do nothing but vacillate and waver if they rest upon our own works. Therefore, righteousness must either depart from us or works must not be brought into account, but faith alone must have place, whose nature it is to prick up the ears and close

---

97. *Institutes*, III.1.3, OS 4:4. Milner examines the idea of "the secret impulse of the Spirit" in Calvin's commentaries. According to Milner, this secret impulse is, for Calvin, a matter of "revelation or inspiration" for the Christian's experience of "an inner certainty of the will of God." Milner, *Calvin's Doctrine of the Church*, 197–203.

98. *Institutes*, III.14.9; *Fatemur, dum nos intercedente Christi iustitia sibi reconciliat Deus, ac gratuita peccatorum remissione donatos pro iustis habet: cum eiusmodi misericordia coniunctam simul esse hanc eius beneficentiam, quod per Spiritum suum sanctum in nobis habitat, cuius virtute concupiscentiae carnis nostrae magis ac magis in dies mortificantur.* OS 4:228.

PART ONE—Calvin's Anthropology

the eyes—that is, to be intent upon the promise alone and to turn thought away from all worth or merit of man.[99]

Calvin thinks that Christians can be assured of their filial identity only in union with Christ. In this spiritual relationship they can find the distinct but harmonious works of each person of the Trinity for their justification and regeneration. As we have seen, one of the ultimate aims of Calvin's anthropology is to offer Christians their identity as children of God which has the dependent nature upon the grace of the triune God.

---

99. *Institutes*, III.13.4, OS 4:219.

The Christian Life as the Eschatological Progress

Introduction: Calvin's Eschatological Idea of the Christian Life

CALVIN THINKS THAT THE WHOLE CHRISTIAN LIFE IS THE COURSE OF REgeneration in which their identity as God's children is manifested. Thus his discussion of the Christian life in the *Institutes* III.6.1 opens with a statement about "the object of regeneration," that is "to manifest in the life of believers a harmony and agreement between God's righteousness and their obedience, and thus to confirm the adoption that they have received as sons."[1]

In Calvin's doctrine of the Christian life, regeneration is understood as an eschatological process. While the course of regeneration begins when believers became God's children by His grace of justification, it will not be completed until the end of their lives:

> Observe, that the design of the gospel is this—that the image of God, which had been effaced by sin, may be stamped anew upon us, and that the advancement of this restoration may be continually going forward in us during our whole life, because God makes his glory shine forth in us by little by little.[2]

---

1. *Institutes*, III.6.1; *Scopum regenerationis esse diximus ut in vita fidelium appareat inter Dei iustitiam et eorum obsequium symmetria et consensus: atque ita adoptionem confirment qua recepti sunt in filios.* OS 4:146. Calvin developed his doctrine of the Christian life from a few lines in the 1536 edition of the *Institutes* to chapters 6–10 in the final edition. Most of these chapters were introduced in the edition of 1539. Furthermore, these chapters were published separately under the title *De vita hominis christiani* in Geneva in 1550.

2. *Comm. 2 Cor.* 3:18, CO 50:47.

PART ONE—Calvin's Anthropology

Many studies have examined Calvin's eschatological understanding of the Christian life. However, as Engel points out, there are unresolved controversies concerning the eschatological elements in Calvin's anthropology, especially over the intellectual background of Calvin's ideas of "immortality" and "resurrection."[3] On the one hand, Quistorp and Selinger argue that Calvin's attachment to the concept of the immortality of the soul shows "a vestige of Platonism" in Calvin's anthropology.[4] On the other hand, Partee and Leithart attempt to demonstrate the biblicism of Calvin's anthropology by underlining his emphasis on the resurrection of the body.[5] It is obvious that Calvin uses Platonic ideas and terms together with biblical concepts in his explanation of the immortality of the soul. For Calvin, while tries to present his anthropology as an explication of the Scripture's teaching about humanity, use of these philosophical ideas and terms does not present a great problem if they can further the principal concern of his doctrine of the Christian life: to provide Christians with consolation for their present life by highlighting God's promise of their preservation in this life and their perfection in the final resurrection.

This chapter aims to illustrate the centrality of this principal concern to Calvin's treatment of the eschatological dimension of the Christian life. To achieve this, I will deal with the two significant points in Calvin's idea of the Christian life: the imperfection of Christians in their present life, which I shall call the "not yet" aspect, and assurance of their future perfection, which I shall call the "already" aspect. For the "not yet" aspect, I will examine Calvin's use of the metaphors of "warfare" and "pilgrimage," the two most frequent metaphors in his explanation of the present condition of Christians. Then I will investigate the "already" aspect of Calvin's eschatological discussion of the condition of Christians at death and in the final resurrection. In the following section, I will examine Calvin's suggestion of three spiritual exercises and of the duty of love toward neighbours, to show that his eschatological concern was a basis of his suggestion of proper methods and attitudes of Christians in managing their life both in the personal and in the communal dimensions. This investigation will show that Calvin's discussion of death and the final resurrection is directed by his

---

3. Engel, *John Calvin's Perspectival Anthropology*, 151–52.

4. Quistorp, *Calvin's Doctrine of the Last Things*, 51–54, 59–60; Selinger, *Calvin Against Himself*, 3ff.

5. Partee, *Calvin and Classical Philosophy*, 61–65.

principal concern to provide Christians with consolation for the present life.

Imperfection in the Present Life of the Christian

The Christian Life as Warfare

Calvin identifies two reasons for the present imperfection in Christians: the inward reason is the sin remaining in them, and outward reason is the tribulations they face in this world. Concerning the inward reason, Calvin argues that although Christians "are purged by sanctification" of the Holy Spirit, they still have daily to "fight against" sin in them as long as they "are besieged by many vices and much weakness" in their present life.[6] Thus Calvin thinks of the Christian life as "warfare": "But since human life on earth is a warfare, those who feel both the stings of sin and the remains of the flesh must feel depression in the world."[7] In his commentary on 1 John 5:4, Calvin argues, "It is, indeed, true, that our warfare continues through life, that our conflicts are daily, nay, that new and various battles are every moment on every side stirred up against us by the enemy."[8]

Calvin thinks of "the flesh" as the main enemy in this spiritual warfare: "We are born so corrupt and depraved, that there is in us as it were an innate hatred to God, so that we desire nothing but what is displeasing to him, so that all the passions of our flesh carry on continual war with his righteousness."[9] As we saw in the previous chapter, Calvin identifies

---

6. Institutes, III.3.14; *Deinde sic nos eius sanctificatione purgari, ut multis vitiis multaque infirmitate obsideamur quandiu inclusi sumus mole corporis nostri. Quo fit ut longo intervallo a perfectione dissiti, proficere semper aliquid, et vitiis irretiti cum illis quotidie luctari necesse habeamus.* OS 4:70. Cf. Institutes, III.3.9, OS 4:63. Comm. Rom. 6:7, CO 49:108, Comm. 1 Cor. 1:9, CO 49:312, Comm. James 4:1, CO 55:414.

7. Psychopannychia, TT 3:433; *Verum, quoniam militia est, vita hominis super terram (Iob. 7,1), necesse est eos, qui sentiunt et aculeos peccati et carnis reliquias, in mundo pressuram habere.* CO 5:188. For Calvin's use of military metaphors, see Leith, *John Calvin's Doctrine of the Christian Life*, 82–85. Wallace, *Calvin's Doctrine of Christian Life*, 265, 317–18. Quistorp, *Calvin's Doctrine of the Last Things*, 29–31. Also see Hall, *With the Spirit's Sword*.

8. Comm. 1 John 5:4, CO 55:363.

9. Comm. 1 John 4:10, CO 55: 354. The devil is the enemy of Christians in this spiritual warfare: "The fact that the devil is everywhere called God's adversary and ours also ought to fire us to an unceasing struggle against him." Institutes, I.14.15, OS 3:165. Comm. Eph. 6:12, CO 51:233–34. Leith argues that "in the light of these [military] metaphors, the word 'hero' is descriptive of the ethos of the Christian life. It is interesting to note that

PART ONE—Calvin's Anthropology

"the flesh" with the sin remaining within Christians.[10] For Calvin, it is not because of their natural infirmity but because of sin remaining in them that Christians are still sinners: "Still further, he [Paul] gives the name of sin to the original depravity which dwells in our hearts, and which leads us to sin, and from which indeed all evil deeds and abominations stream forth."[11]

Calvin understands this spiritual warfare from an eschatological perspective: although the dominating power of sin has already been defeated by the grace of justification, sin itself is not yet totally destroyed in Christians: "God truly carries this [purging believers of all sins] out by regenerating his own people, so that the sway of sin is abolished in them ... But sin ceases only to reign; it does not also cease to dwell in them."[12] As a result, Christians' spiritual warfare against sin remaining in them will not be completed until they take off the "earthly prison of the body."[13] In his use of the Platonic metaphor of prison house for the body, however, Calvin does not define the human body as the cause of sin or the enemy of Christians' spiritual warfare. Rather, he uses this metaphor to illustrate the present imperfection of Christians who are in "the exile from their native land while they are here shut up in the body as in a prison."[14]

Calvin himself frequently uses the word." Leith, *John Calvin's Doctrine of Christian Life*, 85. As we shall see in chapter 6, however, Calvin tends to mentions the devil as the enemy of Christians in the warfare between Christ's Kingdom and Satan's Kingdom.

10. "We accordingly teach that in the saints, until they are divested of mortal bodies, there is always sin; for in their flesh there resides that depravity of inordinate desiring which contends against righteousness." *Institutes*, III.3.10, OS 4:66.

11. *Comm. Rom.* 6:12; *Iam vero peccatum appellat, primam illam pravitatem animis insidentem, quae nos ad peccandum impellit: ex qua proprie maleficia et flagitia omnia scaturiunt.* CO 49:111.

12. *Institutes*, III.3.11, OS 4:66.

13. "For if heaven is our homeland, what else is the earth but our place of exile? If departure from the world is entry into life, what else is the world but a sepulcher? And what else is it for us to remain in life but to be immersed in death? If to be freed from the body is to be released into perfect freedom, what else is the body but a prison?" *Institutes*, III.9.3, OS 4:173. The metaphor "prison" occurs several times in the *Institutes* [1559]: I.15.2; II.7.13, 13.4; III.3.20, 6.5, 9.4, 25.1; IV.1.1, 15.11, 16.19, 17.30.

14. *Comm. 2 Cor.* 5:4; *Gemitus autem fidelium inde nascitur, quod se exsulare hic sciunt extra patriam: quod sicunt se corpore inclusos teneri tanquam ergastulo.* CO 50:62.

The Christian Life as Pilgrimage

The unceasing afflictions of this world are the outward reason for the present imperfection of Christians. Christians cannot enjoy perfect peace amid these afflictions. Calvin's description of the Christians as "pilgrims" who cannot attain perfect peace in their sojourn in this world is significant to this idea:

> As long as we carry about us our flesh, we cannot cast away every care for it; for though our conversation is in heaven, we yet sojourn on earth. The things then which belong to the body must be taken care of, but not otherwise than as they are helps to us in our pilgrimage, and not that they may make us to forget our country.[15]

"Pilgrimage" is one of his favourite metaphors used by Calvin to describe the Christian life, along with other similar travel metaphors such as "journey,"[16] "race"[17] and "sojourn."[18] In the *Institutes* (1559), for example, he uses the travel metaphor more often than any other metaphor to present his ideas. While military metaphors such as "fight," "war," "combat" and "soldier" appear around twelve times, travel metaphors such as "pilgrimage," "race," "sojourn," and "journey" appear more than twenty times.[19] Nevertheless,

---

15. *Comm. Rom.* 13:14, CO 49:256.

16. "Paul confirms . . . that we journey away from God so long as we dwell in the flesh, but that we enjoy his presence outside the flesh." *Institutes*, I.15.2, OS 3:175.

17. "Now this is not to deny a place for growth; rather I say, the closer any man comes to the likeness of God, the more the image of God shines in him. In order that believers may reach this goal, God assigns to them a race of repentance, which they are to run throughout their lives." *Institutes*, III.3.9, OS 4:63.

18. "Hence we likewise by believing 'pass out of death into life' being 'no more strangers and sojourners, but fellow citizens of the saints and of the household of God,' who 'made us sit' with his only-begotten Son 'in heavenly places,' that we may lack nothing for full happiness." *Institutes*, III.25.1, OS 4:432.

19. The travel metaphor frequently appears not only in the *Institutes* but also throughout his writings, especially in his commentaries: *Comm. Rom.* 5:2, 8:23, 13:14; *Gal.* 4:26; *1 Pet.* 1:17. The description of the Christian life as a "pilgrimage" appears in a number of the closing prayers of his lectures on the Prophets: *Comm. Isa* 49:23; *Jer.* 31:13, 41:5; *Ezek.* 2:10, 6:9; *Dan.* 1:8, 2:9, 2:43, 7:8, 7:17, 7:25, 7:27, 8:7, 8:10, 8:12, 11:16, 12:10; *Amos* 2:13, *Obad.* 21; *Hab.* 2:6, 2:19; *Zeph.* 3:9; *Mal.* 3:2. Especially, Calvin uses this metaphor in his commentary on Psalms most frequently in his commentaries: *Comm. Ps.* 4:6, 17:15, 37: Argument, 37:9, 37:18, 49:15, 51:7, 73:16, 89:47, 90:1, 113:2, 119:54, 128:2. Selderhuis properly observes the significance of the metaphor of "pilgrimage" and "solider" concerning Christian life in Calvin's Commentary on the Psalms. Selderhuis,

PART ONE—Calvin's Anthropology

despite their frequency and significance for Calvin, his travel metaphors have not received due attention in the major studies of Calvin's teaching on the Christian life.[20] The significance of each metaphor in Calvin's theology may not actually depend on the frequency of its appearance in the *Institutes*. However, as one of the most popular concepts by which Calvin presents his ideas, the metaphor of pilgrimage offers us an effective way to examine his doctrine of the Christian life.

Calling the Christian life "pilgrimage," Calvin concentrates on the continuous afflictions of Christians as "sojourners": Christians who are pilgrims and sojourners in this world "see things strangely confused in the world," and are "harassed in various ways and distracted by many dangers, which every moment threaten us with death."[21] Tribulation in this world is inevitable for those pilgrims who follow Christ:

> When they see the world opposing Christ with wicked obstinacy, they must be prepared to meet that opposition, and to contend against it undismayed. The unbelief of the world is—we know it—a great and serious hindrance; but it must be conquered, if we wish to believe in Christ.[22]

Calvin claims that it is God's will that Christians suffer tribulation in this life in order "to try their faith that, after having laid aside their desires and forsaken the world, they might serve him."[23] Again, in his understanding of the Christian life as a "pilgrimage," Calvin tries to highlight the imperfect condition of believers from an eschatological perspective: Christians already began their new life when they became members of Christ by becoming united to him, but the perfect status of their life has not yet come in their present life of tribulations and will not come until they reach heaven:

Calvin's Theology of the Psalms, 142–45.

20. In contrast to Leith and Wallace who ignore Calvin's use of travel metaphors, Quistorp begins his discussion of Calvin's idea of the Christian life with this observation on the pilgrim metaphor: "Calvin likes to represent the life of the Christian in its patient hope of future glory as the journey of a pilgrim through foreign lands into the country of promise." Quistorp, *Calvin's Doctrine of the Last Things*, 27.

21. *Comm. Ps.* 37:18, CO 31:367. "He [Peter] calls the present life a sojourning, not in the sense in which he called the Jews to whom he was writing sojourners, at the beginning of the Epistle, but because all the godly are in this world pilgrims." *Comm. 1 Pet.* 1:17, CO 55:225.

22. *Comm. Luke* 2:34, CO 45:92. Hall argues that Calvin always thinks of Christians as a minority within this world. Hall, *With the Spirit's Sword*, 131.

23. *Comm. Isa.* 26:18, CO 36:441.

The Christian Life as the Eschatological Progress

"if we be dead with Christ, as befits his members, we must seek the things that are above, and be pilgrims on earth, so that we may aspire to heaven where our treasure is."[24]

Consolation and Hope for the Christian Life

Calvin argues that the present imperfection of the Christian life would be meaningless and unbearable without God's promise of future perfection. Therefore, in his discussion of death and the final resurrection, the two key eschatological themes, Calvin highlights God's promise to Christians of perfection in the final resurrection. This promise provides them with consolation and hope in their present life.

Calvin's Doctrine of Death

Calvin thinks of death as the end of the Christian's spiritual warfare: "after death comes, since all warfare is ended and our enemies can no longer assault us, we hold it [hope for joy and rest in God] with the greatest of certainty."[25] According to his interpretation of "the house from heaven" in 2 Corinthians 5:2, however, death is only "the commencement" of the blessed state of humanity compared to the final resurrection, which is "the consummation."[26] In Calvin's eschatology, the condition of Christians at the final resurrection is more important than their condition after death. God's promise of future perfection of the entire Christians in salvation history will be accomplished on this last day.

Nevertheless, Calvin's idea of death has received more attention from scholars than his idea of the final resurrection. This is mainly because the immortality of the soul is the subject of his first theological work, *Psychopannychia*. While most scholars have investigated this treatise with the purpose of tracing the roots of Calvin's conversion to the Protestant faith, the eschatological subject of *Psychopannychia* has not received sufficient

---

24. *Institutes*, III.16.2, OS 4:250.

25. John Calvin, *Brief Instruction for Arming All the Good Faithful against the Errors of the Common Sect of the Anabaptist*, 137; CO 7:124. Hereafter referred to as *Against the Anabaptists*.

26. Comm. 2 Cor. 5:2; *Quamquam malo ita accipere, ut initium huius aedificii sit beatus animae status post mortem: consummatio autem sit gloria ultimae resurrectionis.* CO 50:61.

attention.²⁷ Quistorp and Selinger are exceptions because they have examined the eschatological subject of this treatise instead of examination of its implications for Calvin's life. But *Psychopannychia* is the best source for them to criticise Calvin's anthropology. Quistorp argues that Calvin's eschatological ideas in *Psychopannychia* have a "spiritualised" and dualistic tendency in their emphasis on the dignity of the soul over that of the body, and this leads Calvin to fail to rightly recognise the biblical idea of the human being.²⁸ Likewise, Selinger claims that at the beginning of his career as a theologian, Calvin's anthropology suffers from a "tension" between the holistic view of humanity in Scripture and the dualistic view in Platonism.²⁹

It is true that Calvin uses platonic terms and ideas with regard to the condition of the immortal soul after death in *Psychopannychia* and more obviously than in his other writings. However, it should be taken into account that neither the subject nor the methodology of this treatise represents Calvin's whole anthropology. Calvin's prefatory letter of *Psychopannychia* makes it clear that his decision to write this treatise was not in order to introduce his anthropology but was to make an urgent response to the Anabaptists' idea that the soul sleeps after death:

> Long ago, when certain pious persons invited, and even urged me, to publish something for the purpose of repressing the extravagance of those who, alike ignorantly and tumultuously, maintain that the soul dies or sleeps, I could not be induced by all their

27. In investigations of Calvin's *Psychopannychia* for this purpose, on the one hand, some scholars have suggested that Calvin's late or gradual conversion to Protestantism came as late as 1534 on the grounds that there is no "anti-papal" material in this treatise. Ganoczy, *Young Calvin*, 75–91, 245; Tavard, *Starting Point of Calvin's Theology*, 38–39. On the other hand, others have stressed the specific context of *Psychopannychia*, and argue that it is not possible to reconstruct the timing of Calvin's conversion through this treatise. George, "Calvin's *Psychopannychia*," 297–329; Scholl, "Karl Barth as Interpreter of Calvin's Psychopannychia," 291–308; Muller, "Starting Point of Calvin's Theology," 314–41.

28. Quistorp states that Calvin's anthropology often shows "the humanistic bent" which, he believes, hindered Calvin taking seriously enough the corporeal connotations of the Old Testament term "nephesh" and the New Testament term *psyche*. Quistorp, *Calvin's Doctrine of the Last Things*, 64–65.

29. According to Selinger, Calvin holds "an overly spiritualised view" of the soul as the result of "a continuous and significant conflict between dualism and orthodoxy." Selinger, *Calvin against Himself*, 3. Ganoczy, Hwang and Tavard also stress the influence of Platonic dualism and renaissance humanism on his thoughts. Ganoczy, *Young Calvin*, 83–91; Hwang, *Der junge Calvin und seine Psychopannychia*, 262; Tavard, *Starting Point of Calvin's Theology*, 20–39.

The Christian Life as the Eschatological Progress

urgency, so averse did I feel to engage in that kind of dispute . . . The result, however, has been different from what I hoped. These babblers have so actively exerted themselves, that they have already drawn thousands into their insanity. And even the error itself has, I see, been aggravated.[30]

The motive for writing *Psychopannychia* is quite different from that of the first edition of the *Institutes* in 1536. In the prefatory letter to Francis I, Calvin writes:

> My purpose was solely to transmit certain rudiments by which those who are touched with any zeal for religion might be shaped to true godliness . . . The book itself witnesses that this was my intention, adapted as it is to a simple and, you may say, elementary form of teaching.[31]

That Calvin postponed publication of this treatise in 1542 following the advice of the Strasbourg reformers also shows that Calvin did not intend to introduce his anthropology through this treatise.[32] Capito, in particular, advised him not to publish this treatise because it would have caused an unnecessary misunderstanding of Protestant theology with regard to such a controversial issue as the immortality of the soul.[33]

Furthermore, even in this polemical treatise, as Holwerda points out, Calvin does not follow the Platonic idea without a theological focus to highlight God's grace. Calvin argues that the blessed immortality of the believer's soul is not its own nature but "a gift of God, and the life of the soul is continually dependent on the grace and will of God."[34] In this treatise, we can find that the principal concern of Calvin's eschatology is to provide Christians with consolation and hope for their present life based on God's promise of the final resurrection:

30. *Psychopannychia*, TT 3: 414, CO 5:170.

31. *Institutes*, [1536], CO 1:3. For discussion of the purpose of the *Institutes*, see Armstrong, "*Duplex cognitio Dei*, or the Problem and Relation of Structure, Form, and Purpose of Calvin's Theology," 135–51; Hesselink, "Development and Purpose of Calvin's *Institutes*," 71; Jones, *Calvin and the Rhetoric of Piety*, 53ff.; Zachman, "What Kind of Book is Calvin's *Institutes*?"

32. Tavard, *Starting Point of Calvin's Theology*, 8–10; Muller, "Starting Point of Calvin's Theology," 334.

33. Letter of Capito to Calvin, *Epistolae* 1:102–4, CO 10:45–46.

34. Holwerda, "Eschatology and History," 114. The immortality of the souls of the reprobate cannot be called "God's gift" because their souls, "being estranged from God, are perpetually cast down and discarded from his presence." *Psychopannychia*, TT 3:486; CO 7:228.

> We are more miserable than all men if there is no resurrection, because, although we are happy before the resurrection, we are not happy without the resurrection. For we say that the spirits of saints are happy in this that they rest in the hope of a blessed resurrection, which they could not so, were all this blessedness to perish.[35]

Therefore, the platonic terms and ideas in *Psychopannychia* do not prove that Calvin's entire anthropology suffers from the tension between platonic dualism and biblical teaching of humanity. Instead, it should be noted that he presents his first and polemical theological treatise with the concern to provide Christians with consolation in the final resurrection.

The Soul in the Intermediate State

When discussing the condition of the faithful soul after death, Calvin pays attention to its provisional nature: although believers will enjoy tremendous happiness after the termination of their "flesh" at death, this happiness is still provisional in that final consummation is yet to come at the resurrection of their bodies on the last day.

Calvin claims that at death the souls of believers experience "a sudden transition from corrupted nature into a blessed immortality."[36] There are two aspects of this sudden transition: enhancement of their knowledge of God and a closer relationship with God. Christian knowledge of God after death will be far better than their "knowledge of God in faith" in the present life: "And now, indeed, God begins to renew in us his own image, but in what a small measure! Except then we be stripped of all the corruption of the flesh, we shall not be able to behold God face to face."[37] The expression "face to face" in 1 Corinthians 13:12 is the key biblical term by which Calvin presents his idea of the epistemological transformation of Christians after death: "Our faith, therefore, at present beholds God as absent. How so? Because it sees not his face, but rests satisfied with the image in the mirror; but when we shall have left the world, and gone to him, it will behold him

---

35. *Psychopannychia*, TT 3: 472, CO 7:218.

36. *Comm. Phil.* 1:6. CO 52:10. "It [death] will then be the destruction of corruptible nature: it will not be a sleep, in as much as the soul will not quit the body; but there will be a sudden transition from corruptible nature to a blessed immortality." *Comm. 1 Cor.* 15:51, CO 50:561.

37. *Comm. 1 John* 3:2, CO 55:331.

The Christian Life as the Eschatological Progress

as near and before its eyes."[38] After death, Christians will also have a more intimate relationship with God: "For nothing is better than to quit the body, that we may attain near intercourse with God, and may truly and openly enjoy his presence."[39] Calvin stresses the transition of believers to a closer relationship with God after death in his argument against the Anabaptists idea of "soul sleep":

> nothing more fittingly and positively resolves this matter for us than our recalling the union and unity we have with our Lord Jesus . . . Let us hold, I say, to this position, that possessing an inseparable union with our Lord Jesus, we are participants of that permanent life in Him.[40]

However, despite this sudden transformation in knowledge of God and relationship with God, the happiness and peace of the Christian soul after death are still provisional:

> This peace is increased and advanced by death, which, freeing, and as it were discharging them from the warfare of this world, leads them into the place of peace, where wholly intent on beholding God, they have nothing better to which they can turn their eyes or direct their desires. Still, something is wanting which they desire to see, namely, the complete and perfect glory of God, to which they always aspire.[41]

Stating that the condition of the believers' soul after death is not the ultimate perfection, Calvin highlights that their perfection will come only on the last day: "there cannot be a doubt that believers, when they die, make a nearer approach to the enjoyment of the heavenly life. Still, it must be understood that the glory of immortality is delayed till the last day of redemption."[42]

For this purpose, Calvin even speaks of the advancement of Christ's grace on the believers' souls after death. Interpreting "Until the day of Jesus Christ" in Philippians 1:6, Calvin argues,

> The chief thing, indeed, to be understood here is—until the termination of the conflict. Now the conflict is terminated by death. As, however, the Spirit is accustomed to speak in this manner in

---

38. *Comm. 1 Cor.* 13:12, CO 49:514. *Against the Anabaptists*, 141, CO 7:126.
39. *Comm. 2 Cor.* 5:8, CO 50:64.
40. *Against the Anabaptists*, 134–35, CO 7:122.
41. *Psychopannychia*, TT 3:435–36, CO 5:190.
42. *Comm. Luke* 16:22, CO 45:449.

PART ONE—Calvin's Anthropology

reference to the last coming of Christ, it were better to extend the advancement of the grace of Christ to the resurrection of the flesh.[43]

In *Psychopannychia*, he asserts the idea of this "post-mortem advancement of blessedness" to argue against the idea of "soul sleep": "For how do they [Anabaptists] interpret that progress? Do they think that souls are perfected when they are made heavy with sleep as a preparation for their being brought sleek and fat into the presence of God when he shall sit in judgment?"[44] In the same treatise, Calvin argues that Christians will reach the state of perfection at death because the process of regeneration is complete when they become united with God:

> ... our blessedness is always in progress up to that day which shall conclude and terminate all progress, and ... thus the glory of the elect, and complete consummation of hope, look forward to that day for their fulfilment. For it is admitted by all that perfection of blessedness or glory nowhere exists except in perfect union with God.[45]

Since regeneration, the restoration of the *imago Dei* in each Christian, is completed at the moment of death, the spiritual struggle between the flesh and the spirit within them and the tribulations of this world will cease. After death, therefore, there will be no further progress of the regeneration as Christians pass through in their present life. How then can Calvin speak of "advancement of grace" after death while insisting that there is no more "progress" after death? In his eschatology, Calvin seems to think that it is possible to speak of the post-mortem advancement in order to highlight the perfection of all Christians on the last day. For him, whilst regeneration in the present life is a progression of faith in the midst of imperfection, the progress of blessedness after death is characterised by the hope and aspiration for the consummation on the last day:

> For although those who have been freed from the mortal body do no longer contend with the lusts of the flesh, and are, as the

---

43. *Comm. Phil.* 1:6, CO 52:9.

44. *Psychopannychia*, TT 3:444, CO 5:197.

45. *Psychopannychia*, TT 3:463; *Beatitudinem nostram semper in cursu esse, usque ad diem illum, qui omnem cursum claudet et terminabit: ita electorum gloriam, et ultimate spei finem, ad eum ipsum diem spectare, ut impleantur. Nam hoc satis inter omnes convenit, nullam esse vel beatitudinis, vel gloriae perfectionem, nisi perfectam cum Deo coniunctionem.* CO 5:211.

expression is, beyond the reach of a single dart, yet there will be no absurdity in speaking of them as in the way of advancement, inasmuch as they have not yet reached the point at which they aspire,—they do not yet enjoy the felicity and glory which they have hoped for; and in fine, the day has not yet shone which is to discover the treasures which lie hid in hope. And in truth, when hope is treated of, our eyes must always be directed forward to a blessed resurrection, as the grand object in view.[46]

Although there is no further speculative discussion to clarify this postmortem advancement of believers' souls in Calvin's theology, it is at least certain that he intends to emphasise the importance of the final resurrection as the perfection of the whole Christians.[47]

The Final Resurrection

In Calvin's anthropology, the climax of the Christian life is the final resurrection. He thinks that the entire progress of Christians is completed by this event. In his *Treatise against the Libertines,* Calvin points out four aspects of the perfection gained by Christians on the last day: firstly, they will see the glory of God "fully face to face." Secondly, both their soul and body will enjoy perfect happiness in the presence of God. Thirdly, their bodies "will be transfigured into the glory of our Lord Jesus." Finally, all creatures will be finally "united in company with" Christians.[48]

As we have seen, the first and second points are accomplished in the Christian's soul by death. Thus there is no difference in the state of

46. *Comm. Phil.* 1:6; *Tametsi enim qui ex corpore mortali sunt liberati, non amplius militent cum carnis concupiscentiis, sintque extra teli iactum, ut aiunt: tamen nihil erit absurdi, si dicantur esse in profectu: quia nondum pertigerunt quo adspirant, nondum potiuntur felicitate et gloria quam sperarunt, denique nondum illuxit dies qui revelat absconditos in spe thesauros. Atque adeoquum de spe agitur, semper ad beatam resurrectionem, tanquam ad scopum, referendi sunt oculi.* CO 52:9–10.

47. Probably, Calvin's opposition to indulgences and the Roman Catholic doctrine of purgatory hinders him from developing the idea of the advancement after death. However, for Calvin the problem of indulgences and purgatory mainly concerns the issue of *sola gratia Christi* rather than an anthropological issue about human condition after death: "purgatory is a deadly fiction of Satan, which nullifies the cross of Christ inflicts unbearable contempt upon God's mercy, and overturns and destroys our faith. For what means this purgatory of theirs but that satisfaction for sins is paid by the souls of the dead after their death?" *Institutes*, III.5.6, OS 4:138.

48. John Calvin, *Against the Fantastic and Furious Sect of the Libertines who are called "Spirituals,"* 297–98, CO 7:224–25.

PART ONE—Calvin's Anthropology

Christians at these points between their death and the last day except that their body also enjoy blessings in these regards. Firstly, Calvin again uses the expression "face to face," which appears in his explanation about believer's knowledge of God after death, with reference to the perfect knowledge gained by them on the last day:

> For though we very truly hear that the Kingdom of God will be filled with splendor, joy, happiness, and glory, yet when these things are spoken of, they remain utterly remote from our perception, and, as it were, wrapped in obscurities, until that day comes when he will reveal to us his glory, that we may behold it face to face.[49]

Secondly, Calvin's explanation about the perfect relationship to be had with God on the last day is similar to his thoughts about this relationship immediately after death:

> If the Lord will share his glory, power, and righteousness with the elect—nay, will give himself to be enjoyed by them and, what is more excellent, will somehow make them to become one with himself, let us remember that every sort of happiness is included under this benefit.[50]

Thus the differences between the states of perfection in the status of Christians at death and on the last day are seen in the third and fourth aspects. Concerning the third aspect, Calvin argues that, "although we shall retain the substance of our bodies, there will be a change, that its condition may be far more excellent." This "far more excellent" condition is the incorruptible nature of the body: "Therefore, that we may be raised, the corruptible body will not perish or vanish but, having laid aside corruption, will put on incorruption."[51] In his *Institutes* and commentary on 1 Corinthians, however, Calvin is satisfied with simply mentioning the significance of the renewal of the body as the completion of salvation without any further speculation on the new relationship between the soul and the resurrected body:

> He [God] accomplishes the salvation of his people only when death and the grave are reduced to nothing. For no one will deny that in that passage [1 Cor. 15:58] there is a description of completed

---

49. *Institutes*, III.25.10, OS 4:453.
50. *Institutes*, III.25.10, OS 4:453.
51. *Institutes*, III.25.8, OS 4:450. Cf. *Comm. 1 Cor.* 15:35, CO 51:555.

salvation. As, therefore, we do not see such a destruction of death, it follows, that we do not yet enjoy that complete salvation, which God promises to his people, and that, consequently, it is delayed until that day.[52]

With respect to the fourth aspect of perfection, Quistorp argues that due to the "chief concern with the doctrine of justification," Calvin's eschatology "lacks very largely the cosmic breadth which is characteristic of the Biblical expectation of the end."[53] Of course, Calvin does not totally ignore the cosmic dimension of the consummation. In his commentary on 1 Corinthians 15:27, for example, he mentions the restoration of Christ's lordship over the world: "First, that all things must be brought under subjection to Christ before he restores to the Father the dominion of the world, and secondly, that the Father has given all things into the hands of his Son in such a way as to retain the principal right in his own hands."[54] Nevertheless, he goes no further in his treatment of the cosmic dimension of the last judgment. In the *Institutes* III.25, Calvin simply mentions the restoration of the whole universe with reference to Romans 8:19–22 thus:

> For since Adam by his fall brought into confusion the perfect order of nature, the bondage to which the creatures have been subjected because of man's sin is heavy and grievous to them. Not that they are endowed with any perception, but they naturally long for the undamaged condition whence they have fallen.[55]

In his commentary on Romans 8:19–22, Calvin clarifies the limits of proper inquiry into the restoration of the universe on the last day:

> But what that perfection will be, as to beasts as well as plants and metals, it is not meet nor right in us to inquire more curiously; for the chief effect of corruption is decay. Some subtle men, but hardly sober-minded, inquire whether all kinds of animals will be immortal; but if reins be given to speculations where will they at

---

52. *Comm. 1 Cor.* 15:54; *His verbis significat Deus, tunc se demum servare suos fideles, quum mors et infernus in nihilum rediguntur. Nemo enim negabit, eo loco descriptionem esse perfectae salutis. Quum ergo talem mortis interitum nondum cernamus, sequitur, necdum plena salute nos potiri, quam Deus populo suo promittit: et ideo in illum diem differri.* CO 50:563.

53. Quistorp, *Calvin's Doctrine of the Last Things*, 11–12.

54. *Comm. 1 Cor.* 15:27, CO 51:549. "For in the cross of Christ . . . the whole world was renewed and all things restored to order." *Comm. John* 13:31, CO 47:316. For the cosmic dimension of Calvin's eschatology, see Holwerda, "Eschatology and History," 121ff.

55. *Institutes*, III.25.2, CO 4:434.

PART ONE—Calvin's Anthropology

length lead us? Let us then be content with this simple doctrine—
that such will be the constitution and the complete order of things,
that nothing will be deformed or fading.[56]

When he treats the last two aspects of the final resurrection, therefore, Calvin has a certain reservation about developing any further speculation with regard to either the condition of the resurrected body or the restoration of the universe. It is sufficient and legitimate for Calvin to recognise in the biblical teachings of the perfection of the whole universe, the dramatic transformation, through grace, of the Christians' state on the last day:

> Thus the condemnation of mankind is imprinted on the heavens, and on the earth, and on all creatures. It hence also appears to what excelling glory the sons of God shall be exalted; for all creatures shall be renewed in order to amplify it, and to render it illustrious.[57]

Consolation through the Promise of God

In the *Institutes* III.25, where he deals with the final resurrection, Calvin argues that any speculation beyond the teaching of Scripture is not only unlawful but also harmful:

> We also feel how we are titillated by an immoderate desire to know more than is lawful. From this, trifling and harmful questions repeatedly flow forth—trifling, I say, for from them no profit can be derived. But this second kind is worse because those who indulge in them entangle themselves in dangerous speculations: accordingly, I call these questions "harmful."[58]

Quistorp suggests that Calvin worries too much about the misuse of the idea of cosmic perfection both "in the hands of the Catholics in a speculative sense" and "in the hands of the fanatics for apocalyptic purposes," and, as a result, he is reluctant to present a further discussion of the cosmic dimension of the last things.[59] It is not quite certain to what extent such polemical situations prevented Calvin from presenting a speculation on cosmic perfection because Calvin himself does not mention this polemical

56. *Comm. Rom.* 8:21, CO 49:153.
57. *Comm. Rom.* 8:21, CO 49:153.
58. *Institutes*, III.25.10, CO 4:452–53.
59. Quistorp, *Calvin's Doctrine of the Last Things*, 11.

The Christian Life as the Eschatological Progress

context in either the *Institutes* III.25 or his *Commentary on Romans* 8:19-22. Yet, it is obvious that no speculative discussion of cosmic perfection is presented by Calvin in these two texts. It is enough for him to highlight the implication of future perfection for the present life of the Christian: "But he [Paul] introduces all parts of the world, by a sort of personification, as being endued with reason; and he does this in order to shame our stupidity, when the uncertain fluctuation of this world, which we see, does not raise our minds to higher things."[60]

Calvin thinks that "scripture goes no farther than to say that Christ is present with them, and receives them into paradise that they may obtain consolation, while the souls of the reprobate suffer such torments as they deserve."[61] He holds the same view about the perfect condition of the Christian on the last day:

> Meanwhile, since Scripture everywhere bids us wait in expectation for Christ's coming, and defers until then the crown of glory, let us be content with the limits divinely set for us; namely, that the souls of the pious, having ended the toil of their warfare, enter into blessed rest, where in glad expectation they await the enjoyment of promised glory, and so all things are held in suspense until Christ the Redeemer appear.[62]

When referring to the biblical notion of cosmic restoration, it is again consolation and hope that Calvin tries to highlight: "And, that their courage may not fail in this race, Paul joins all creatures to them as companions. For because formless ruins are seen everywhere, he says that everything in heaven and on earth strives after renewal."[63] In his comment on Romans 8:19, Calvin makes this point clearer:

> For, to omit various interpretations, I understand the passage to have this meaning—that there is no element, and no part of the world which, being touched, as it were, with a sense of its present misery, does not intensely hope for a resurrection. He indeed lays down two things—that all are creatures in distress,—and yet that

---

60. *Comm. Rom.* 8:20, CO 49:152.

61. *Institutes*, III.25.6, CO 4:442. "As far as I am concerned, I not only refrain personally from superfluous investigation of useless matters, but I also think that I ought to guard against contributing to the levity of others by answering them." *Comm. 2 Cor.* 5:8, CO 50:64.

62. *Institutes*, III.25.6, CO 4:442.

63. *Institutes*, III.25.2, OS 4:433.

they are sustained by hope. And it hence also appears how immense is the value of eternal glory, that it can excite and draw all things to desire it.[64]

In his eschatology, Calvin draws attention to the twofold promise of God: He will preserve His children throughout their life and finally complete His work of regeneration at the end. This promise is the sole foundation on which Christians gain consolation and hope during their present pilgrimage of continuous warfare and afflictions. Christians can be assured of their final victory by remembering that Christ will protect them until the end of their life:

> Thus it is that we may patiently pass through this life with its misery, hunger, cold, contempt, reproaches, and other troubles—content with this one thing: that our King [Christ] will never leave us destitute, but will provide for our needs until, our warfare ended, we are called to triumph.[65]

In their present life of pilgrimage, Christians can have consolation by reminding themselves that God preserves them at any rate: "For if, while they are pilgrims in the world, they bear a close resemblance to dead men, much less does any appearance of life exist in them after the death of the body. But God is faithful to preserve them alive in his presence, beyond the comprehension of men."[66]

Christians find consolation in God's promise not only for living but also when facing death. Death is, of course, a fearful and detestable experience even for Christians: "we have naturally an aversion to the quitting of this life, considered in itself, as no one willingly allows himself to be stripped of his garments."[67] Yet "true faith" of Christians "begets not merely contempt of death, but even a desire for it." Calvin argues thus that it is "a token of unbelief, when dread of death predominates in us above the joy and consolation of hope."[68] Christians, therefore, are those who find the consolation of hope in death. Commenting on 2 Timothy 4:6, Calvin argues that Paul here "affirms that to Christ's combatants death is desirable,

---

64. *Comm. Rom.* 8:19, CO 49:151–52.
65. *Institutes*, II.15.4, OS 3:476.
66. *Comm. Luke* 20:38, CO 45:607.
67. *Comm. 2 Cor.* 5:4, CO 50:62.
68. *Comm. 2 Cor.* 5:8, CO 50:64.

because it puts an end to their labours."[69] However, it is God's promise of the final victory which provides Christians with the unshakable foundation of their hope of future perfection:

> After Paul's example let us now eagerly triumph in the midst of our battles, because He [God] who has promised us a future life is able to preserve what has been entrusted; and so let us exult that the crown of righteousness has been laid up for us, which the righteous Judge [Christ] shall give to us. Thus it will come to pass that whatever annoyances we suffer will foreshow to us the life to come.[70]

The Promise of God and the Human Response

Confirmation of Future Perfection by the Grace of the Trinity

Calvin argues that Christians can confirm their future perfection and obtain consolation and hope for their present life not by their own efforts, but solely by the grace of the Triune God. This shows that the consistent focus of Calvin's eschatology is also the focal point of his anthropology: to highlight the distinct but complementary works of each person of the Trinity in the process of salvation. Most scholars who have noted this focus in Calvin's eschatology have indicated his emphasis on the significance of Christ's role in providing Christians with hope of their future perfection.[71] Calvin himself, however, explains this grace of hope from a trinitarian perspective, which underscores not only the work of Christ, but also the promise of the Father and the confirmation given by the Holy Spirit. Calvin's trinitarian perspective is evident in his explanation that Christ's resurrection provides the foundation of the resurrection of the believer's body:

---

69. *Comm.* 2 *Tim.* 4:6, CO 52:389.
70. *Institutes*, III.25.4, OS 4:438.
71. For example, Holwerda and Quistorp approach Calvin's eschatology from a christological perspective: "Jesus Christ stands at the centre of Calvin's perspective on the Christian life. Everything said about self-denial, cross-bearing, and contempt of this life, as well as everything Calvin says about the history of the world and its future, is determined by the person and work of Jesus Christ." Holwerda, "Eschatology and History," 121. "The hope of Christians is rooted in their fellowship with Christ. Through faith they are incorporated in His body. As members of His body they have an eternal destiny." Quistorp, *Calvin's Doctrine of the Last Things*, 20ff.

PART ONE—Calvin's Anthropology

Therefore, Christ rose again that he might have us as companions in the life to come. He was raised by the Father, inasmuch as he was Head of the church, from which the Father in no way allows him to be severed. He was raised by the power of the Holy Spirit, the Quickener of us in common with him. Finally, he was raised that he might be the resurrection and the life.[72]

Calvin posits the omnipotence of the Father, who raised Christ for Christians, as the foundation of Christian assurance of the resurrection: "Scripture provides two helps by which faith may overcome this great obstacle: one in the parallel of Christ's resurrection, the other in the omnipotence of God."[73] According to Calvin, it is Christ's resurrection that confirms the Father's promise. He maintains that Christ was not raised up again for his own sake but for ours so that we might be "companions in the life to come."[74] *The Genevan Catechism* of 1542 stresses the significance of Christ's resurrection for the assurance of the future resurrection of believers and the basis of their present life: "For by it [Christ's resurrection] righteousness is obtained for us; it is a sure pledge of our future immortality; and even now by its virtue we are raised to newness of life, that we may obey God's will by pure and holy living."[75] Calvin also points out the significance of Christ's ascension in confirming God's promise of the resurrection.[76] Finally, God's promise is sealed and effectuated in the hearts of Christians by the Holy Spirit. Calvin defines the sealing work of the Holy Spirit as being to "give life to us, on pilgrimage in the world and resembling dead men, so as to assure us that our salvation is safe in God's unfailing care."[77]

In his idea of the Christian life, therefore, Calvin highlights the grace of the triune God which provides Christians with consolation in the present

72. *Institutes*, III.25.3, OS 4:436.

73. *Institutes*, III.25.3, OS 4:435.

74. *Institutes*, III.25.3, OS 4:435. "Christ did not die, or rise again for himself, but for us: hence his resurrection is the foundation of ours, and what was accomplished in him, must be fulfilled in us also." *Comm. 1 Cor.* 15:13, CO 50:542.

75. *Catechism of the Church of Geneva*, LCC 22:100, CO 6:35.

76. "Carried up into heaven, therefore, he [Christ] withdrew his bodily presence from our sight [Acts 1:9], not to cease to be present with believers still on their earthly pilgrimage, but to rule heaven and earth with a more immediate power. But by his ascension he fulfilled what he had promised: that he would be with us even to the end of the world, as his body was raised up above all the heavens, so his power and energy were diffused and spread beyond all the bounds of heaven and earth." *Institutes*, II.16.14, CO 2:381–82. *Catechism of the Church of Geneva*, LCC 22:101, CO 6:36.

77. *Institutes*, III.1.3, OS 4:4.

The Christian Life as the Eschatological Progress

life by promising them unfailing guidance and certain victory in the future. This is Calvin's principal concern that directs his discussions of eschatological issues with regard to the Christian life and death.

The Three Spiritual Exercises as the Human Response

Leithart observes that Calvin sees the motives for the Christian response to the grace of God as being hope and consolation through the promise of God.[78] For Calvin, the course of regeneration is a life of repentance, which consists of mortification of the flesh and vivification of the spirit.[79] Although both mortification and vivification are divine works of the Holy Spirit, they call for a human response:

> Those who walk after the Spirit are not such as have wholly put off all the emotions of the flesh, so that their whole life is redolent with nothing but celestial perfection; but they are those who sedulously labour to subdue and mortify the flesh, so that the love of true religion seems to reign in them.[80]

Furthermore, the inevitable imperfections and tribulations within their present lives calls for Christians to respond with as much effort as possible to the grace of regeneration:

> But no one in this earthly prison of the body has sufficient strength to press on with due eagerness, and weakness so weighs down the greater number that, with wavering and limping and even creeping along the ground, they move at a feeble rate. Let each one of us, then, proceed according to the measure of his puny capacity and set out upon the journey we have begun. No one shall set out so inauspiciously as not daily to make some headway, though it be light.[81]

In Calvin's view, the indispensability of the regenerating grace of the Holy Spirit and the inevitability of their own imperfections mean that Christians should not be idle or passive in their present lives.[82] Since the

---

78. Leithart, "Stoic Elements in Calvin's Doctrine of the Christian Life," 31.

79. "Therefore, in a word, I interpret repentance as regeneration, whose sole end is to restore in us the image of God that had been disfigured and all but obliterated through Adam's transgression." *Institutes*, III.3.9, OS 4:63.

80. *Comm. Rom.* 8:1, CO 49:136.

81. *Institutes*, III.6.5, OS 4:150.

82. "And this is the case, when we renounce carnal lusts, so as to devote ourselves, as

object of regeneration is to manifest "in [the] life of believers a harmony and agreement between God's righteousness and their obedience," Christians should be encouraged to respond actively to the grace of regeneration when they recognise their identity as God's children. In the *Institutes*, Calvin suggests that the motive for leading the Christian life is gratitude for having received the grace of the triune God:

> Ever since God revealed himself Father to us, we must prove our ungratefulness to him if we did not in turn show ourselves his sons . . . Ever since he engrafted us into his body, we must take especial care not to disfigure ourselves, who are his members, with any spot or blemish . . . Ever since the Holy Spirit dedicated us as temples to God, we must take care that God's glory shine through us, and must not commit anything to defile ourselves with the filthiness of sin.[83]

Calvin proposes three spiritual exercises as a human response to this grace on a personal level: self-denial, bearing of the cross, and meditation on the future life. Both self-denial and bearing of the cross are responses to the Holy Spirit's work of mortification:

> There is, however, a twofold participation and fellowship in the death of Christ. The one is inward—what the Scripture is wont to term the mortification of the flesh, or the crucifixion of the old man . . . the other is outward—what is termed the mortification of the outward man. It is the endurance of the cross.[84]

Calvin regards self-denial as the foremost spiritual exercise of the Christian life in response to the Spirit's twofold work of mortification:

> Let this [self-denial] . . . be the first step that a man departs from himself in order that he may apply the whole force of his ability in the service of the Lord. I call "service" not only what lies in obedience to God's Word but what turns the mind of man, empty of its own carnal sense, wholly to the bidding of God's Spirit.[85]

---

those who are bound, to the righteousness of God. Thus indeed we ought to reason, not as some blasphemers are wont to do, who talk idly, and say—that we must do nothing, because we have no power. But it is as it were to fight against God, when we extinguish the grace offered to us, by contempt and negligence." *Comm. Rom.* 6:12, CO 49:111.

83. *Institutes*, III.6.3, OS 4:148.

84. *Comm. Phil.* 3:10, CO 52:50. For the benefits that bearing the cross brings to Christian humbleness before God, see *Institutes*, III.8.3; OS 4:163.

85. *Institutes*, III.7.1, OS 4:151. CO 2:505. For general studies of Calvin's doctrine of

The Christian Life as the Eschatological Progress

The aim of self-denial is the total submission of the Christian to the authority of God: "Therefore, we are ready to seize and grasp God's grace when we have utterly cast out confidence in ourselves and rely only on the assurance [certainty] of his goodness."[86] Thus in pointing out the difference between the Christian idea of self-denial and that of the philosophers, Calvin argues that self-denial is a total and radical submission and subjection of the believer's whole being to God:

> While it [self-denial] is the first entrance to life, all philosophers were ignorant of this transformation, which Paul calls "renewal of the mind" . . . But the Christian philosophy bids reason give way to, submit and subject itself to, the Holy Spirit so that the man himself may no longer live but hear Christ living and reigning within him.[87]

Calvin speaks of the most significant benefits of the exercise of self-denial as being "peaceful repose" in the condition of "impatience and loathing" and "the strength of patience" in the midst of afflictions by "the various diseases, plagues, and calamities of war, ice and hail."[88] To gain these benefits from the exercise of self-denial, Christians should always "look to the Lord so that by his guidance we may be led to whatever lot he has provided for us."[89] In his discussion of self-denial in the *Institutes* III.7.3, Calvin argues that God's promise of the final resurrection gives Christians an additional motive for practising self-denial:

> Consequently, Paul, in order to extricate our minds from all snares, recalls us to the hope of blessed immortality, reminding us that we strive not in vain. For, as Christ our Redeemer once appeared, so in his final coming he will show the fruit of the salvation brought forth by him. In this way he scatters all the allurements that becloud us and prevent us from aspiring as we ought to heavenly glory. Nay, he teaches us to travel as pilgrims in this world that our celestial heritage may not perish or pass away.[90]

---

self-denial, see Wallace, *Calvin's Doctrine of the Christian Life*, 49–100; Leith, *John Calvin's Doctrine of the Christian Life*, 74–86; Leithart, "Stoic Elements in Calvin's Doctrine of the Christian Life," 191–208.

86. *Institutes*, III.12.8; *Gratiae ergo Dei apprehendae ac obstinendae, abiecta quidem prorsus nostri fiducia, freti vero sola bonitatis eius certitudine, idonei sumus.* OS 4:215.

87. *Institutes*, III.7.1, OS 4:151.

88. *Institutes*, III.3.9–10, OS 4:65.

89. *Institutes*, III.3.9, OS 4:65.

90. *Institutes*, III.7.3, OS 4:153.

PART ONE—Calvin's Anthropology

If self-denial applies to the inner life of Christians, bearing the cross is a spiritual exercise by which Christians can respond outwardly to the Holy Spirit's work of mortification. This exercise is especially useful for believers who currently suffer from persecution and tribulations:

> Hence also in harsh and difficult conditions, regarded as adverse and evil, a great comfort comes to us: we share Christ's sufferings in order that as he has passed from a labyrinth of all evils into heavenly glory, we may in like manner be led through various tribulations to the same glory.[91]

In bearing the cross during their present life, Christians can find encouragement and comfort from the biblical teaching that, "we shall not be partakers of the life and glory of Christ, unless we have previously died and been humbled with him."[92] But Christians cannot endure the cross without having received God's promise of protection:

> That God has promised to be with believers in tribulation they experience to be true, while, supported by his hand, they patiently endure—an endurance quite unattainable by their own effort. The saints, therefore, through forbearance experience the fact that God, when there is need, provides the assistance that he has promised.[93]

The exercise of meditation on the future life depends, of course, on God's promise of future life. He argues that the chief benefit of this exercise is to remind Christians that their perfection is to be found not in the present life, but in the life to come:

> From this at the same time, we conclude that in this life we are to seek and hope for nothing but struggle; when we think of our crown, we are to raise our eyes to heaven. For this we must believe: that the mind is never seriously aroused to desire and ponder the life to come unless it be previously imbued with contempt for the present life.[94]

---

91. *Institutes*, III.8.1, OS 4:161. "There is another fellowship as to the death of Christ, of which the apostle often speaks, as he does in 2 Corinthians 4, that is, the bearing of the cross, which is followed by a joint-participation also of eternal life." *Comm. Rom.* 6:12, CO 49:111.

92. *Comm. 2 Tim.* 2:11–12, CO 52:365.

93. *Institutes*, III.8.3, OS 4:163.

94. *Institutes*, III.9.1, OS 4:171.

Calvin does not forget to highlight that Christians can obtain consolation by anticipating their future perfection through this spiritual exercise. Thus his discussion of the meditation of the future life in the *Institutes* III starts with this statement: "Whatever kind of tribulation presses upon us, we must ever look to this end: to accustom ourselves to contempt for the present life and to be aroused thereby to meditate upon the future life."[95]

Calvin suggests these three spiritual exercises as a means of providing Christians with a way in which to find consolation and hope solely in God's promise of protection and perfection. God's promise of future happiness "is our sole comfort. If it be taken away, either our minds must become despondent or, to our destruction, be captivated with the empty solace of this world."[96]

Love of Neighbour

While these three spiritual exercises concern the personal life of the Christian, the duty to love one's neighbour is the response to the Holy Spirit's work of mortification which concerns their communal life: "the mortification will take place in us only if we fulfil the duties of love."[97] Calvin thinks that the spiritual exercise of self-denial is closely related to the obligation to love one's neighbour: "Unless you give up all thought of self and, so to speak, get out of yourself, you will accomplish nothing" in the duty of loving neighbours.[98] All human beings are to be regarded as "neighbours," but Christians should love their fellow believers first, because God commands them to love the members of the same body above others: "There are duties which we owe to all men arising out of a common nature; but the tie of a more sacred relationship, established by God himself, binds us to believers."[99]

Throughout his discussion of this duty, Calvin stresses that the motive for loving one's neighbour is not to earn salvation by merit. Indeed, the good works of Christians towards their neighbours "are most unworthy if they be judged by their own merit."[100] Calvin suggests a twofold motive

---

95. *Institutes*, III.9.1, OS 4:171.
96. *Institutes*, III.9.6, OS 4:176.
97. *Institutes*, III.7.7, OS 4:157.
98. *Institutes*, III.7.5, OS 4:155.
99. *Comm. Gal.* 6:10, CO 50:263. *Institutes*, III.7.5, OS 4:155, *Comm.* 1 *Cor.* 10:16, CO 49:464.
100. *Institutes*, III.7.6, OS 4:156.

PART ONE—Calvin's Anthropology

for love of one's neighbour: the pious desire to worship God and the hope of reward in heaven. Concerning the former motive, Calvin argues in his commentary on Galatians 5:14 that "Piety to God, I acknowledge, ranks higher than love of the brethren." Thus Christian love towards one's neighbour is meaningless unless its motive is to prove "worship of God to be real." Calvin declares in consequence that, "Love to men springs only from the fear and love of God."[101] In his thoughts on the latter motive, Calvin's believes Christ's teaching in Matthew 6:21, that "Where our treasure is, there resides our heart," is significant. In the *Institutes*, Calvin refers to this teaching and argues thus:

> But if we believe heaven is our country, it is better to transmit our possessions thither than to keep them here where upon our sudden migration they would be lost to us. But how shall we transmit them? Surely, by providing for the needs of the poor; whatever is paid out to them, the Lord reckons as given to himself... For what is devoted to our brothers out of the duty of love is deposited in the Lord's hand.[102]

Christians can share their possessions with their neighbour because they trust the promise of God of future reward that incites them to love their neighbours by good works:

> For what is devoted to our brothers out of the duty of love is deposited in the Lord's hand. He, as he is a faithful custodian, will one day repay it with plentiful interest... from these you can duly infer nothing except the pure inclining of God's mercy toward us. To quicken us to well-doing, although the services we offer him are unworthy even of his glance, he permits none of them to be lost.[103]

---

101. *Comm. Gal.* 5:14; *Ergo caritas erga homines non nisi ex timore et amore Dei nascatur.* CO 50:251. "True love towards man does not flow except from the love of God, and it is its evidence, and as it were its effects." *Comm. Rom.* 13:8, CO 49:252.

102. "For what is devoted to our brothers out of the duty of love is deposited in the Lord's hand." *Institutes*, III.18.6, OS 4:276.

103. *Institutes*, III.18.6, OS 4:276–77. However, Calvin is very careful in arguing that future reward does not mean merit for our salvation: "The use of the term 'reward' is no reason for us to suppose that our works are the cause of our salvation. First, let us be heartily convinced that the Kingdom of Heaven is not servants' wages but sons' inheritance [Ephesians 1:18], which only they who have been adopted as sons by the Lord shall enjoy [cf. Galatians 4:7], and that for no other reason than this adoption [cf. Ephesians 1:5–6]." *Institutes*, III.18.2, OS 4:271.

Calvin argues thus that "by acts of charity we obtain favour with God, who has promised, that 'to the merciful he will show himself merciful' (Psalm 18:25)."[104] God's promise of future reward is a gift of grace, providing the suffering Christians with assurance of salvation by reminding them of God's mercy:

> Let us always remember that this promise, like all others, would not bear fruit for us if the free covenant of his mercy had not gone before, upon which the whole assurance of our salvation depended. Now, relying on this, we ought to have firm confidence that, however unworthy our services, a reward will not be lacking from God's generosity.[105]

As Lane points out, however, this reward is not given to believers "according to strict justice," but because of God's "grace and generosity" who overlooks the inadequacies of their good works: "Our works are pleasing only through pardon."[106] Therefore, in his exhortation to love, Calvin does not forget to point out God's promise of reward in the future life as being a motive for Christians" duty to love neighbours in their life.

Conclusion: God's Promise of the Future for the Present Life

In Calvin's doctrine of the Christian life, the condition of perfection of the Christian at the end of the whole salvation history has its meaning not in some unaccomplished mystery of the future life but in providing consolation, hope and motive during their present life. In this respect, Calvin holds an eschatological perspective in his anthropology: while their perfection has not yet come, Christians are already assured of it by trusting in the promise of God in their present life.

---

104. *Comm. Luke* 16:9; *sed benigne erogando favorem apud Deum acquire docet, qui se misericordibus et homanis vicissim misercordem fore promisit.* CO 45:404.

105. *Institutes*, III.18.7, OS 4:277.

106. *Institutes*, III.18.5, OS 4:275. "This recompense, therefore, does not depend on considerations of merit, but on God's gracious acceptance, and is so far from being inconsistent with the righteousness of faith, that it may be viewed as an appendage to it." *Comm. 1 Tim.* 6:19, CO 52:334. Concerning the relationship between justification and reward, Lane describes Calvin's idea of God's approval of the good works of Christians after justification as "double justification." Lane, *Justification by Faith in Catholic-Protestant Dialogue*, 33–37.

PART ONE—Calvin's Anthropology

Therefore, the future life has its significance in the present life. Calvin thus urges Christians to express gratitude for the present earthly life immediately after speaking of the necessity of contempt for the world—as part of the spiritual exercise of meditation on the future life: "Indeed, this life, however crammed with infinite miseries it may be, is still rightly to be counted among those blessings of God which are not to be spurned."[107] What Christians should hold in contempt is not the present life itself, but the "evil fetters" and "enticing allurement" of the world:

> Accordingly, if we have any concern for eternity, we must strive diligently to strike off these evil fetters. Now, since the present life has very many allurements with which to entice us, and much show of pleasantness, grace, and sweetness wherewith to wheedle us, it is very much in our interest to be called away now and again so as not to be captivated by such ponderings.[108]

In conclusion, it is right to say that Calvin's ethical teachings are presented in his eschatological understanding of Christian life. From this eschatological perspective, he tries to provide Christians with consolation and hope in the promise of the triune God.

---

107. *Institutes*, III.9.3, OS 4:173.
108. *Institutes*, III.9.2, OS 4:172.

PART TWO

Calvin's Ecclesiology

4

The Church as the Mother of All Believers

Introduction: The Functional Identity of the Church

CALVIN PRESENTS HIS ECCLESIOLOGY FROM HIS FUNCTIONAL UNDERstanding of the Church. This perspective is represented by the title of the *Institutes* IV: "The external means or aids by which God invites us into the society of Christ and holds us therein."[1] Under this title, those ecclesiological discussions, which had been dispersed throughout previous editions of the *Institutes*, were consolidated into his most mature and fullest ecclesiological discussion in the final edition of the *Institutes*.[2]

However, scholars have found difficulty in understanding the structure of the first chapter of the *Institutes* IV mainly because Calvin suggests here a series of distinctions of the Church, such as the distinction between the invisible and the visible; the true and the false; and the individual and the universal Church, without a sufficient explanation of each definition. Loeschen complains that the structure of this chapter is "an organised chaos."[3] Among those distinctions, as Wiley indicates, the distinction between the invisible and the visible has caused the most serious difficulty in

---

1. *De externis mediis vel adminiculis, quibus Deus in Christi societatem nos invitat, et in ea retinet.* OS 5:1.

2. As Milner points out, it is in the 1543 edition of the *Institutes* that the largest part of Calvin's ecclesiological discussion is composed. Milner, *Calvin's Doctrine of the Church*, 1. However, his ecclesiological discussions were placed dispersedly through the various chapters until the 1559 Latin edition, in which he finally extracted and combined the discussions into an independent presentation of his ecclesiology in book IV. For discussion of the historical and exegetical contexts of the development of Calvin's *Institutes*, see Benoit, "History and Development of the *Institutio*," 102–17; McKee, "Exegesis, Theology, and Development in Calvin's *Institutio*: A Methodological Suggestion," 154–74.

3. Loeschen, *The Divine Community*, 160–61.

PART TWO—Calvin's Ecclesiology

understanding Calvin's idea of the Church, not only in the *Institutes* IV.1, but also in this book as a whole.[4] To recognise Calvin's overriding idea of the Church in this chapter, we need to note its title: "The true Church with which as mother of all the godly we must keep unity."[5] The meaning of this title is explicated in the body thus:

> I shall start, then, with the church, into whose bosom God is pleased to gather his sons, not only that they may be nourished by her help and ministry as long as they are infants and children, but also that they may be guided by her motherly care until they mature and at last reach the goal of faith . . . so that, for those to whom he is Father the church may also be Mother. And this was so not only under the law but also after Christ's coming, as Paul testifies when he teaches that we are the children of the new and heavenly Jerusalem [Gal. 4:26].[6]

According to this statement Calvin emphasises, on one hand, the nourishing help and the motherly care given to believers by the Church by means of the concept of "the mother Church." But, on the other hand, he also seems to speak of the mystical identity of the Church by referring to the Church as "the new and heavenly Jerusalem." Since Calvin mentions both identities alongside his idea of the Church as mother in his ecclesiological discussion, one of the major problems in his ecclesiology in the *Institutes* IV is to determine which identity Calvin speaks of when he calls the Church "the mother of all believers": the visible—functional Church or the invisible—spiritual Church.

This chapter will argue that Calvin presents his idea of the Church as mother not to show the mystical identity of the Church, but to explain its functional identity in the light of his anthropological idea of the Christian identity as children of God. To justify this argument, the first section will investigate Calvin's general use of the "mother" metaphor and his discussion of two important ecclesiological topics from a functional perspective:

---

4. Wiley, "Church as the Elect," 108.

5. *De vera Ecclesia, cum qua nobis colenda est unitas: quia piorum omnium mater est.* OS 5:1.

6. *Institutes*, IV.1.1; *Incipiam autem ab Ecclesia: in cuius sinum aggregari vult Deus filios suos, non modo ut eius opera et ministerio alantur quamdiu infantes sunt ac pueri, sed cura etiam materna regantur donec adolescent, ac tandem perveniant ad fidei metam . . . ut quibus ipse est Pater, Ecclesia etiam mater sit: neque id sub Lege modo, sed etiam post Christi adventum, teste Paulo, qui novae et caelestis Hierosolymae nos esse filios docet [Galat. 4.d.26].* OS 5:1.

the necessity and unity of the Church. In the second section, I will investigate the foci in his idea of the Church as the mother of all believers: the imperfection of the human ministers and the earthly signs; and the necessity of the work of the Holy Spirit in effectuating the ministries of the Church for God's work of regeneration. This investigation will show that Calvin highlights God's grace of accommodation for His children in his idea of the Church as the mother of all believers. The third section will examine Calvin's discussion of the two major ministries of the mother Church, preaching and the sacraments, to illustrate that his idea of functions of the Church as "the mother all believers" is based on the anthropological idea of the present imperfection of the Christians as children of God.

Calvin's Functional Idea of the Church as Mother

A Functional Perspective in Calvin's Use of the "Mother" Metaphor

As shall be seen in the next two subsections, Calvin's idea of the Church as mother is employed in dealing with the two major issues of the first chapter of the *Institutes* IV: the necessity of the Church for salvation and its unity. As Kroon has noted, despite its significance, Calvin's use of the mother metaphor in describing the Church has not been examined either sufficiently or precisely.[7] In particular, two classic studies of Calvin's theology, those by Wendel and Niesel, have not treated this metaphor adequately. Wendel simply notes that "Calvin is using for his own purpose the well-known definitions of St. Cyprian and St. Augustine, and is repeating, in accord with general tradition and with Luther, that the Church is our mother and that apart from her there is no salvation."[8] Niesel offers a more detailed treatment than Wendel by devoting a section of his study to the topics concerning this metaphor.[9] But his examination of this metaphor is too brief to answer the question about the identity of the Church that described by means of the "mother" metaphor in Calvin's ecclesiology. Milner's thorough study of Calvin's doctrine of the Church says even less about this metaphor than Wendel and Niesel. He refers to Calvin's idea of the Church as the mother only once in a footnote, simply mentioning that this

---

7. Kroon, *Honour of God and Human Salvation*, 150.
8. Wendel, *Calvin*, 294–95.
9. Niesel, *Theology of Calvin*, 182–87.

PART TWO—Calvin's Ecclesiology

metaphor shows Calvin's emphasis on "the organic connection between the church and its members."[10] This contrasts sharply with his treatment of Calvin's other metaphors, such as *Corpus Christi* and *Regnum Dei*, with which Milner deals in a chapter entitled "The Church as the Kingdom and Body of Christ."[11]

The only full-scale study of this metaphor in Calvin's theology is Léopold Schümmer's monograph *L'Ecclesiologie de Calvin à la lumière de l'Ecclesia Mater* (1981). In his study, Schümmer tries to demonstrate that Calvin explains the mystical identity of the Church in her marital relationship with God the Father, or her identity as the Spouse of Christ, by calling the Church the "mother."[12] However, Schümmer's theological analysis of Calvin's idea of the Church as the mother seems to be based more on his own systematised idea than on Calvin's idea of the Church. For in the three passages, which Schümmer uses as his proof texts, Calvin does not actually speak of the mystical identity of the Church as the spouse of God using this metaphor. For example, Schümmer quotes the following statement in the *Institutes* II.8.18 in order to argue that Calvin's idea of the mother Church indicates the mystical identity of the Church:

> God very commonly takes on the character of a husband to us. Indeed, the union by which he binds us to himself when he receives us into the bosom of the church is like sacred wedlock, which must rest upon mutual faithfulness. As he performs all the duties of a true and faithful husband, of us in return he demands love and conjugal chastity.[13]

However, Calvin's use of the imagery of spiritual marriage does not refer to the mystical identity of the Church but to the mystical union between God, a husband, and Christians, His spouses. As we shall see, not only in this passage but in the two other proof texts of Schümmer, the *Institutes* IV.1,

10. Milner, *Calvin's Doctrine of the Church*, 2.

11. Ibid., 164–89.

12. "Dire de l'Eglise qu'elle est mere des fidèles, c'est tirer les conclusions terrestres et toujours actuelles de la paternitè de Dieu en Christ. Dieu étant père, le Christ étant le Fils qui manifeste le père, l'Eglise, comme épouse de Christ, est mère." Schümmer, *L'Ecclesiologie de Calvin à la lumière de l'Ecclesia Mater*, 9.

13. *Institutes*, II.8.18; *Personam mariti erga nos induere, usitatissimum est Deo; siquidem coniunctio qua nos sibi devincit dum in Ecclesiae sinum recipit, sacri cuiusdam coniugii instar habet, quod mutua fide stare oportet. Ipse ut omnibus fidelis ac veracis mariti officiis defungitur, ita vicissim a nobis stipulatur amorem ac castitatem coniugalem.* OS 3:360.

The Church as the Mother of All Believers

and Calvin's *Sermon on Galatians* 4:26, Calvin does not use the metaphor "mother" to imply any claims about the mystical identity of the Church as the spouse of God.[14]

In order to ascertain Calvin's intention in using this metaphor in his ecclesiology, we need to examine the general use of this metaphor in his writings, because he uses the metaphor of "motherhood" for various topics besides the Church. Although there are several variations in the meaning of this metaphor according to the different contexts in which it is used, Calvin generally and consistently refers to something as "mother" if he thinks that it has been a "source" or a "fountainhead" of something else. In the *Institutes*, for example, Calvin calls obedience the "mother of all virtue": "Augustine also very truly calls the obedience that is paid to God sometimes the mother and the guardian of all virtues, sometimes their sources."[15] He also defines election as the mother of faith: "Besides, if election, as Paul testifies, is the mother of faith, I turn back upon their head the argument that faith is not general because election is special."[16] At times, Calvin uses this metaphor with negative connotations. In analysing original sin, for example, he calls ambition "the mother" of obstinate disobedience.[17] Likewise, he describes disobedience as "the mother" of all stubbornness.[18] He even invokes this metaphor with negative connotations in his ecclesiological discussion. For example, he calls envy and pride "the mother" of all heresies:

> It is true, that the Church cannot but be torn asunder by false doctrine, and thus heresy is the root and origin of schism, and it is also true that envy or pride is the mother of almost all heresies, but at the same time it is of advantage to distinguish in this way between these two terms.[19]

When he calls the Church "mother" in his ecclesiological discussions of the *Institutes* IV, Calvin uses the metaphor more generally, denoting the Church as the divinely appointed "source" from which God's grace of salvation operates, rather than implying a particular connotation for the mystical identity of the Church. In his commentary on Acts 15:1, Calvin argues, "Jerusalem was honoured not without cause among all churches, because

14. Schümmer, *L'Ecclesiologie de Calvin*, 29–32.
15. *Institutes*, II.8.5, OS 3:347.
16. *Institutes*, III.22.10, OS 4:391.
17. *Institutes*, II.1.4, OS 3:232.
18. *Comm. Eph.* 2:2, CO 51:161.
19. *Comm. 1 Cor.* 11:19, CO 49:481.

they reverenced it even as their mother, For the Gospel was deducted, as it were, by pipes and conduits from that source."[20] In the *Institutes* IV, Calvin uses this metaphor to describe the Church in order to illustrate her character as the unique source of the divine grace of regeneration: "For there is no other way to enter into life unless this mother conceive us in her womb, give us birth, nourish us at her breast, and lastly, unless she keep us under her care and guidance until, putting off mortal flesh, we become like the angels."[21] Therefore, it is hardly persuasive to argue with Schümmer that Calvin speaks of the Church as "the mother" to denote her mystical identity as the spouse of God. Rather, when he calls the Church "the mother" to signify that the Church is the unique source of grace, Calvin concentrates on the vital role played by the Church in God's work of regeneration. It will become clear in the following examinations of Calvin's discussion of the necessity and unity of the Church as "mother" that he uses this metaphor from such a functional perspective.

The Necessity of the Church for Salvation

In Calvin's ecclesiology, the Church is necessary for salvation not because of its mystical identity, but because of its divinely appointed role in teaching the Word of God. By calling the Church mother, Calvin upholds the necessity of the Church for salvation as firmly as Cyprian: "Furthermore, away from her bosom one cannot hope for any forgiveness of sins or any salvation, as Isaiah [Isa. 37:32] and Joel [Joel 2:32] testify."[22] In the *Institutes* IV.2.3, Calvin insists that God's grace of salvation is given only by the truth of the Word: "For the Lord nowhere recognises any temple as his save where his Word is heard and scrupulously obeyed."[23] In the next passage, the absolute indispensability of the Word for human salvation is sharply contrasted with the outward form of the Church: "Accordingly, after Paul has expounded the doctrine, he disposes this difficulty, denying those Jews (as enemies of truth) to be the church, even though they lacked nothing which could otherwise be desired for the outward form of the church."[24] However, Calvin here does not speak of the mystical identity of the Church.

20. *Comm. Acts* 15:1, CO 48:336.
21. *Institutes*, IV.1.4, OS 5:7.
22. *Institutes*, IV.1.4, OS 5:8.
23. *Institutes*, IV.2.3, OS 5:33.
24. *Institutes*, IV.2.3, OS 5:33.

The Church as the Mother of All Believers

Calvin's idea of the Church as the mother would be inconsistent with his emphasis on the necessity of the Word for salvation if he mentions the necessity of the Church without the notion of her role with regard to the Word. In his sermon on Galatians 4:26-31, which describes the New Jerusalem as the true mother of the believers, Calvin says thus: "God governs his people through his Word. It is this message which he has bestowed as a deposit and priceless treasure for the salvation of his church, to bring us regeneration and nourish our spiritual lives."[25]

Calvin's idea that the nature of the true Church is determined by its role in salvation makes evident his functional idea of the Church as mother. In the same sermon on Galatians 4:26–31, Calvin interprets Paul's allegory of the heavenly Jerusalem being the mother of the faithful as teaching about the true and the false Church:

> We need to be discerning, and not like animals who are led by the reins across the field. We need to be aware of what constitutes the true church . . . Wherever, his Word is preached faithfully without any human additions, his own people will be found. This will occur where the gospel is unadulterated, and where people are led directly to God seek in him all that they lack.[26]

In his commentary on the same passage in Galatians, Calvin charges the Roman Church with being a false mother because she is failing in her task of taking care of God's children: "But the Papists are fools and twice children; for their mother is an adulteress, who brings forth to death the children of the devil; and how foolish is the demand, that the children of God should surrender themselves to her to be cruelly slain!"[27] For Calvin, the authenticity of the true Church depends on the faithful performance of its function in teaching God's Word.

In the *Institutes*, Calvin makes two points in clarifying his idea that teaching the Word, the "priceless treasure," is entrusted to the Church. Firstly, Christians as God's children are conceived and born by the preaching ministry of the Church: "God breathes faith into us only by the instrument

---

25. *Serm. Gal.* 4:26–31; "Voilà donc comme Dieu veut gouverner ses fideles, c'est à sçavoir quand il y aura sa parole, comme un depost et un thresor inestimable de salut pour son Eglise, à fin que nous en soyons tous regenerez et nourris." CO 50:646. English translations of Calvin's sermons on Galatians are quoted from John Calvin, *Sermons on Galatians*.

26. *Serm. Gal.* 4:26–31, CO 50:647.

27. *Comm. Gal.* 4:26, CO 50:323.

of his gospel . . . Likewise, the power to save rests with God but (as Paul again testifies) He displays and unfolds it in the preaching of the gospel."[28] Secondly, they are nourished and cared for by God through the education of the Church: "We see how God, who could in a moment perfect his own, nevertheless desires them to grow up into manhood solely under the education of the church."[29] Thus both the beginning and sustenance of the life of the Christian are possible only through the Church's ministry of the Word. This is the basis for Calvin's claim that "out of the Church, there is no salvation." With regard to this point, Niesel aptly argues that Calvin claims the necessity of the Church for salvation because he thinks that "God wills to let Himself be found only where His Word is proclaimed."[30]

The Unity of the Church

In his idea of the Church as the mother of all believers, Calvin shares with Cyprian a concern for the unity of the Church. However, there is a difference in focus between them: while Cyprian refers to the mystical and perfect Church, Calvin speaks of the visible Church and its maternal functions as the reason for the unity of the Church.

In *De Unitate Ecclesiae*, Cyprian claims thus: "The spouse of Christ cannot be defiled; she is uncorrupt and chaste." With his idea of the perfection of the Church as the spouse of God, Cyprian contends that belonging to the mother church is the prerequisite of becoming children of God: "No longer can he have God for his father who has not the Church for his mother."[31] For Cyprian, there is only one perfect Church, whose unity is maintained by the consensus of the bishops who have the presiding authority over the Church: "This unity we ought to hold and to maintain especially we, the Bishops, who preside over the Church, that we may prove the episcopate itself one and indivisible."[32] In Cyprian's mind, unity is the feature of the universal Church which is most necessary for the Christian,

---

28. *Institutes*, IV.1.5; *Fidem nobis Deus inspirat, sed Evangelii sui organo . . . Sicuti etiam penes Deum sua residet potentia ad servandum: sed eam in Evangelii praedicatione (eodem Paulo teste) depromit atque explicat.* OS 5:8.

29. *Institutes*, IV.1.5, OS 5:8.

30. Niesel, "The Reformed View," 247–56.

31. Cyprian, *De Unitate Ecclesiae* VI.19.

32. Cyprian, *De Unitate Ecclesiae* V.17.

The Church as the Mother of All Believers

because of the prerequisite to be a member of the mother Church, that is, the "Episcopal Church" to achieve salvation.

In the *Institutes*, Calvin makes a similar statement to Cyprian's idea: "for those to whom he [God] is Father the church may also be Mother."[33] However, his intentions in using this phrase differ from those of Cyprian. When Cyprian refers to the Church as mother, he is indicating the mystical and perfect Church without considering any division between the visible and invisible Church. Calvin, however differentiates between the two and is referring to the visible Church: "But because it is now our intention to discuss the visible church, let us learn even from the simple title "mother" how useful, indeed how necessary, it is that we should know her."[34] In Calvin's ecclesiology, the visible Church is distinct from the invisible Church not only because it is a visible institution, but also because it is imperfect and even impure, due to the presence of hypocrites—unlike the invisible and spiritual Church. Calvin thinks that the visible and institutional Church is imperfect because hypocrites "who have nothing of Christ but the name and outward appearance" are mingled with the faithful.[35] For him, the mystical identity of the "Church" as the spouse of God is identical not with the visible Church, but with the invisible or spiritual identity of the Church as the fellowship of the elect. Therefore, it is the visible Church that Calvin deals with the idea of "the mother" Church in his ecclesiology.

Thus Calvin stresses the maternal function of the visible Church, especially its preaching ministry, in the light of his idea of Christian unity:

> We must hold to what we have quoted from Paul - the church is built up solely by outward preaching, and that the saints are held together by one bond only: that with common accord, through learning and advancement, they keep the church order established by God.[36]

He believes that the obligation to maintain Christian unity, within the visible mother Church, does not arise from consensus of the legitimate

---

33. *Institutes*, IV.1.1; *ut quibus ipse est Pater, Ecclesia etiam mater sit*. OS 5:1.

34. *Institutes*, IV.1.4; *Verum quia nunc de visibili Ecclesia disserere propositum est, discamus vel uno matris elogio quam utilis sit nobis eius cognitio, imo necessaria*. OS 5:7.

35. *Institutes*, IV.1.7, OS 5:12.

36. *Institutes*, IV.1.5; *Nobis vero quod ex Paulo citavimus tenendum est, Ecclesiam non aliter aedificari quam externa praedicatione, nec alio vinculo inter se retineri sanctos, nisi dum uno consensu discendo et proficiendo ordinem Ecclesiae a Deo praescriptum colunt*. OS 5:10.

PART TWO—Calvin's Ecclesiology

bishops, but from God's will to regenerate His children through the ministry of the Church:

> He [God] alone should rule and reign in the church as well as have authority or pre-eminence in it, and this authority should be exercised and administered by his Word alone. Nevertheless, because he does not dwell among us in visible presence, we have said that he uses the ministry of men to declare openly his will to us by mouth, as a sort of delegated work, not by transferring to them his right and honor, but only that through their mouths he may do his own work—just as a workman uses a tool to do his work.[37]

All believers should be united in their Church because it is only by the ministry of the Word, which God appoints in the Church, that they can be regenerated: "through his unfailing kindness, he desired that his Word should be proclaimed here below, and committed that responsibility to those whom he has called. It is for this reason that the church is referred to here as 'the mother of all.'"[38]

In his reply to Cardinal Sadolet, Calvin argues that unity of the Church should be pursued only in the bond of the truth: "My conscience told me how strong the zeal was with which I burned for the unity of thy Church, provided thy truth made the bond of concord."[39] He argues further that the unity of the Church is maintained only through Christ, who gathers Christians together by "the Word and Spirit":

> The only true bond of ecclesiastical unity consists in this, that Christ the Lord, who has reconciled us to God the Father, gathers us out of our present dispersion into the fellowship of his body, that so, through his one Word and Spirit, we may join together with one heart and one soul.[40]

---

37. *Institutes*, IV.3.1, OS 5:42. Calvin uses Cyprian's idea of the universal bishopric in *De unitate Ecclesiae* to argue against the primacy of the Roman see: "'Nor is the unity of the body severed; it spreads its branches through the whole earth; it pours forth its overflowing streams; yet there is one head and one source,' etc. Again: 'The Bride of Christ cannot be an adulteress; she knows one house; with chaste modesty she guards the sanctity of one marriage bed.' You see that he makes the universal bishopric Christ's alone, who takes the whole church under himself." *Institutes*, IV.6.17, OS 5:103.

38. *Serm. Gal.* 4:26–31; "[M]ais tant y a que par sa bonté infinie il veut que sa parole soit preschee ici bas, et en a ordonné la charge à ceux qu'il appelle: et pour ceste cause l'Eglise est nommée la mere de tous." CO 50:645.

39. *Reply to Sadolet*, LCC 22:250, CO 5:410.

40. *Reply to Sadolet*, LCC 22:256; . . . *non aliud esse ecclesiasticae unitatis vinculum, quam si Christus Dominus, qui nos Deo patri reconciliavit, in corporis sui societatem nos*

The Church as the Mother of All Believers

For this reason, Calvin argues that "under cover of being a church, the 'Papists' have audaciously assumed that they have the authority to add and detract from the Word of God."[41]

Accordingly, Calvin maintains that the unity of the visible Church is required, even though she is not perfect enough to be called the spouse of Christ, because of her divinely appointed function for the regeneration of His children: "This is how the church bears us as her children, through the incorruptible seed we have been speaking about . . . we are not to be like those who claim be believers without ever reading and listening to the preached Word."[42] In Calvin's ecclesiology, therefore, it is not the Church that has the authority over the doctrine of the Word, but, conversely, pure doctrine that guarantees the legitimacy and authenticity of the mother Church.

The Accommodating Grace of God

Calvin thinks that preaching and the sacraments are the two crucial functions of the Church as the mother of all believers. In his ecclesiology, these two ministries are identified as the outward marks of the true Church: "Wherever we see the Word of God purely preached and heard, and the sacraments administered according to Christ's institution, there it is not to be doubted, a church of God exists."[43] In his discussion of these two ministries of the Church, Calvin underlines the dependent nature of those human and earthly instruments of the Church's motherly functions in order to highlight the accommodating grace of God. It is God who regenerates His children by those human and earthly instruments in the ministries of the Church.

The Dependent Nature of the Human Ministers

Calvin maintains that the preaching ministry of the Church is dependent in nature not only because preachers cannot effectively teach the congregation

---

ab ista dissipatione recolligat: ut ita uno eius verbo ac spiritu in cor unum et animam unam coalescamus. CO 5:416.

41. *Serm. Gal.* 4:26–31, CO 50:644.
42. *Serm. Gal.* 4:26–31, CO 50:646.
43. *Institutes*, IV.1.9, OS 5:13.

PART TWO—Calvin's Ecclesiology

by themselves but also because the congregation cannot obtain benefit from the preaching without the effectuating work of the Holy Spirit.

It is certain that Calvin stresses the importance of the preaching ministry by claiming that divine grace works together dynamically with human efforts in preaching. He says in his commentary on 2 Corinthians 3:6 thus:

> It is in consequence of there being such a connection and bond of union between Christ's grace and man's effort, that in many cases *that* is ascribed to the minister which belongs exclusively to the Lord. For in that case it is not the mere individual that is looked to, but the entire dispensation of the gospel, which consists, on the one hand, in the secret influence of Christ, and, on the other, in man's outward efforts.[44]

Leith describes this idea in Calvin's theology as "the sacramental doctrine of preaching" which enables Calvin "both to understand preaching as a very human work and to understand it as the work of God."[45]

For Calvin, not every act of preaching leads the audience to experience Christ's presence: "It is one thing for Christ to connect his influence with a man's doctrine, and quite another for the man's doctrine to have such efficacy of itself."[46] Calvin compares "letter" and "spirit" to these two kinds of preaching: ineffective and effective:

> By the term "letter," therefore, is meant literal preaching—that is, dead and ineffectual, perceived only by the ear. By the term "spirit," on the other hand, is meant spiritual doctrine, that is, what is not merely uttered with the mouth, but effectually makes its way to the souls of men with a lively feeling.[47]

Calvin thinks that the effectiveness of the preaching ministry depends solely on the Holy Spirit, even though there is the dynamics between divine works of grace and human efforts in preaching:

44. *Comm.* 2 *Cor.* 3:6, CO 50:40.

45. "In preaching, the Holy Spirit uses the words of the preacher as an occasion for the presence of God in grace and in mercy," and "in this sense, the actual words of the sermon are comparable to the element in the sacraments." Leith, "Doctrine of the Proclamation of the Word," 210–12.

46. *Comm.* 2 *Cor.* 3:6; *Aliud autem est, Christum adiungere hominis doctrinae suam virtutem, quam hominis doctrinam per se tantum valere.* CO 50:40.

47. *Comm.* 2 *Cor.* 3:6; *Litera ergo perinde valet ac literalis praedicatio, hoc est, mortua et ineffecax, quae tantum auribus percipitur. Spiritus autem est doctrina spiritualis, hoc est, quae non ore tantum pronuntiatur, sed efficaciter in animas usque vivo sensu penetrat.* CO 50:39.

> I indeed admit that the power does not proceed from the tongue of man, nor exists in mere sound, but that the whole power is to be ascribed altogether to the Holy Spirit: there is, however, nothing to hinder the Spirit from putting forth His power in the word preached.[48]

With regard to this point, Leith aptly notes that in Calvin's idea of preaching, "the words of the sermon are at best frail, human words, but words that can by the power of the Holy Spirit become the occasion of the presence of God."[49] Calvin talks about the imperfection of all preachers, including himself, in his sermons on Galatians:

> God bestows great honour upon the church here, when he calls her the mother of all believers . . . It does not mean that the truth needs to be maintained by sinners like ourselves, inclined as we are to fickleness and inconstancy, and prone to falsehood. How could the truth of God rest upon the shoulders of men, unstable as we are?[50]

In his discussion of the preaching ministry of the Church, Calvin notes the importance of the proper attitude of the congregation:

> Among the many excellent gifts with which God has adorned the human race, it is a singular privilege that he deigns to consecrate to himself the mouths and tongues of men in order that his voice may resound in them. Let us accordingly not in turn dislike to embrace obediently the doctrine of salvation put forth by his command and by his own mouth.[51]

At this point, Parker argues, "The preacher is only the half of the Church's activity of proclamation . . . Calvin certainly expected the congregation to be active in the business of the Church's preaching."[52] Calvin even declares that it is a mark of being God's children to "profit from the Word":

> If we desire to be children of God, and to bear the true marks of a believer; if we desire to be acknowledged as such even by angels, we need to maintain order in the church . . . This, then, is the first

---

48. *Comm. Heb.* 4:12, CO 55:51. For the authority of the preached Word, see *Comm. Ezek.* 2:2, CO 40:62, *Comm. 2 Cor.* 3:6, CO 50:40, Parker, *Calvin's Preaching*, 57–64.
49. Leith, "Doctrine of the Proclamation of the Word," 210–12.
50. *Serm. Gal.* 4:26–31, CO 50:643.
51. *Institutes*, IV.1.5, OS 5:10.
52. Parker, *Calvin's Preaching*, 48.

PART TWO—Calvin's Ecclesiology

point, that while we are in this world, we must make it our business to profit from the Word of God. Herein lies the key to spiritual life; for if God has granted us regeneration, we are to nourish ourselves with the teaching of Scripture for the rest of our lives.[53]

Nevertheless, without the Holy Spirit, the preached Word will not be able to penetrate the believers' minds: "Paul shows the Spirit to be the inner teacher by whose effort the promise of salvation penetrates into our minds, a promise that would otherwise only strike the air or beat upon our ears."[54] The right human response is important for Christians to receive the benefits of the Word. Yet it is the Holy Spirit's work of illumination that enables Christians to receive the benefits of the Word:

> Accordingly, without the illumination of the Holy Spirit, the Word can do nothing. From this, also, it is clear that faith is much higher than human understanding. And it will not be enough for the mind to be illumined by the Spirit of God unless the heart is also strengthened and supported by his power.[55]

Therefore, Calvin maintains that the ministry of the Word, both in preaching and listening, depends on the work of the Holy Spirit.

The Dependent Nature of the Earthly Signs

Likewise, Calvin stresses that Christians must distinguish the earthly signs from the realities designated by them, and recognizes the dependent nature of those signs lest they should receive the sacraments without any benefit:

> Since the Supper is nothing but a visible witnessing of that promise contained in the sixth chapter of John, namely, that Christ is

---

53. *Serm. Gal.* 4:26–31; "[M]ais si nous desirons d'estre reputez enfans de Dieu et avoir la vraye marque, par laquelle nous soyons cognus devant les Anges, que nous souffrions d'estre enseignez, et que nous gardions en toute reverence et humilité l'ordre de l'Eglise . . . Voilà donc pour un item, que cependant que nous sommes en ce monde, nous taschions à profiter en la parole de Dieu, d'autant que c'est là où gist toute nostre vie spirituelle, et comme Dieu nous regenerez, qu'asussi nous serons là nourris iusques en la fin, comme c'est la seule pasture de nos ames." CO 50:647.

54. *Institutes*, III.1.4; *Ostendit enim internum esse doctorem, cuius opera in mentes nostras penetrat salutis promissio, quae alioqui aerem duntaxat vel aures nostras feriret.* OS 4:5.

55. *Institutes*, III.2.33; *Proinde, sine Spiritus sancti illuminatione, verbo nihil agitur. Unde etiam liquet fidem humana intelligentia multo superiorem esse. Nec satis fuerit mentem esse Dei Spiritu illuminatam, nisi et eius virtute cor obfirmetur ac fulciatur.* OS 4:44.

The Church as the Mother of All Believers

the bread of life come down from heaven [John 6:51], visible bread must serve as an intermediary to represent that spiritual bread—unless we are willing to lose all the benefit which God, to sustain our weakness, confers upon us.[56]

Calvin's rejection of the doctrine of transubstantiation is based on his idea of the dependent nature of the visible signs. In a theological or philosophical sense, the integrity of Christ's physical existence is the reason for his rejection of this doctrine: since Christ's body is now in heaven, it cannot be divided or dispersed in the bread and wine of the Supper.[57] From a practical point of view, Calvin insists that this doctrine misleads participants into believing that the imperfect earthly elements by themselves have some divine power, and this doctrine ultimately diminishes God's grace by which spiritual blessings are bestowed through those earthly elements:

> It is our duty to put no confidence in other creatures which have been destined for our use by God's generosity and beneficence, and through whose ministry he lavishes the gifts of his bounty upon us: nor to admire and proclaim them as the causes of our good. In the same way, neither ought our confidence to inhere in the sacraments, nor the glory of God be transferred to them. Rather, laying aside all things, both our faith and our confession ought to rise up to him who is the author of the sacraments and of all things.[58]

Calvin distinguishes the efficacy of the sacraments from their validity when he explains the effectiveness of the sacraments to the reprobate:

---

56. *Institutes*, IV.17.14; *Interim repeto, quum Coena nihil aliud sit quam conspicua eius promissionis testificatio quae Ioannis sexto habetur, nempe Christum esse panem vitae qui e caelo descendit: panem visibilem intercedere oportet quo spiritualis ille figuretur: nisi nobis perire volumus omnem fructum quem in hac parte sustinendae nostrae imbecillitati Deus indulget.* OS 5:359–360.

57. "Let us never allow these two limitations to be taken from us: Let nothing be withdrawn from Christ's heavenly glory—as happens when he is brought under the corruptible elements of this world, or bound to any earthly creatures. Let nothing inappropriate to human nature be ascribed to his [Christ's] body, as happens when it is said either to be infinite or to be put in a number of places at once." *Institutes*, IV.17.19, OS 5:365. See Wandel, *Eucharist in the Reformation: Incarnation and Liturgy*, 160–64.

58. *Institutes*, IV.14.12; *Et ut nostrum est in caeteris creaturis, quae Dei liberalitate et beneficentia usibus nostris destinatae sunt, quarumque ministerio bonitatis suae munera nobis largitur, nihil fiduciae defigere, nec quasi boni nostri causas admirari et praedicare: ita neque in Sacramentis haerere fiducia nostra debet, nec Dei gloria in ipsa transferri: sed omissis omnibus, ad ipsum et Sacramentorum et rerum omnium authorem surgere et fides et confessio debent.* OS 5:269.

PART TWO—Calvin's Ecclesiology

"Yet it is one thing to be offered, another to be received. Christ proffers this spiritual food and gives this spiritual drink to all. Some feed upon them eagerly, others haughtily refuse them."[59] He claims that the benefits of the sacraments "avail and profit nothing unless received in faith, just as Christ is offered and held forth by the Father to all unto salvation, yet not all acknowledge and receive him."[60] Concerning this point, Riggs argues that for Calvin the promise of God, the substance of the sacrament, "could be refused by the person to whom they were offered; yet, the promises themselves were not without full divine power."[61] In the *Institutes*, Cavlin proposes what kind of faith believers should have to receive a sacrament effectively:

> Accordingly, in this passage [Acts 8:37], to "believe with all our heart" is not to believe Christ perfectly, but only to embrace him from the heart and with a sincere mind; not to be sated with him, but to hunger, thirst, and aspire to him with fervent affection.[62]

As with the effectiveness of the preaching ministry, however, it is again the Holy Spirit, who enables Christians to possess Christ fully through participation in the sacraments:

> The sacraments properly fulfil their office only when the Spirit, that inward teacher, comes to them, by whose power alone hearts are penetrated and affections moved and our souls opened for the sacraments to enter in. Therefore, I make such a division between Spirit and sacraments that the power to act rests with the former, and the ministry alone is left to the latter—a ministry empty and

---

59. *Institutes*, IV.17.33; *Aliud tamen est offerri, aliud recipi. Spiritualem hunc cibum omnibus porrigit Christus, potumque spiritualem propinat: alii avide vescuntur, alii fastidiose respuunt, an horum reiectio faciet ut cibus et potus suam naturam perdant? . . . vel (si cum Augustino loqui magis placet) nego plus referre homines ex Sacramento quam vase fidei colligunt. Ita Sacramento nihil decedit: imo illibata manet eius veritas et efficacia, quanvis ab externa eius participatione inanes descendant impii.* OS 5:393.

60. *Institutes*, IV.14.17, OS 5:275.

61. Riggs, *Baptism in the Reformed Tradition*, 60–62.

62. *Institutes*, IV.14.8; *Itaque in hoc loco ex toto corde credere, non est perfecte Christo credere: sed ex animo duntaxat et syncere mente illum amplecti: non eo saturum esse, sed ardenti affectu esurire, sitire, et ad eum suspirare.* OS 5:265. For the analysis of the development of Calvin's doctrine of baptism in the editions of the *Institutes*, Riggs argues that "Calvin came to express himself more cautiously" by changing the term "completed" (*consummari*) for the description of the proper faith for baptism in the 1539 edition to the term "comes to maturity" (*conscendere ad maturitatem*) in the 1559 edition of the *Institutes*. Riggs, *Baptism in the Reformed Tradition*, 58–59.

trifling, apart from the action of the Spirit, but charged with great effect when the Spirit works within and manifests his power.[63]

It can be seen therefore, that Calvin feels strongly that both human ministers and the outward signs of the sacraments are imperfect in themselves, and that their effectiveness in Christians' hearts therefore depends solely on the work of the Holy Spirit. It means that Christians cannot receive the benefits of those ministries without the inner work of the Holy Spirit.[64]

God's Grace of Accommodation

Why, then, does God use those dependent and imperfect human ministers and earthly sacraments to regenerate His children if it is not those instruments, themselves, but the Holy Spirit's work that effectuates the grace of God's in Christians? Calvin's answer to this question is that God wishes to regenerate His children, and will do so through those earthly and human instruments which are suited to the dullness and weaknesses of Christians. Hence, the Father's grace of accommodation towards His children is the most important focus in Calvin's functional understanding of the Church as mother.

According to Dowey's definition, in Calvin's theology the term accommodation refers to "the process by which God reduces or adjusts to human capacities what he wills to reveal of the infinite mysteries of his being, which by their very nature are beyond the power of the mind of man to grasp."[65] Following Dowey, most scholars, who consider the role of "accommodation" in Calvin's theology, tend to concentrate on its place in his doctrine of God.[66] However, scholars have not fully appreciated the ecclesiological

63. *Institutes*, IV.14.9, OS 5:266.

64. Ward explores the application of Calvin's emphasis on the active participation and the response of believers to the ministry of preaching: "Calvin's ideal of preaching in community makes strong and explicit allowance for the active participation on the part of the congregation" because Calvin thinks "this congregation is to be a community able to judge the acceptable degree of departure from the Word." R. Holder, "*Ecclesia, Legenda atque Intelligenda Scriptura*," 270–89.

65. Dowey, *Knowledge of God in Calvin's Theology*, 3.

66. Since Dowey points out the importance of the concept of "accommodation" in Calvin's theology, this topic has received further attention from scholars. Willis, "Rhetoric and Responsibility in Calvin's Theology," 53; Battles, "God was accommodating Himself to Human Capacity," 21–26; Milet, *Calvin et la dynamique de la parole*, 247–55; Wright, "Calvin's Pentateuchal Criticism," 33–50; "Calvin's Accommodating God," 3–19; Balserak, *Divinity Compromised*.

context of this idea that it is a crucial element in his discussion of the two main ministries of the Church: preaching and the sacraments.

Firstly, preaching of the Word by human ministers shows the accommodating grace of God, who "provides for our weakness in that he prefers to address us in human fashion through interpreters in order to draw us to himself, rather than to thunder at us and drive us away." Calvin argues, "Although God's power is not bound to outward means, he has nonetheless bound us to this ordinary manner of teaching."[67] In his exhortation of the proper Christian response of humility to the ministries of the preaching, Calvin highlights God's grace of accommodation:

> For who would not dread the presence of his power? Who would not be stricken down at the sight of such great majesty? Who would not be confounded at such boundless splendor?... It was for this reason, then, that he hid the treasure of his heavenly wisdom in weak and earthen vessels in order to prove more surely how much we should esteem it.[68]

Secondly, establishment of the ministry of the sacraments in the Church is also a sign of God's grace of accommodation. In the sacraments, God is prepared to condescend to the dullness of human understanding by using earthly elements to enable believers to experience spiritual blessings:

> For God's truth is of itself firm and secure enough, and it cannot receive better confirmation from any other source than from itself. But as our faith is slight and feeble, unless it be propped on all sides and sustained by every means, it trembles, wavers, totters, and at last gives way. Here our merciful Lord, according to his infinite kindness, so tempers himself to our capacity that, since we are creatures who always creep on the ground, cleave to the flesh, and, do not think about or even conceive of anything spiritual, he condescends to lead us to himself even by these earthly elements, and to set before us in the flesh a mirror of spiritual blessings.[69]

---

67. *Institutes*, IV.1.5, OS 5:10.

68. *Institutes*, IV.3.1, OS 5:43.

69. *Institutes*, IV.14.3; *Siquidem Dei veritas per se satis solida certaque est: nec aliunde meliorem confirmationem quam a se ipsa accipere potest. Verum ut exigua est et imbecilla nostra fides, nisi undique fulciatur, ac modis omnibus sustenetur, statim concutitur, fluctuatur, vacillat, adeoque labascit. Atque ita quidem hic se captui nostro pro immensa sua indulgentia attemperat misericors Dominus, ut quando animales sumus, qui humi semper adrepentes, et in carne haerentes, nihil spirituale cogitamus, ac ne concipimus quidem, elementis etiam istis terrenis nos ad se deducere non gravetur, atque in ipsa carne proponere bonorum spiritualium speculum.* OS 5:260.

Calvin thinks that it is the union of believers with Christ which should be clarified by the sacraments: in baptism "we are not only engrafted into the death and life of Christ, but so united to Christ himself that we become sharers in all his blessings."[70] In the Lord's Supper "godly souls can gather great assurance and delight" because "in it they have a witness of our growth into one body with Christ such that whatever is his may be called ours."[71] However, since the mystery of Christian union with Christ belongs to a spiritual knowledge which is beyond human understanding, God provides believers with the visible signs by which union with Christ can be experienced and the benefits from this union obtained: "Since, however, this mystery of Christ's secret union with the devout is by nature incomprehensible, he shows its figure and image in visible signs best adapted to our small capacity."[72] Therefore, it is God's accommodation to take care of His children that Calvin tries to manifest in his discussion of the two maternal roles of the visible Church.

The Two Ministries of the Church for the Children of God

In Calvin's emphasis on God's grace of accommodation in establishing the two ministries of the Church, his anthropological idea, that the Christian is a child of God the Father, is significant: "For by its ministry and labor God willed to have the preaching of his Word kept pure and to show himself the Father of a family, while he feeds us with spiritual food and provides everything that makes for our salvation."[73] Thus, his functional idea of the Church as mother of believers does not presuppose the marital relationship between God and the Church. Instead this idea is based on his focus on the father-child relationship between God and Christians, who are entrusted by God to the care of the Church, their mother. In the following section, I shall look at Calvin's explanation of the two ministries of the Church as the

---

70. *Institutes*, IV.15.6, OS 5:289.

71. *Institutes*, IV.17.2, OS 5:343.

72. *Institutes*, IV.17.1; *Quoniam vero mysterium hoc arcanae Christi cum piis unionis natura incomprehensibile est, figuram eius et imaginem in signis visibilibus exhibet ad modulum nostrum aptissimis.* OS 5:342. "But the sacraments bring the clearest promise; and they have this characteristic over and above the word because they represent them for us as painted in a picture from life." *Institutes*, IV.14.5, OS 5:262.

73. *Institutes*, IV.1.10, OS 5:52.

PART TWO—Calvin's Ecclesiology

maternal functions of the Church to argue that his explanation is based on his anthropological idea of the Christians being children of God.

The Ministry of Preaching

In his discussion of the preaching ministry, Calvin describes the Church as a mother who teaches the Word of God to His children because they are still dull in their understanding. Commenting on 1 Corinthians 13:11, "When I was a child," Calvin argues, "education is necessary for childhood; it does not comport with mature age. So long as we live in this world, we require, in some sense, education. We are far from having attained, as yet, the perfection of wisdom."[74] His notion of a good teacher's duty to accommodate himself to the limitations of his pupils in teaching the truth of the gospel echoes his emphasis on God's grace of accommodation:

> For Christ is at once "milk to babes," and "strong meat to those that are of full age," the same truth of the gospel is administered to both, but so as to suit their capacity. Hence it is the part of a wise teacher to accommodate himself to the capacity of those whom he has undertaken to instruct, so that in dealing with the weak and ignorant . . . in short, he drops in his instructions by little and little, lest it should run over, if poured in more abundantly.[75]

Preaching of the Word is the most important function of the mother Church because it is the means by which God reveals His will to His children: "The word goeth out of the mouth of God in such a manner that it likewise goeth out of the mouth of men for God does not speak openly from heaven, but employs men as his instruments that by their agency he may make known his will."[76] The Word brings faith to Christians only when they hear it.[77] They can hear the Word by both private reading and attendance at public sermons: "we must be diligent in hearing God's Word; we must resort to preaching; we must read in private; we must listen to

---

74. *Comm. 1 Cor.* 13:11; *pueritiae necessaria est paedagogia: virili aetati non congruit. Nos quantisper degimus in hoc mundo, indigemus paedagogia: procul adhuc distamus a plena sapientia.* CO 49:513–14.

75. *Comm. 1 Cor.* 3:2, CO 49:347.

76. *Comm. Isa.* 55:11, CO 37:291, "The Word of God is not distinguished from the word of the prophet." *Comm. Hag.* 1:12, CO 44:94.

77. "God breathes faith into us only by the instrument of his gospel, as Paul points out that, 'faith comes from hearing' [Rom. 10:17]." *Institutes*, IV.1.5, OS 5:8.

good exhortation, and to all doctrine by which we may profit; we must give good heed to these things."⁷⁸ However, attendance at public sermons is even more important for Christians than private reading, because it is God's will that His children be edified and preserved together in the Church. The Geneva Catechism says thus:

> M: You affirm then that it is not enough for each to read privately at home, and that all ought to meet in common to hear the same doctrine?
>
> S: They must meet when they can—that is, when an opportunity is given . . . and the order which he [God] hath recommended to his church is not what two or three only might observe, but all should obey in common. Moreover, he declares this to be the only method of edifying as well as preserving.⁷⁹

Despite what Gerrish regards "strange neglect" of the preaching in the *Institutes* IV, Calvin does not ignore its importance entirely: "He [Paul] therefore contends that there is nothing more notable or glorious in the church than the ministry of the gospel, since it is the administration of the Spirit and of righteousness and of eternal life."⁸⁰

In his commentary on Ephesians 4:12, Calvin explicitly relates the preaching ministry with the maternal function of the Church:

> But Paul expressly states, that, according to the command of Christ, no real union or perfection is attained but by the outward preaching. We must allow ourselves to be ruled and taught by men . . . The church is the common mother of all the godly, which bears, nourishes and brings up children of God, kings and peasants alike; and this is done by the ministry.⁸¹

---

78. *Serm. Eph.* 4:11-14; "Il est vray que nous devons mettre toute peine à ce que nostre foy soit confermee, il nous faut estre diligens à ouir la parole de Dieu, frequenter les predications, lire en privé, ouir de bonnes exhortations et toute doctrine qui nous pourra profiter: il faut que nous soyons attentif à cela." CO 51:574.

79. *Catechism* [1545], TT 2:82–83, OS 2:127.

80. *Institutes*, IV.3.3; *Contendit ergo nihil Evangelii ministerio in Ecclesia magis praeclarum aut gloriosum esse, quum sit administratio Spiritus et iustitiae et vitae aeternae.* OS 5:45. Gerrish's suggestion is probably the most plausible way in which to understand this strange neglect of the preaching ministry in the *Institutes*, IV: "Perhaps Calvin felt that the word of the gospel, as the theme of his entire work, could not be reduced to a single chapter, any more than grace could be." Gerrish, *Grace and Gratitude*, 103.

81. *Comm. Eph.* 4:12; *Paulus autem aperte hic testatur, non alio modo, secundum Christi praescriptum, rite coagmentari nos et perfici, quam per externam praedicationem,*

PART TWO—Calvin's Ecclesiology

In his sermon on the same biblical passage, Calvin encourages his audience to be good students in the school of God: "So then, let us be lowly that we may be the scholars of our God, and this lowliness means a ridding of ourselves of all pride, and an abasing of ourselves, knowing that we have such things as are given to us by God and no more."[82] For Calvin, therefore, both the mother and school metaphors for the Church have the same practical implication with regard to the preaching ministry. By means of the metaphor of "school," just as the metaphor of "mother," Calvin obviously tries to explain practical role of the Church for God's children, not its mystical identity. In the *Institutes* IV.1.4, having just named the Church as the mother of all believers, Calvin says, "Our weakness does not allow us to be dismissed from her school until we have been pupils all our lives."[83]

The Ministry of the Sacraments

While the preaching ministry concerns the Church's maternal role of teaching, the ministry of sacraments represents her role of caring: "sacraments are truly named the testimonies of God's grace and are like seals of the good will that he feels toward us, which by attesting that good will to us, sustain, nourish, confirm, and increase our faith."[84] Calvin's choice of such terms as "sustain," "nourish," and "increase" when describing the benefits of the sacraments shows that he thinks of the Church providing maternal care for the children of God through this ministry.

We can see Calvin's idea of how the sacraments function as part of the maternal care of the Church in his explanation of the relationship between preaching and the sacraments. As mentioned above, Calvin stresses the priority of the Word over the sacrament by calling a sacrament an "appendix"

---

dum per homines patimur nos regi et doceri . . . Et certe ecclesia communis est piorum omnium mater, quae tam reges quam plebeios gignit in Domino, nutrit et gubernat: quod fit ministerio. CO 51:199.

82. Serm. Eph. 4:11–14; "Et ainsi que nous soyons humbles pour estre escoliers de notre Dieu: et ceste humilité là emporte que nous soyons despuillez de toute arrogance pour estre là abatus, sçachant que nous n'avons sinon ce qui nous est donné de Dieu, et non plus." CO 51:574. English translation is from *John Calvin's Sermons on the Epistle to the Ephesians.*

83. *Institutes*, IV.1.4; *Neque enim patitur nostra infirmitas a schola nos dimitti donec toto vitae cursu discipuli fuerimus.* OS 5:7.

84. *Institutes*, IV.14.7; *sacramenta vere nominari testimonia gratiae Dei, ac veluti quaedam benevolentiae, qua erga nos affectus est, sigilla: quae ipsam nobis obsignando, fidem nostram hoc modo sustinent, alunt, confirmant, adaugent.* OS 5:264.

of the Word.[85] On this point, Avis argues, "Even when Calvin discusses the marks of Word and sacrament, he seems prepared to resolve the latter into the former."[86] However, Calvin's idea of the superiority of the Word does not diminish the importance of the sacraments as one of the external means of grace. For him, both the sacraments and preaching offer the same spiritual blessing to Christians: "let it be regarded as a settled principle that the sacraments have the same office as the Word of God: to offer and set forth Christ to us and in him the treasures of heavenly grace."[87] Furthermore, a sacrament is a more useful aid for the weak faith of the children of God than preaching because a sacrament is "a visible Word for the reason that it represents God's promises as painted in a picture and sets them before our sight, portrayed graphically and in the manner of images."[88]

The idea of the sacraments as being part of the maternal care of the Church leads Calvin to stress the continuous benefits of both baptism and the Lord's Supper for Christians because of the weakness of their faith. First, baptism, even though it is administered only once in a lifetime, has a continuous benefit for Christians throughout their course of regeneration. In their course of regeneration, baptism encourages Christians to fight against their "flesh" by reminding them of their "mortification in Christ, and new life in him."[89] These continuous benefits of baptism are necessary for children of God because the perversity of sin still remains in them:

85. "Now, from the definition that I have set forth we understand that a sacrament is never without a preceding promise but is joined to it as a sort of appendix, with the purpose of confirming and sealing the promise itself, and of making it more evident to us and in a sense ratifying it." *Institutes*, IV.14.3, OS 5:260.

86. Avis, *Church in the Theology of the Reformers*, 31.

87. *Institutes*, IV.14.17; *Quamobrem fixum maneat, non esse alias Sacramentorum quam verbi Dei partes: quae sunt offerre nobis ac proponere Christum, et in eo caelestis gratiae thesaurus.* OS 5:274.

88. *Institutes*, IV.14.6, OS 5:263. Gerrish argues that "Calvin himself describes the word as *verbum sacramentale*, the 'sacramental word.'" In Calvin's theology, according to Gerrish, the word has not only the "pedagogical" function of directing us to have the knowledge of the Creator, but also the "sacramental" functions of gathering us "together in the assembly of believers to hear the doctrine of salvation." Gerrish, *Grace and Gratitude*, 76–86. With regard to the inseparability between the preaching and the sacraments, DeVries says, "He could not imagine a Eucharist without the proclamation of the gospel in preaching. But neither did he believe that preaching alone, without a celebration of the Eucharist, was sufficient for regular worship." Although Calvin does not affirm the insufficiency of the preaching without the sacrament, he emphasises the common and essential function of both ministries for regeneration. DeVries, *Jesus Christ in the Preaching of Calvin and Schleiermacher*, 20.

89. *Institutes*, IV.15.5, OS 5:288.

PART TWO—Calvin's Ecclesiology

> The other point is that this perversity never ceases in us, but continually bears new fruits—what we have previously described as "works of the flesh"—just as a glowing furnace continually emits flame and sparks, or a spring ceaselessly gives forth water.[90]

In baptism, moreover, Christians can confirm their identity and its privilege that they now become sharers in all of Christ's blessings in their union with Christ: "our faith receives from baptism the advantage of its sure testimony to us that we are not only engrafted into the death and life of Christ, but so united to Christ himself that we become sharers in all his blessings."[91] Calvin even argues for the continuous benefits that infant baptism brings not only for the parents, but also for the infants:

> The children receive some benefit from their baptism: being engrafted into the body of the church, they are somewhat more commended to the other members. Then, when they have grown up, they are greatly spurred to an earnest zeal for worshiping God, by whom they were received as children through a solemn symbol of adoption before they were old enough to recognize him as Father.[92]

The Lord's Supper is God's method of nourishing his children continuously through the maternal care of the Church:

> God has received us, once for all, into his family, to hold us not only as servants but as sons. Thereafter, to fulfill the duties of a most excellent Father concerned for his offspring, he undertakes also to nourish us throughout the course of our life. And not content with this alone, he has willed, by giving his pledge, to assure us of this continuing liberality. To this end, therefore, he has, through the hand of his only-begotten Son, given to his church another sacrament, that is, a spiritual banquet.[93]

---

90. *Institutes*, IV.15.11; *Alterum est, quod haec perversitas nunquam in nobis cessat, sed novos assidue fructus parit, ea scilicet quae ante descripsimus opera carnis: non secus atque incensa fornax flammam et scintillas perpetuo efflat, aut scaturigo aquam sine fine egerit.* OS 5:292–293.

91. *Institutes*, IV.15.6, OS 5:289.

92. *Institutes*, IV.16.9, OS 5:313. Calvin argues that the benefits of infant baptism for the infants appear in a secret way by the work of the Holy Spirit: "Accordingly, in infant baptism nothing more of present effectiveness must be required than to confirm and ratify the covenant made with them by the Lord. The remaining significance of this sacrament will afterward follow at such time as God himself foresees." *Institutes*, IV.16.21, OS 5:326. Also see Wright, "Development and Coherence in Calvin's *Institutes*," 226–37.

93. *Institutes*, IV.17.1, OS 5:342.

The Church as the Mother of All Believers

Calvin compares the Supper to medicine for the sick and alms to the poor because of its continuous benefits for the Christians' weaknesses:

> This sacred feast is medicine for the sick, solace for sinners, alms to the poor; but would bring no benefit to the healthy, righteous and rich—if such could be found. For since in it Christ is given to us as food, we understand that without him we would pine away, starve, and faint—as famine destroys the vigour of the body.[94]

Like baptism, the Lord's Supper is beneficial for Christians "to exercise us in the remembrance of Christ's death" and "grow in union with Christ."[95] In discussing Calvin's idea of the benefits of baptism and the Supper, Wallace properly says that, "Baptism . . . mainly bears witness to our initiation in to this union, while the Lord's Supper is a sign of our continuation in this union."[96]

As those passages above demonstrate, Calvin's emphasis on the importance of the sacraments for Christians in the course of regeneration is based on his anthropological idea that Christians are children of God who still need the continuous nourishing care of the mother Church. Firstly, the weak and dull nature of Christians calls for a visible support in addition to preaching: "because we are of flesh, they [sacraments] are shown us under things of flesh, to instruct us according to our dull capacity, and to lead us by the hand as tutors lead children."[97] Secondly, God gives His children the sacraments as "the pillars of our faith" and "the mirror of His grace," to show that He "manifests himself to us as far as our dullness is given to perceive, and attests his good will and love toward us more expressly than by

---

94. *Institutes*, IV.17.42; . . . *has sacras epulas aegrotis esse pharmacum, peccatoribus solatium, pauperibus largitionem: quae sanis, iustis et divitibus, siqui reperiri possent, nullum afferrent operaepretium. Nam quum in illis Christus nobis in cibum detur: inteligimus, nos sine ipso tabescere, liqui, deficere: qualiter inedia, corporis vigorem extinguit.* OS 5:407.

95. *Institutes*, IV.17.37, OS 5:401. Calvin's exhortation to the frequent celebration of the Supper results from the idea of the continuous benefits of the Lord's Supper: "Rather, it was ordained to be frequently used among all Christians in order that they might frequently return in memory to Christ's passion, by such remembrance to sustain and strengthen their faith, and urge themselves to sing thanksgiving to God and to proclaim his goodness; finally, by it to nourish mutual love, and among themselves give witness to this love, and discern its bond in the unity of Christ's body." *Institutes*, IV.17.44, OS 5:410.

96. Wallace, *Calvin's Doctrine of the Word and Sacraments*, 150.

97. *Institutes*, IV.14.6, OS 5:263.

word."[98] In his definition of the sacraments, Calvin indicates the necessity of the sacraments for nurturing the weak faith of the Christians:

> It seems to me that a simple and proper definition would be to say that it is an outward sign by which the Lord seals on our consciences the promises of his good will toward us in order to sustain the weakness of our faith; and we in turn attest our piety toward him in the presence of the Lord and of his angels and before men.[99]

Although there are distinct features of these two sacraments, Calvin lays a great emphasis on the common feature of both baptism and the Supper as expression of the continuous maternal care of the Church which God provides for Christians. This concentration on the continuous benefits of the sacraments reflects his anthropological idea that Christians are children who need the continuous care of the Church as their nurturing mother.

Conclusion: The Need of the Christian for the Maternal Care of the Church

The focal point of Calvin's concept of the Church as mother is her maternal roles on behalf of Christians. What matters most is the mother-child relationship between the Church and the individual Christian rather than the mystical relationship between God and the Church. In confirming the identity of the Church as the mother of all believers, therefore, Calvin consistently mentions the need of Christians for the maternal care of the Church in the course of their regeneration:

> Since, however, in our ignorance and sloth (to which I add fickleness of disposition) we need outward helps to beget and increase faith within us, and advance it to its goal, God has also added these aids that he may provide for our weakness. And in order that the

---

98. *Institutes*, IV.14.6; . . . *manifestat quantum nostrae habetudini agnoscere datum est, suamque erga nos benevolentiam et amorem expressius quam verbo testatur*. OS 5:263. For discussion of the relationship between the Word and the sacrament, see Gerrish, "Gospel and Eucharist: John Calvin on the Lord's Supper," 106–17.

99. *Institutes*, IV.14.1; *Videtur autem mihi haec simplex et propria fore definitio, si dixerimus externum esse symbolum, quo benevolentiae erga nos suae promissiones conscientiis nostris Dominus obsignat, ad sustinendam fidei nostrae imbecillitatem: et nos vicissim pietatem erga eum nostram tam coram eo et Angelis quam apud homines testamur.* OS 5:259.

preaching of the gospel might flourish, he deposited this treasure in the church.[100]

It seems obvious from this statement that Calvin's functional understanding of the mother Church is presented in the light of his anthropological idea of the identity of Christians as the children of God: since Christians remain imperfect as children in their present life, they still need maternal guidance and care; and God, their Father, appoints the ministry of the Church as the means to provide this care to His children. This pragmatic, rather than mystical, interpretation is the key to understanding Calvin's insistence in the *Institutes*, IV.1.1 that "for those to whom God is father the church may also be Mother."

---

100. *Institutes*, IV.1.1, OS 5:1.

5

The Church as the Body of Christ

Introduction: The Spiritual Identity of the Church

WHILE CALVIN'S USE OF THE "MOTHER" METAPHOR CONCERNS THE FUNCtional identity of the visible Church, his use of the biblical metaphor "the body of Christ" concerns the spiritual identity of the invisible Church.[1] According to Calvin, the Church is distinct from other societies because of its spiritual and mystical identity as the body of Christ:

> It is usual, however, for any society of men, or congregation, to be called a body, as one city constitutes a body, and so, in like manner, one senate, and one people . . . Among Christians, however, the case is very different; for they do not constitute a mere political body, but are the spiritual and mystical body of Christ.[2]

For Calvin, however, this spiritual identity of the Church should not remain merely a mystical and spiritual ideal. The characteristics of the spiritual identity of the invisible Church as the body of Christ provide theological principles to guide the practical aspects of the visible Church, in particular its government. Commenting on Colossians 1:18, the biblical notion of Christ as "the head of the body, the Church," Calvin argues, "in my opinion, he [Paul] speaks chiefly of government. He shews therefore that it is Christ

---

1. In his study on the metaphor of *Corpus Christi* in the Reformed tradition MacGregor argues, "The language, though Biblical, is figurative; nevertheless, Calvin used it with an eye to the ontological fact of the relation that exists between Christ and the Church." MacGregor, *Corpus Christi*, 43-65.

2. *Comm. 1 Cor.* 12:12; *Caeterum hoc usitatum est, quamlibet hominum societatem aut collegium vocari corpus: sicuti civitas una corpus efficit, senatus item et plebs . . . Verum inter Christianos longe alia est ratio: neque enim corpus politicum duntaxat efficiunt: sed sunt spirituale et arcanum Christi corpus.* CO 49:201.

alone that has authority to govern the Church, that it is he to whom alone believers ought to have an eye, and on whom alone the unity of the body depends."[3]

This chapter will examine Calvin's use of the biblical metaphor "the body of Christ" to analyse his idea of the spiritual identity of the Church, that is, the corporative dimension of the union of the individual Christians with Christ, and the applications of this idea in his proposal of church government. Thus this chapter has two purposes. The first purpose is to show the relationship between Calvin's ecclesiology and his anthropology. In both doctrines Calvin takes a trinitarian perspective when focusing on the union of Christians with Christ and is concerned with providing believers with the assurance of their salvation. The second purpose is to demonstrate that Calvin attempts to find the theological foundations of his proposal for church government within the principles of the spiritual Church as the body of Christ. For these purposes, I shall first point out three principles of *Corpus Christi*, which are highlighted in Calvin's commentary on Ephesians 4:16: Christ's headship, the communication of diverse gifts, and the necessity of mutual love.[4] I shall then investigate the *Institutes* IV.3 and the *Draft Ecclesiastical Ordinances* (1541) in order to indicate that the three principles of *Corpus Christi* are reflected in three important points in Calvin's proposal for church government: election and examination of pastors, fourfold ecclesiastical office, and charity and mutual care. In conclusion, the meaning and position of ecclesiology in Calvin's theology will be briefly evaluated.

Union with Christ and *Corpus Christi*

"Engrafting into the Body of Christ"

In Calvin's ecclesiology, the spiritual identity of the Church as the body of Christ is established when believers are collectively "engrafted into his body." The biblical notion of "engrafting into Christ's body" is an important

---

3. *Comm. Col.* 1:18, CO 52:86.

4. McKee demonstrates the importance of Ephesians 4 in the development of Calvin's idea of the fourfold ministry: while the role of preaching ministry, is briefly mentioned in the 1536 edition, Calvin's interpretation of *Ephesians* 4:11 is expanded in the *Institutes* of 1543 to argue that the human ministry of the Word is necessary for the Church because it is "the chief sinew by which believers are held together in the body of Christ." McKee, *Elders and the Plural Ministry*, 133–36.

PART TWO—Calvin's Ecclesiology

expression for Calvin to explain the benefit that Christians obtain from Christ for their salvation.[5] At the beginning of the *Institutes* III, Calvin uses a number of diverse expressions from Scripture to describe the relationship of Christians with Christ, including the relationship between Christ, as Head, and Christians, as members, and that of being "engrafted into him":

> Therefore, to share with us what he [Christ] has received from the Father, he had to become ours and to dwell within us. For this reason, he is called "our Head" [Ephesians 4:15], and "the first-born among many brethren" [Romans 8:29]. We also, in turn, are said to be "engrafted into him" [Romans 11:17], and to "put on Christ" [Galatians 3:27]; for, as I have said, all that he possesses is nothing to us until we grow into one body with him.[6]

These two expressions are emphasised, in particular, in the latter part of the same book when Calvin underlines the spiritual benefits that Christians gain from being in union with Christ:

> Therefore, that joining together of Head and members, that indwelling of Christ in our hearts - in short, that mystical union - are accorded by us the highest degree of importance, so that Christ, having been made ours, makes us sharers with him in the gifts with which he has been endowed. We do not, therefore, contemplate him outside ourselves from afar in order that his righteousness may be imputed to us but because we put on Christ and are engrafted into his body - in short, because he deigns to make us one with him.[7]

However, among various expressions for the Christian's relationship with Christ in Calvin's theology, the notion "engrafting into Christ's body" does not only have soteriological implications but also has ecclesiological implications. For Calvin, the beginning of Christian identity through grace coincides with the beginning of their membership of Christ's body, the Church: "Christ, when he illumines us into faith by the power of his Spirit,

---

5. For comment on the way in which Calvin uses the terms "union with Christ" and "engrafting into Christ's body," interchangeably, see chapter 2, note 41 of this study.

6. *Institutes*, III.1.1, OS 4:1.

7. *Institutes*, III.11.10; *Coniunctio igitur illa capitis et membrorum, habitatio Christi in cordibus nostris, mystica denique unio a nobis in summo gradu statuitur: ut Christus noster factus, donorum quibus praeditus est nos faciat consortes. Non ergo eum extra nos procul speculamur, ut nobis imputetur eius iustitia: sed quia ipsum induimus, et insiti sumus in eius corpus, unum denique nos secum efficere dignatus est: ideo iustitiae societatem nobis cum eo esse gloriamur.* OS 4:191.

The Church as the Body of Christ

at the same time so engrafts us into his body that we become partakers of every good."[8] Calvin's ecclesiological discussion in the *Institutes* IV makes it clear that he identifies "engrafting into the body of Christ" with membership of the Church under the headship of Christ:

> It is not sufficient, indeed, for us to comprehend in mind and thought the multitude of the elect, unless we consider the unity of the church as that into which we are convinced we have been truly engrafted. For no hope of future inheritance remains to us unless we have been united with all other members under Christ, our Head.[9]

"Being engrafted into Christ's body" and this related to Christ, as Head, gives Christians a powerful motive for holiness in their lives:

> Ever since he engrafted us into his body, we must take especial care not to disfigure ourselves, who are his members, with any spot or blemish. Ever since Christ himself, who is our Head, ascended into heaven, it behoves us, having laid aside love of earthly things, wholeheartedly to aspire heavenward.[10]

This motive for holiness concerns not only their personal lives, but also their corporate life within the Church:

> But Scripture goes even farther by comparing them to the powers with which the members of the human body are endowed. No member has this power for itself nor applies it to its own private use; but each pours it out to the fellow members ... So too, whatever a godly man can do he ought to be able to do for his brothers, providing for himself in no way other than to have his mind intent upon the common upbuilding of the church.[11]

While union with Christ or "engrafting into Christ's body" in the *Institutes* III is mainly concerned with relationships of the individual Christian with Christ, the focus of these notions in the *Institutes* IV turns to the

---

8. *Institutes*, III.2.35, OS 4:46. "[W]e cannot possess our wealth and secure the peaceful and lawful enjoyment of it [salvation] in any other way than by dwelling in Christ, who is the sole heir of the world, and without being ingrafted into his body." *Comm. Isa.* 65.22, CO 37:431.

9. *Institutes*, IV.1.2, OS 5:4. I will deal with the eschatological implications of the spiritual identity of the Church, which are mentioned in this statement, in the next chapter.

10. *Institutes*, III.6.3, OS 4:148.

11. *Institutes*, III.7.5, OS 4:155; III.20.19, OS 4:324.

PART TWO—Calvin's Ecclesiology

corporate relationship of Christians to Christ within the Church.[12] At this point, we can see that Calvin's idea of the spiritual identity of the Church, which is constituted by the relationship between Christ and Christians as the head and members, is presented in the light of his anthropological understanding of Christian identity in union with Christ. For both the identity of the Christian and the spiritual identity of the Church, he concentrates on the intimate relationship between Christians and Christ in both their personal and communal lives.

The Trinitarian Perspective

Presenting his idea of the spiritual identity of the Church in the light of his idea of Christian identity, Calvin adopts a trinitarian perspective in his ecclesiological discussions (both in the *Institutes* IV and in his commentaries on the Pauline Epistles) just as he does in his anthropological discussion (in the *Institutes* III).

The trinitarian perspective of Calvin's definition of the universal Church developed over successive editions of the *Institutes*. Until the 1539 edition of the *Institutes*, the universal Church had been defined thus:

> First, we believe the holy Catholic Church—that is the whole number of the elect, whether angels or men; of men, whether dead or still living; of the living, in whatever lands they live, or wherever among the nations they have been scattered—to be one church and society, and one people of God. Of it, Christ, our Lord, is Leader and Ruler, and as it were Head of the one body, according as, through divine goodness, they have been chosen in him before the foundation of the world, in order that all might be gathered into God's Kingdom.[13]

In the 1543 edition, however, this definition was replaced by the following statement about the distinction between the invisible and the visible

---

12. Loeschen correctly notes that Calvin discusses the experience and life of the visible Church mainly in the *Institutes* III "even though that term was never used" in this Book. Loeschen, *The Divine Community*, 161.

13. *Institutes* [1536]; *Primum credimus sanctam ecclesiam catholicam, hoc est, universum electorum numerum, sive angeli sint, sive homines; ex hominibus, sive mortui, sive adhuc vivant; ex viventibus, quibuscumque in terris agant, aut ubivis gentium dispersi sint: unam esse ecclesiam ac societatem et unum Dei populum cuius Christus, Dominus noster, dux sit et princeps, ac tanquam unius corporis caput; prout in ipso divina bonitate electi sunt, ante mundi constitutionem, ut in regnum Dei omnes aggregentur.* OS 1:86.

Church which includes a more explicit allusion to the distinct persons of the Trinity:

> Sometimes by the term "church" it means that which is actually in God's presence, into which no persons are received but those who are children of God by grace of adoption and true members of Christ by sanctification of the Holy Spirit. Then, indeed, the church includes not only the saints presently living on earth, but all the elect from the beginning of the world. Often, however, the name "church" designates the whole multitude of men spread over the earth who profess to worship one God and Christ.[14]

The development of the definition of the Church from 1539 to 1543 editions shows that Calvin sought deliberately to explain the spiritual identity of the Church from a clearer trinitarian perspective in elucidating the idea of the invisibility of the spiritual Church. In this definition, he mentions explicitly the Father's grace of adoption, integration in Christ, and the sanctification of the Holy Spirit.

Not only in his definition of the invisible Church but also in his ecclesiology as a whole, it is underlined that both the establishment and the sustenance of the Church depend on the distinctive roles of each person of the Trinity. The Father is "the origin" or "the first author" of the Church because the Church is established by His election: "We must thus consider both God's secret election and his inner call. For he alone knows who are his and, as Paul says, encloses them under his seal [Eph. 1:13], except that they bear his insignia by which they may be distinguished from the reprobate."[15] The Son is called "the Head" because he furnishes the whole body with spiritual benefits and sustains the safety of the Church: "the Church does not stand otherwise than in the event of all things being furnished to her by Christ, the Head and, accordingly, that her entire safety consists in him."[16] The Holy Spirit is "the band." In his commentary on "the fellowship of the Spirit" in 2 Corinthians 13:13, Calvin points out

---

14. *Institutes*, IV.1.7; *Interdum quum Ecclesiam nominant, eam intelligent quae re vera est coram Deo, in quam nulli recipiuntur nisi qui et adoptionis gratia filii Dei sunt, et Spiritus sanctificatione, vera Christi membra. Ac tunc quidem non tantum sanctos qui in terra habitant comprehendit, sed electos omnes qui ab origine mundi fuerunt. Saepe autem Ecclesiae nomine universam hominum multitudinem in orbe diffusam designat, quae unum se Deum et Christum colere profitetur.* OS 5:12.

15. *Institutes*, IV.1.2, OS 5:2.

16. *Comm. Col.* 2:19; *non aliter stare ecclesiam, quam si omnia illi a Christo capite subministrentur: itaque in eo totam eius incolumitatem contineri.* CO 51:113.

PART TWO—Calvin's Ecclesiology

that the Spirit's role as the bond between Christ and the Christian is not only to communicate Christ's benefits to individual Christians, but also to maintain unity between members of the Church:

> The fellowship of the Holy Spirit is added because it is only under his guidance that we come to possess Christ, and all his benefits. He seems, however, at the same time, to allude to the diversity of gifts, of which he had made mention elsewhere, because God does not give the Spirit to every one in a detached way, but distributes to each according to the measure of grace, that the members of the Church, by mutually participating one with another may cherish unity.[17]

In his ecclesiological discussion in the *Institutes* IV, Calvin says that the distinct roles of the three persons of the Trinity work harmoniously to bestow divine grace upon members of the Church: "Consequently, we must firmly believe that by God's generosity, mediated by Christ's merit, through the sanctification of the Spirit, sins have been and are daily pardoned to us who have been received and engrafted into the body of the Church."[18] Calvin's use of the trinitarian perspective to explain the establishment and sustenance of the Church shows that he believes the spiritual identity of the Church as the body of Christ to be a manifestation of the corporative union between Christians and Christ.

The Concern for the Assurance of Salvation in the Church

In his ecclesiology, Calvin highlights the grace of each person of the Trinity, who initiates and sustains the body of Christ: the Father's election, the son's headship and the Spirit's fellowship. Just as in his anthropological discussion of Christian identity, his ultimate concern is to provide Christians with a secure foundation for their salvation in the Church.

Among the distinct but harmonious work of each person of the Trinity for the Church, however, some scholars have argued that Calvin's attempt

---

17. *Comm. 2 Cor.* 13:13, CO 50:156.

18. *Institutes*, IV.1.21; *Quare certo statuendum, divina liberalitate, intercedente Christi merito, per Spiritus sanctificationem, peccatorum gratiam nobis factam esse ac quotidie fieri, qui in Ecclesiae corpus asciti et inserti sumus.* OS 5:25. Milner argues that Calvin presents his understanding of the church as a dialectical tension between the static character of the headship of Christ and the dynamic character of the gifts of the Spirit. However, he does not explicitly recognise the trinitarian perspective in Calvin's ecclesiology. Milner, *Calvin's Doctrine of the Church*, 150.

to root the spiritual identity of the Church in God's election of believers is methodologically problematic.[19] For example, MacGregor argues that Calvin's definition of the Church in terms of election introduces "a great methodological error" because Calvin brings "the eternal order" into the definition of "the temporal order." Macgregor places the Church in the temporal order because of the presence of the reprobate in the Church, which would be impossible in the eternal order.[20] MacGregor's criticism, however, is not justified, because Calvin is speaking of the spiritual identity of the invisible Church when he focuses on election. Calvin posits that the invisible Church is included in "the eternal order," which embraces not only the elect of this world but also the departed saints and the angels.[21] However, it is still useful for us to examine this issue to understand Calvin's idea of the spiritual identity of the Church.

In his ecclesiological discussions in the *Institutes* IV, Calvin upholds his definition of the invisible Church in terms of God's election in order to provide Christians with assurance of their salvation in the body of Christ. Since Calvin affirms Cyprian's statement that "away from her [the visible Church's] bosom one cannot hope for any forgiveness of sins or any salvation,"[22] he feels the need to maintain the idea of the invisible Church in the *Institutes* to argue that even in the most wretched condition of the visible Church, Christians can be assured of their salvation because their membership of the invisible Church continues: "Although the melancholy desolation which confronts us on every side may cry that no remnant of

---

19. Thus Loeschen raises a question of Calvin's distinction between the visible and invisible Church in the *Institutes*, IV, 1–8: "[O]ne gets the feeling that Calvin was surprised and unprepared for the issues that occurred to his own self-conscious and systematic mind" while he here mainly deals with the visible Church. Loeschen, *The Divine Community*, 160–61.

20. MacGregor, *Corpus Christi*, 48–50.

21. Ibid., 50. After painstaking analysis of Calvin's idea of the invisible Church in terms of God's secret election through the consecutive editions of the *Institutes*, Wiley briefly suggests five reasons for this idea: to comfort persecuted and isolated Christians; to secure the foundation of church discipline; to find the basis of the continuous reformation of the Church; to maintain the unity of the Church; and to emphasise God's grace. Wiley, "The Church as the Elect," 112–13.

22. *Institutes*, IV.1.4, OS 5:7. Calvin also insists on the necessity of the church for salvation in the Catechism of 1541: "[I]f we would not render Christ's death ineffective and reduce to nothing all that has hitherto been said. For the one effect of all this is that there be a Church." *Catechism*, 102.

PART TWO—Calvin's Ecclesiology

the Church is left, let us know that Christ's death is fruitful, and that God miraculously keeps his Church as in hiding places."[23]

Likewise, in his soteriological discussions in the *Institutes* III, one of the ultimate aims of Calvin's doctrine of election is to secure the assurance of salvation:

> The fact that, as we said, the firmness of our election is joined to our calling is another means of establishing our assurance. For those whom Christ has illumined with the knowledge of his name and has introduced into the bosom of his church, he is said to receive into his care and keeping.[24]

Calvin adopts a trinitarian perspective again in his discussion of election in his idea that the grace of the triune God confirms Christians in assurance of their election. It is significant that, in his discussion of election in the *Institutes* III, Calvin ascribes a distinct role to each person of the Trinity with regard to the benefit of election for Christians: "if we seek God's fatherly mercy and kindly heart, we should turn our eyes to Christ, on whom alone God's Spirit rests."[25] Already in Calvin's soteriological presentation of the doctrine of election in the *Institutes* III, we can observe the ecclesiological implications of this doctrine. When speaking of the way in which the Father elects and adopts His children, Calvin stresses that their election and adoption will lead to a familial unity not only with God but also with other children of God: "God designates as his children those whom he has chosen, and appoints himself their Father. Further, by calling, he receives them into his family and unites them to him so that they may together be one."[26]

Calvin insists that Christians cannot find the "ground for firmness and confidence" of their salvation without Christ's teaching and promise confirming the Father's election: "in order to free us of all fear and render us victorious amid so many dangers, snares, and mortal struggles, he

---

23. *Institutes*, IV.1.2, OS 5:4. Niesel points out that Calvin's definition of the invisible Church in terms of God's election "gives to the church its peace and certainty and the impetus which it needs for its ministry in this world." Niesel, *The Theology of Calvin*, 190–191.

24. *Institutes*, III.24.6, OS 4:417.

25. *Institutes*, III.24.5; *Primum, si paternam Dei clementiam propitiumque animum quaeramus, ad Christum convertendi sunt oculi, in quo solo Patris anima acquiescit*. OS 4:416.

26. *Institutes*, III.24.1, OS 4:411. Wiley points out that "in so far as Calvin's doctrine of election is soteriological, it is also ecclesiological." Wiley, "The Church as the Elect," 110–12.

The Church as the Body of Christ

[Christ] promises that whatever the Father has entrusted into his keeping will be safe [John 10:28-29]."[27] When discussing Christ's vital role in confirming the election of the Christians, Calvin repeatedly speaks of the head-member relationship between Christ and Christians within the Church:

> We must, in order that election may be effectual and truly enduring, ascend to the Head, in whom the Heavenly Father has gathered his elect together, and has joined them to himself by an indissoluble bond . . . yet in the members of Christ a far more excellent power of grace appears, for, engrafted to their Head, they are never cut off from salvation.[28]

When he discusses the way in which the Holy Spirit illuminates believers in order to confirm their election by God, Calvin seems to bear in mind the preaching ministry of the Church and two different responses to it: the elect are sanctified by the Holy Spirit when they hear the Word; but the reprobate reject it.[29] On the one hand, the elect can confirm their salvation when the Spirit illuminates their mind "in the faith of the gospel":

> Hence, in order that we may know that we are elected by God, there is no occasion to inquire as to what he decreed before the creation of the world, but we find in ourselves a satisfactory proof if he has sanctified us by his Spirit,—if he has enlightened us in the faith of his gospel.[30]

---

27. *Institutes*, III.21.1, OS 4:369-70.

28. *Institutes*, III.21.7, OS 4:377. "For since it is into his [Christ's] body the Father has destined those to be engrafted whom he has willed from eternity to be his own, that he may hold as sons all whom he acknowledges to be among his members, we have a sufficiently clear and firm testimony that we have been inscribed in the book of life if we are in communion with Christ." *Institutes*, III.24.5, OS 4:416.

29. "Besides, even the very nature and dispensation of the call clearly demonstrate this fact [that God calls the elect only by grace], for it consists not only in the preaching of the Word but also in the illumination of the Spirit." *Institutes*, III.24.2, OS 4:412. "Even though the preaching of the gospel streams forth from the wellspring of election, because such preaching is shared also with the wicked, it cannot of itself be a full proof of election. But God effectively teaches his elect that he may lead them to faith." *Institutes*, III.24.1, OS 4:410.

30. *Comm. 2 Thess.* 2:13; *Ergo ut sciamus nos a Deo electos esse, non est quod sciscitemur quid ante mundi creationem decreverit: sed in nobis reperiemus legitimam probationem, si nos spiritu suo sanctificaverit, si in fidem evangelii sui illuminaverit.* CO 52:206. "That effect [of our election] is the sanctification of the Spirit, even effectual calling, when faith is added to the outward preaching of the gospel, which faith is begotten by the inward operation of the Spirit." *Comm. 1 Pet.* 1:2, CO 55:208.

PART TWO—Calvin's Ecclesiology

On the other hand, the reprobate are exposed to the testimony of God's love but shut themselves off from the sanctification of the Spirit:

> When he [God] first shines with the light of his Word upon the undeserving, he thereby shows a sufficiently clear proof of his free goodness. Here, then, God's boundless goodness is already manifesting itself but not to the salvation of all; for a heavier judgment remains upon the wicked because they reject the testimony of God's love. And God also, to show forth his glory, withdraws the effectual working of his Spirit from them.[31]

The reason for Calvin's definition of the invisible Church in terms of God's election in his ecclesiology is not different from his soteriological concern of the doctrine of election in the *Institutes* III, in which he already hints at the ecclesiological implications of this doctrine: to provide Christians with a secure foundation of the assurance of their salvation not only in their personal life but also in their communal life in the Church. In addition to his trinitarian perspective, this concern also shows his idea that the spiritual identity of the Church is the corporative dimension of the relationship of the individual Christians with Christ.

Three Ecclesiological Foci of the Metaphor of *Corpus Christi*

As we have seen, Calvin's term "engrafting into Christ's body," his trinitarian perspective, and his concern for the assurance of salvation manifest that his idea of the Church as the body of Christ is he corporative dimension of the relationship between individual Christians and Christ. This poses some interesting questions. If Calvin understands the Church as merely another dimension of Christian identity, where is Calvin's ecclesiology? Is it simply a subsidiary doctrine of his anthropology or soteriology? Although Calvin's idea of the invisible Church is closely related to his anthropology or soteriology, one can hardly say that there is not really any ecclesiology at all, because Calvin points out the principles of the actual community of Christians in his idea of the spiritual identity of the Church as the body of Christ. As we shall see in the next section, he attempts to realise the principles of the invisible Church, the main subject of the *Institutes* III as we saw in the

---

31. *Institutes*, III.24.2, OS 4:412.

The Church as the Body of Christ

previous section, within the concrete and institutional aspects of the visible Church, the main subject of the *Institutes* IV.

In his commentary on Ephesians 4:16, we can observe three foci to which Calvin pays attention to in order to sustain the health of the spiritual community of the body of Christ: Christ's headship, the communication of diverse gifts between the members and the necessity of mutual love:

> There are three things here which deserve our attention. The first is what has been stated. All the life or health which is diffused through the members flows from the head; so that the members occupy a subordinate rank. The second is that by the distribution made, the limited share of each renders the communication between all the members absolutely necessary. The third is that without mutual love, the health of the body cannot be maintained.[32]

These three foci in his idea of the Church as *Corpus Christi* provide Calvin with the theological principle by which he suggests a method to sustain the healthy condition of the visible Church can be sustained.

The Headship of Christ

Calvin argues that in Scripture Christ is called "the head" because he is the source of vital energy both for the individual Christian and for the Church. In his commentary on Colossians 1:18, Calvin writes that Christ, "in rising again had made the commencement of the Kingdom of God, then do we truly begin to have a being in the sight of God, when we are renewed, so as to be new creatures."[33] In the same commentary, he also argues, "as in the human body it [the head] serves as a root, from which vital energy is diffused through all the members, so that life of the Church flows out from Christ."[34]

In the first place, the headship of Christ is essential for the unity of the Church:

32. *Comm. Eph.* 4:16; *Verum tria notanda sunt. Primum, illud quod dixi, quidquid vitale est aut salubre quod per membra spargitur, id a capite manare: ut in membris nihil sit praeter administrationem. Secundum, quod talis sit distributio, ut inter se communicare opus habeant propter finitam cuiusque mensuram. Tertio, quod sine mutua caritate salvum esse nequeat corpus.* CO 51:203.

33. *Comm. Col.* 1:18; *Quia igitur Christus resurgendo regnum Dei auspicatus est, merito dicitur principium: quia tunc vere incipimus esse coram Deo, quum renovamur ut simus novae creaturae.* CO 52:87.

34. *Comm. Col.* 1:18, CO 52:86.

> For we are called for this end that we may unite together in one body, since Christ has ordained a fellowship and connection between the faithful similar to that which exists between the members of the human body; and as men could not of themselves come together into such an union, he himself becomes the bond of this connection.[35]

Calvin relates "Christ's headship" of the Church to his authority as in the declaration in his commentary on Ephesians 1:22: "The metaphor of a head denotes the highest authority." That Christ has the highest authority means that "all others, whether angels or men, must rank as members; so that he who holds the highest place among his fellows is still one of the members of the same body."[36] In his commentary on 1 Corinthians 1:12, Calvin focuses on the supreme authority of Christ for the unity of the Church: "In short, the unity of the Church consists more especially in this one thing—that we all depend upon Christ alone, and that men thus occupy an inferior place, so as not to detract in any degree from his pre-eminence."[37] Using this idea, Calvin argues against the claims of the Roman Catholics that the pope is "the ministerial head" of the Church: "He [Paul] shews, therefore, that it is Christ that alone has authority to govern the Church, that it is he to whom alone believers to have an eye, and on whom alone the unity of the body depends."[38] His interpretation of "Christ's headship" in Colossians 1:19 is also accompanied by polemics against what he calls "the kingdom of the Pope": "As, however, we do not there [in the Roman Church] see what Paul here requires in the Church, what shall we say, but that it is a humpbacked body, and a confused mass that will fall to pieces of itself."[39]

Therefore, the foremost focus of Calvin's idea of the Church as the body of Christ is the vital role of Christ in maintaining the unity and health

---

35. *Comm. Rom* 12.4; *Vocati enim sumus hac lege, ut tanquam in unum corpus coalescamus: quandoquidem eam quae est inter humani corporis membra societatem ac connexionem inter omnes suos fideles instituit Christus: et quia in tantam unitatem per se homines convenire non poterant, illius coniunctionis vinculum ipse factus est.* CO 49:237. Cf. *Comm. 1 Cor.* 3:23; 11:28; 13:4; *Comm. Eph.* 1:10; 2:25.

36. *Comm. Eph.* 1:22, CO 51:159. "As the members of the same body have distinct offices, and all of them are distinct, for no member possesses all powers, nor does it appropriate to itself the offices of others." *Comm. Rom.* 12:4, CO 49:237.

37. *Comm. 1 Cor.* 1:12, CO 49:316.

38. *Comm. Col.* 1:18, CO 52:87.

39. *Comm. Col.* 2:19, CO 52:113.

of Church in the truth of the Word as a result of his highest authority as its Head.

The Communication of Diverse Gifts

The second focus of the biblical notion of *Corpus Christi* for Calvin is that God distributes diverse gifts to every member of Christ's body in order to preserve the unity and health of the Church:

> He [Paul] means, that God has not acted at random, or without good reason, in assigning different gifts to the members of the body; but because it was necessary that it should be so, for the preservation of the body; for if this symmetry were taken away, there would be utter confusion and derangement.[40]

Calvin perceives that the diversity of the gifts might provoke divisions among the members, and that this division would harm the health of the visible Church. Therefore, these gifts should be exercised according to each member's limited measure, for the common good of the Church: "I admit then that the society of the godly cannot exist, except when each one is content with his own measure, and imparts to others the gifts which he has received, and allows himself by turns to be assisted by the gifts of others."[41] This means, firstly, that no member should be proud of his gifts: "The words 'grace' and 'gifts' remind us that, whatever may be our attainments, we ought not to be proud of them, because they lay us under deeper obligations to God."[42] Secondly, the members should not envy or despise each other's gifts:

> Hitherto he [Paul] has been showing, what is the office of the less honourable [more vile] members—to discharge their duty to the body, and not envy the more distinguished members. He enjoins it upon the more honourable members, not to despise the inferior members, which they cannot dispense with.[43]

This "divinely appointed symmetry," established only by the proper exercise of the diverse gifts, is necessary for the benefit of the whole body: "God has appointed this symmetry and that with a view to the advantage

---

40. *Comm. 1 Cor.* 12:19, CO 49:503.
41. *Comm. Rom.* 12:6, CO 49:238.
42. *Comm. Eph.* 4:7, CO 50:193.
43. *Comm. 1 Cor.* 12:21, CO 49:504.

PART TWO—Calvin's Ecclesiology

of the whole body, because it cannot otherwise maintain its standing."[44] The mutual connection of the members is necessary for maintaining this symmetry:

> The unity of the body is of such a nature as cannot be maintained but by a diversity of members; and . . . while the members differ from each other in offices and functions, it is in such a way as to have a mutual connection with each other for the preservation of the one body.[45]

Calvin's idea of the sharing of diverse gifts and mutual communication between the members relies upon the idea that all these gifts are endowed by God for the common good of the Church.[46]

Mutual Love

Concerning the third focus in his idea of the Church as the body of Christ, Calvin argues that mutual love is indispensable to the unity of the Church: "The first commendation of love is this—that, by patient endurance of many things, it promotes peace and harmony in the Church."[47] The communication of diverse gifts does not contribute to the health and the edification of the Church unless it is carried out in mutual love:

> Let there be mutual affection, mutual fellow-feeling, mutual concern. Let us have a regard to the common advantage, in order that we may not destroy the Church by malignity, or envy, or pride, or any disagreement; but may, on the contrary, every one of us, strive to the utmost of his power to preserve it.[48]

---

44. *Comm. 1 Cor.* 12:24, CO 49:503. "Here then we have the main design which the Apostle had in view, that all things do not meet in all, but that the gifts of God are so distributed that each has a limited portion, and that each ought to be so attentive in imparting his own gifts to the edification of the Church, that no one, by leaving his own function, may trespass on that of another." *Comm. Rom.* 12:6, CO 49:238.

45. *Comm. 1 Cor.* 12:20, CO 49:503. "On no one has God bestowed all things. Each has received a certain measure. Being thus dependent on each other, they find it necessary to throw their individual gifts into the common stock, and thus to render mutual aid." *Comm. Eph.* 4:7, CO 50:192.

46. "As, then, he has taught above, that everything that an individual has received from God should be made subservient to the common good, so now he declares that offices are distributed in such a manner, that all may together, by united efforts, edify the Church, and each individual according to his measure." *Comm. 1 Cor.* 12:27, CO 49:506.

47. *Comm. 1 Cor.* 13:4, CO 49:510.

48. *Comm. 1 Cor.* 12:27; *sit mutuus amor, mutual . . . mutua sollicitudo: moveat nos*

Calvin does not speak of love in terms of mere sympathy or charity between human individuals. Rather, what Calvin refers to as "mutual love" is a more profound love based on faith, the conviction of God's grace of salvation.[49] For Calvin, love is the corollary of the conviction of the mind. He asked thus: "how can mind be aroused to taste the divine goodness without at the same time being wholly kindled to love God in return?"[50] Since he thinks of the mutual love and mutual connection in the Church as being love which is based on faith, Calvin argues that the symmetry and growth, the two characteristics of the spiritual Church described in Ephesians, "consist in unity of faith":

> There is first required a fitting together, that believers may embrace and accommodate themselves to each other by mutual intercourse; otherwise there would not be a building, but a confused mass. The chief part of the symmetry consists in unity of faith, next follows progress or increase.[51]

Calvin's emphasis on the necessity of faith for the harmony of the Church in love echoes his idea of the relationship between faith and love: "for it is faith alone that first engenders love in us."[52] He also claims, "For, though he means that love with which Christ hath loved us, and of which he hath given us a proof by his death, yet he connects with us that mutual love which springs from the conviction of having received so great a blessing."[53]

---

communis utilitas, ne malignitate, aut invidia, aut superbia, aut ullo dissidio ecclesiam perdamus: sed potius singuli in eius consecrationem pro sua virili incumbant. CO 49:505. "This is accomplished by love; and where it does not reign, there is no 'edification,' but an absolute scattering of the church." *Comm. Eph.* 4:16, CO 51:203.

49. For Calvin, faith is the knowledge of God's grace for Christians: "Now we shall possess a right definition of faith if we call it a firm and certain knowledge of God's benevolence toward us." *Institutes,* III.2.7, OS 4:16.

50. *Institutes,* III.2.41; *Ad talem vero divinae bonitatis gustum percipiendum quomodo se attollat animus, quin simul ad redamandum Deum totus accendatur?* OS 4:51.

51. *Comm. Eph.* 2:21; *Primum requiritur coaptatio, ut se invicem complectantur fideles, et se alii aliis mutuale communicatione accommodent: alioqui non aedificium esset, sed confusa moles. Sed praecipua symmetria in fidei unitate consistit, deinde sequitur profectus, vel incrementum.* CO 51:176.

52. *Institutes,* III.2.41; *Quod enim tradunt Scholastici, charitatem fide ac spe priorem esse, merum est deliramentum: quandoquidem sola est fides quae in nobis charitatem primum generat.* OS 4:52.

53. *Comm. John* 21:15, CO 46:451. In the next statement in the same commentary, Calvin associates this idea with the ministers of the Church: "Those who are called to govern the Church ought, therefore, to remember that, if they are desirous to discharge their office properly and faithfully, they must begin with the love of Christ."

PART TWO—Calvin's Ecclesiology

When, therefore, he refers to mutual love, as the indispensable condition for the peace and harmony of the Church, Calvin does not speak merely of a human affection for each other but of a more profound love, arising from the conviction that believers have received the grace of God and from the gratitude shown to God as a result.

Corpus Christi and Church Government

In order to understand how Calvin tries to realise his idea of the Church as *Corpus Christi* in practice, it is useful for us to investigate the three main elements in his outline of church government in the *Institutes* IV.3: the election and examination of ministers; the assignment of each ecclesiastical office according to the gifts of candidates; and the restoration of the office of deacons. In the *Institutes* IV.4, these are the three points from which Calvin attacks the Roman Church and with which he tries to justify the Reformed Church with regard to church government.[54]

A number of studies have investigated Calvin's idea of church government from both theological and historical perspectives. Niesel, Wendel, Milner and Loeschen have dealt with the theological basis of Calvin's idea of church government, focusing mainly on either the Christological or the dialectical features of his ecclesiology.[55] Another scholarly tradition has sought to elucidate the historical context of Calvin's ecclesiology. Monter and Kingdon have presented helpful examinations of the historical context of Geneva with regard to Calvin's idea of church government.[56] Kroon,

---

54. He attacks the loss of recognition of the proper gifts of preaching in the Roman Church in sections 1–4, its abuse of the property of the Church and the office of deacon in sections 5–9, and the procedure of the priests' ordination in section 10–15.

55. Niesel evaluates Calvin's ecclesiology as "a testimony to God's revelation in Jesus Christ, and not a characterization of the essence of religious fellowship." Niesel, *The Theology of Calvin*, 195. Wendel analyses the *Institutes* and sketches Calvin's idea of church government in its historical context. Wendel, *Calvin*, 291–311. Ganoczy argues that the dialectic between the "divine- interior-invisible" and the "human-visible-exterior" elements is the dominant perspective by which Calvin presents his ideas of church government. Ganoczy, *Calvin*, 302ff. Milner attempts to interpret Calvin's idea of church government according to his framework of the dialectic between the *ordinatio Dei* and the freedom of the Spirit. Milner, *Calvin's Doctrine of the Church*, 150–52. Loeschen argues that Calvin understands the church as both "being" and "becoming" at the same time. Loeschen, *The Divine Community*, 181–88.

56. Monter, *Calvin's Geneva*, 137–39; Kingdon, "The Control of Morals in Calvin's Geneva," 3–16.

van't Spijker and Hammann have offered comparative studies of Calvin and Bucer, on their ideas of church government and demonstrate how Bucer influenced Calvin.[57] Höpfl is representative of those who approach this topic from the perspective of political theory.[58] McKee's study of Calvin's idea of the fourfold ministry seeks to show the context of the exegetical history in which Calvin developed his ideas.[59] Although those historical studies have provided useful insights and resources to studies of Calvin's ecclesiology, there has been little attention to the role of Calvin's idea of the Church as the body of Christ in providing him with the theological basis of his proposals for church government.

The *Institutes* IV.3 is one of the most useful sources for us to see Calvin's idea of church government, not only because it contains the theological reflections and scriptural supports of his idea of church government, but also because most of this chapter was written in 1543, two years later than Calvin's plan of church government in the *Ordinances*.[60] The *Ordinances* is also useful for understanding Calvin's idea of church government because his practical proposals for church government are succinctly presented in this document. In his letter to Farel in September 1541, Calvin wrote that he had started drafting an article concerning ecclesiastical polity as a whole, and the purpose of this article was to establish a settled church government according to Scripture and the model of the ancient Church: "Immediately I had offered my service to the Senate, I declared that a Church could not hold together unless a settled government should be agreed on, such as is

---

57. Kroon, *Studien zu Martin Bucers Obrigkeitsverständnis*, 91ff., 123ff., 160ff.; Spijker, *The Ecclesiastical Offices in the Thought of Martin Bucer*, 159-60, 399-402, 419ff.; Hammann, *Entre la secte et la cité*, 282, 285-88.

58. Höpfl approaches Calvin's ecclesiology from the perspective of political theory and argues that the development of the Calvin's theology is influenced more by his political experience and practical needs than scriptural factors or inconsistent theological convictions. Höpfl, *Christian Polity of John Calvin*, 1, 76, 106-8, 128, 154-55.

59. McKee, *Elders and the Plural Ministry*, 15-25, 115-19, 123-29, 211-22.

60. Höpfl, *The Christian Polity of John Calvin*, 103-27. It is not certain when Calvin wrote this chapter about church government, which was the eighth chapter of the 1543 edition of the *Institutes*. However, it is possible to say that there were some interactions between Calvin's experiences around the events of his return to Geneva and his theological writings about church government in the 1543 edition of the *Institutes*. The *Bibliotheca Calviniana* suggests that most of the newly added part of the 1543 edition must have been written around January, 1542. Peter and Gilmont, *Bibliotheca Calviniana*, 130-31. Also see OS 3:xix-xx.

PART TWO—Calvin's Ecclesiology

prescribed to us in the Word of God, and such as was in use in the ancient Church."[61]

However, the aim of the investigation in this section is neither to judge the faithfulness of Calvin's ideas about church government to Scripture and the ancient Church nor to evaluate their success in his proposal to the Church of Geneva. Instead, I shall try to show that the three principles identified by Calvin of the spiritual identity of the Church as the body of Christ, namely, Christ's headship, the communication of diverse gifts, and mutual love, provide the theological foundations for the three significant points in his proposal on church government.

The Election and Examination of Ministers

Calvin's suggestion that pastors should be elected by a multi-stage process including the consent of the people reflects his focus on Christ's headship in the Church. In his commentary on Ephesians 1:22, "And gave him [Christ] to be the head over all things to the church," Calvin argues that the title "Head" given to Christ is "not a mere honorary title but is accompanied by the entire command and real government of the universe."[62] In particular, Christ's headship should be realised in the government of the visible Church: "though all things are regulated by the will and power of Christ, yet the subject of which Paul particularly speaks [in Ephesians 1:22-23] is the spiritual government of the Church."[63] Arguing against Roman Catholics' claim of the primacy of the Pope, Calvin explicitly refers to Christ's headship as the fundamental principle of church government: "For it has Christ as its sole Head, under whose sway all of us cleave to one another, according to that order and that form of polity which he has laid down."[64]

The method of electing pastors is one of the most important issues in Calvin's plan for church government, because pastors are considered to

---

61. *Letters* 1:260, Calvin to Farel; *Ubi operam meam senatui detuli, exposui non posse consistere ecclesiam, nisi certum regimen constitueretur quale ex verbo Dei nobis praescriptum est et in veteri ecclesia fuit observatum.* CO 11:281. For the historical context of the Ordinances, see Parker, *John Calvin*, 82–84.

62. *Comm. Eph.* 1:22; *Significat autem non esse nudum honorem quod caput ecclesiae constitutus est: quia simul plena rerum omnium potestas et administratio illi sit commissa.* CO 51:159.

63. *Comm. Eph.* 1:22; *Nam utcunque Christus omnia perficiat nutu virtuteque sua: tamen specialiter loquitur hic Paulus de spirituali ecclesiae gubernatione.* CO 51:160.

64. *Institutes*, IV.6.9, OS 5:97.

The Church as the Body of Christ

discharge the highest office in the Church: "I have accordingly pointed out above that God often commended the dignity of the ministry by all possible marks of approval in order that it might be held among us in highest honor and esteem, even as the most excellent of all things."[65] Yet it is more important for Calvin that the pastors' authority comes not from themselves but from the Word that has been entrusted to their office by God:

> We admit, therefore, that ecclesiastical pastors are to be heard just like Christ himself, but they must be pastors who execute the office entrusted to them. And this office, we maintain, is not presumptuously to introduce whatever their own pleasure has rashly devised, but religiously and in good faith to deliver the oracles which they have received at the mouth of the Lord.[66]

Because of these ideas, he argues that all members of the Church, including pastors, should be subordinated to Christ and the Word:

> Let that humility be ours which, beginning with the lowest and paying respect to each in his degree, yields the highest honour and respect to the Church in subordination, however, to Christ the Church's head; let that obedience be ours, which while it disposes us to listen to our elders and superiors, tests all obedience by the Word of God; in a word, let our Church be one whose supreme concern it is humbly and religiously to venerate the Word of God, and submit in obedience to it.[67]

Subordination of the members of the Church to Christ's headship should be expressed in church government by establishing a lawful way to elect pastors according to the Word:

> Nor is there reason for our opponents to philosophize subtly over a comparison of heavenly and earthly hierarchy . . . it is not safe to be wise beyond measure concerning the former, and in establishing the latter we should not follow any other pattern than that which the Lord himself has sketched in his Word.[68]

---

65. *Institutes*, IV.3.3, OS 5:44.

66. *Reply to Sadolet*, LCC 22:242; *Audiendos ergo fatemur, non secus ac Christum ipsum, ecclesiasticos pastores, sed qui munus sibi iniunctum exsequantur. Id porro ipsum esse dicimus, non quae a se ipsis placita temere excuderint, confidenter ingerere, sed quae ex ore Domini oracular acceperint, religiose ac bona fide proferre.* CO 5:404.

67. *Reply to Sadolet*, LCC 22:241, CO 5:403.

68. *Institutes*, IV.6.10, OS 5:98.

PART TWO—Calvin's Ecclesiology

That is because Christ, as the Head of the Church, rules his Kingdom by the Word: "the church is Christ's Kingdom, and he reigns by his Word alone."[69]

For Calvin, the multi-stage process of the election of pastors, including the consent and approval of the people, is the proper way by which the entire Church will be subordinate to the authority of the Word.[70] The concrete electoral procedure is prescribed in the *Ordinances* thus:

> The order is that ministers first elect such as ought to hold office; afterwards that he be presented to the Council; and if he is found worthy the Council receive and accept him, giving him certification to produce finally to the people when he preaches, in order that he be received by the common consent of the company of the faithful.[71]

As MacGregor indicates, Calvin thinks that this multi-stage process was proposed to allow the people "a period of time" to oppose the ordination of those who were found to be improper for the pastoral duty.[72] The *Ordinances* thus posits the process of rejecting an unsuitable candidate for the office of pastors: "If he be found unworthy, and show this after due probation, it is necessary to proceed to a new election for the choosing of another."[73]

This suggestion may reflect the historical and political situation in Geneva.[74] Calvin himself, however, argues that this method is being proposed because he believes it to be the most lawful way by which the teaching of Scripture can be represented: "Therefore, this is the most lawful way, that those be chosen by common voices (*communibus suffragiis*) who are to take upon them any public function in the Church."[75] Commenting on Titus 1:5 where Paul urges Titus to appoint presbyters or elders for each church, Calvin argues: "Not that they [Paul and Barnabas] alone, in an authoritative

---

69. *Institutes*, IV.2.4, OS 5:36. I will deal with Calvin's idea of the Church as the Kingdom of Christ in the next chapter.

70. "We therefore hold that this call of a minister is lawful according to the Word of God, when those who seemed fit are created by the consent and approval of the people." *Institutes*, IV.3.15, OS 4:56.

71. *Ordinances*, LCC 22:59, OS 2:329.

72. MacGregor, *Corpus Christi*, 60.

73. *Ordinances*, LCC 22:59, OS 2:329.

74. Monter demonstrates that the struggle between the people and the Prince-Bishop appointed by the Duke of Savoy had made the Genevan people sensitive to the issue of who had the authority to elect or appoint pastors. Monter, *Calvin's Geneva*, 29–92. Also see Ganoczy, *Calvin*, 312–13; Höpfl, *Christian Polity of John Calvin*, 104–12.

75. *Comm. Acts*, 6:3, CO 48:120.

The Church as the Body of Christ

manner, appointed pastors which the churches had neither approved nor known; but that they ordained fit men, who had been chosen or desired by the people."[76]

The *Ordinances* prescribes the necessity for the continuous examination of pastors after ordination for the same purpose: "Now as it is necessary to examine the ministers well when they are to be elected, so also it is necessary to have good supervision to maintain them in their duty."[77] According to the *Ordinances*, elders take part in the examination of pastors on both moral and doctrinal matters:

> If there appears difference of doctrine, let the ministers come together to discuss the matter. Afterwards, if need be, let them call the elders to assist in composing the contention. Finally, if they are unable to come to friendly agreement because of the obstinacy of one of the parties, let the case be referred to the magistrate to be put in order.[78]

In his treatise *The Necessity of Reforming the Church*, which was dedicated to Charles V in 1543, Calvin argues that the restoration of "the apostolic rule and the practice of the primitive Church" in the election of pastors by such a process is essential to the reformation of church government: "the magistracy and people had a discretionary power of approving or refusing the individual who was nominated by the clergy, in order that no man might be intruded on those unwilling or not consenting."[79] Calvin states the same idea in his commentary on Ephesians 4:11 which shows clearly how he rejects the practice of selecting priests in the Roman Church:

> In truth, he [Paul] plainly rejects it [the idea of the earthly head] as without foundation, when he ascribes superiority to Christ alone, and represents the apostle, and all the pastors, as indeed inferior to Him, but associated on an equal level with each other. There is no

---

76. *Comm. Titus* 1:5, CO 53:409. Calvin quotes Acts 14:23 as another scriptural basis for affirming the necessity of the people's approval in election of pastors: "Thus also Luke relates that Paul and Barnabas ordained elders in every church (Acts 14:23)."

77. *Ordinances*, LCC 22:60, OS 2:330.

78. *Ordinances*, LCC 22:60, OS 2:330.

79. *Necessity of Reforming the Church*, LCC 22:207–8, CO 6:491. To support his argument, Calvin then quotes the statements of the fourth African Council, Leo, Cyprian and Gregory to criticize the practice of appointing priests in the Roman Church: "In their election, no account is taken either of life or doctrine. The right of voting is wrested from the people."

PART TWO—Calvin's Ecclesiology

passage of Scripture by which that tyrannical hierarchy, regulated by one earthly head, is more completely overturned.[80]

In Calvin's view, this "tyrannical hierarchy" of the Roman Church has been brought about by the immoderate enforcement of clerical power so as to rob the people of their right to choose their pastors.[81] However, Calvin himself is well aware of the danger of the appropriation of ecclesiastical authority by the people without restraint. Accordingly, he stresses the moderation of pastors in the course of election:

> And this is the mean between tyranny and confused liberty, that nothing be done without the consent and approbation of the people, yet so that the pastors moderate and govern that their authority may be as a bridle to keep under the people, lest they pass their bounds too much.[82]

For Calvin, therefore, realisation of Christ's headship in church government is totally different from both "tyranny and confused liberty."[83] The desirable ecclesiastical government is established only "by the ministry of the Word," and it "is not a contrivance of men, but an appointment made by the Son," the head of the Church.[84]

---

80. *Comm. Eph.* 4:11, CO 51:198.

81. "Now all the people's right in electing a bishop has been taken away. Votes, assent, subscriptions, and all their like have vanished: the whole power has been transferred to the canons alone. They confer the episcopate on whom they please; they introduce him directly before the people, but to be adored, not to be examined." *Institutes*, IV.5.2, OS 5:74.

82. *Comm. Acts* 6:3, CO 48:120.

83. It is significant that Calvin holds a similar opinion about the desirable form of civil government: "The fall from kingdom to tyranny is easy; but it is not much more difficult to fall from the rule of the best men to the faction of a few; yet it is easiest of all to fall from popular rule to sedition. For if the three forms of government which the philosophers discuss be considered in themselves, I will not deny that aristocracy, or a system compounded of aristocracy and democracy, far excels all others." *Institutes*, IV.20.8, OS 5:479. Ganoczy argues that Calvin "pursued a 'via media' between the extreme harmfulness of the two contrasting tyrannies: that of the one person and that of the anonymous crowd." But Ganoczy does not note the idea of the headship of Christ as the theological basis of Calvin's practical suggestions of "via media" concerning the methods of electing pastors. Ganoczy, *Calvin: Théologien de l'église et du ministère*, 317–18.

84. *Comm. Eph.* 4:11; *Denique regimen ecclesiae, quod verbi ministerio constat, non ab hominibus excogitatum, sed a filio Dei positum esse docet.* CO 51:196.

The Fourfold Ecclesiastical Office

The fourfold ecclesiastical office is the second most important idea in Calvin's proposal of church government purposed in the *Ordinances*: "There are four orders of office instituted by our Lord for the government of his Church: First, pastors, then doctors; next, elders, and fourth deacons."[85] This idea is closely related to Calvin's ecclesiological focus on the communication of diverse gifts among Church members in interpreting the metaphor of *Corpus Christi*.

These four ecclesiastical offices may be divided into two categories: the teaching and the non-teaching offices. Pastors and teachers constitute the teaching offices:

> Next come pastors and teachers, whom the church can never do without. There is, I believe, this difference between them: teachers are not put in charge of discipline, or administering the sacraments, or warning and exhortations, but only of Scriptural interpretation—to keep doctrine whole and pure among believers. But the pastoral office includes all these functions within itself.[86]

Although Calvin distinguishes between the offices of pastors and teachers in the *Ordinances*, he admits the practical difficulty in dividing them: "It may sometimes happen that the same person is both a pastor and a teacher, but the duties to be performed are entirely different."[87] Calvin uses the term "bishop"(*Episcopus*) as a label for the office of pastors. He thinks that the scriptural term of "bishop" is used to denote a person who discharges the duty of the Word:

> He [Paul] names the pastors separately, for the sake of honor. We may, however, infer from this that the name of bishop is common to all the ministers of the Word, inasmuch as he assigns several bishops to one Church. The titles, therefore, of bishop and pastor, are synonymous.[88]

---

85. *Ordinances*, LCC 22:58, OS 2:328.
86. *Institutes*, IV.3.4, OS 5:46.
87. *Comm. Eph.* 4:11, CO 51:198.
88. *Comm. Phil.* 1:1, CO 52:7. However, following scriptural usage, Calvin does not sharply distinguish the offices usually referred to as "bishop" from "presbyter." But he applies the title "bishop" to anyone who discharges the office of the Word: "But in indiscriminately calling those who rule the church 'bishop,' 'presbyters,' 'pastors' and 'ministers.' I did so according to Scriptural usage, which interchanges these terms. For to all who carry out the ministry of the Word, it accords the title of 'bishop.'" *Institutes*, IV.3.8, OS 5:50.

PART TWO—Calvin's Ecclesiology

Elders and deacons constitute the "non-teaching" offices. According to the *Ordinances*, in contrast to the pastors, elders govern without teaching. In his commentary on 1 Timothy 5:17, Calvin claims that the idea of the two kinds of elder comes from Scripture: "there were at that time two kinds of elders; for all were not ordained to teach. The words plainly mean that there were some who "rule well" and honourably, but who did not hold the office of teachers."[89] The office of deacon also belongs in this category because their duty is the administration of welfare in the church: "Now we see to what end deacons were made. The word itself is indeed general, yet is it properly taken for those which are stewards for the poor."[90]

On the one hand, Calvin stresses the dignity of the teaching office: "He [Paul] therefore contends that there is nothing more noble or glorious in the church than the ministry of the gospel, since it is the administration of the Spirit and of righteousness and of eternal life."[91] Yet, on the other hand, he sharply distinguishes between the ministry and the ministers with respect to the dignity of the office of the Word. He emphasises that the dignity of the ministry of the Word does not imply the superior status of pastors to other members in the church. In discussing Calvin's high evaluation of the office of pastor, Höpfl argues that aggressive clericalism is the most significant feature of 1543 edition of the *Institutes*. However, this argument is hardly persuasive without qualification if we take Calvin's proposal of restricting the authority of pastors into consideration:

> . . . as pastors are not sent forth by him [God] to rule the Church with a wanton and lawless authority, but are restricted to a certain rule of duty which they must not exceed, so the Church is ordered to see that those who are appointed over her on these terms faithfully comply with their vocation.[92]

When Höpfl argues, "on Calvin's account, ministerial government of the church is divinely ordained, and the subordination of laity to clergy inevitably follows," he does not properly take into account that Calvin tries to distinguish between the dignity of "ministers" and that of "the ministerial

89. *Comm.* 1 *Tim.* 5:17, CO 52:315.
90. *Comm. Acts* 6:3, CO 48:121.
91. *Institutes*, IV.3.3; OS 5:45. Cf. *Comm. Titus* 1:5; "It is a point which ought to be carefully observed; that churches cannot safely remain without the ministry of pastors, and that consequently, wherever there is a considerable body of people, a pastor should be appointed over it." CO 53:409.
92. *Reply to Sadolet*, LCC 22:242, CO 5:404.

office."⁹³ In Calvin's view, the nobility of the teaching office does not depend on human quality. Instead, it is the Word, the objective of their office, which makes the office of pastor noble and honourable in the Church.⁹⁴

When discussing the gifts required for the office of pastor, Calvin refers to the inner calling of God: "Therefore, if a man were to be considered a true minister of the church, he must first have been duly called, then he must respond to his calling, that is, he must undertake and carry out the tasks enjoined."⁹⁵ In the *Ordinances* he also remarks that this inner calling is the prerequisite for the office of pastor: "Now in order that nothing happen confusedly in the Church, no one is to enter into this office without a calling."⁹⁶

However, Calvin perceives the practical difficulty for the congregation to be confirmation of the divine calling for each candidate for the ministry: "I pass over that secret call, of which each minister is conscious before God, and which does not have the church as witness."⁹⁷ In an attempt to overcome this difficulty, Calvin suggests that since God's secret calling must be accompanied by the appropriate gifts, the people will be able to recognise the suitability of a person for the teaching office by testing his gifts:

> Those whom the Lord has destined for such high office, he first supplies with the arms required to fulfil it, that they may not come empty-handed and unprepared. Accordingly, Paul, in his letter to the Corinthians, when he undertook to discuss these offices, first reviewed the gifts in which those who perform the offices ought to excel.⁹⁸

Taking this idea further, he charges the Roman Church with failing to consider whether or not a potential priest has the right gifts for preaching:

---

93. Höpfl, *Christian Polity of John Calvin*, 108.

94. "Whenever then God bids those pastors to be heard whom he sets over his Church, his will is, as it has been before stated, that he himself should be heard through their mouth. In short, whatever authority is exercised in the Church ought to be subjected to this rule—that God's law is to retain its own preeminence, and that men blend nothing of their own, but only define what is right according to the Word of the Lord." *Comm. Haggai* 2:10–14, CO 44:111.

95. *Institutes*, IV.3.10, OS 5:52.

96. *Ordinances*, LCC 22:58, OS 2:328.

97. *Institutes*, IV.3.11, OS 5:52.

98. *Institutes*, IV.3.11, OS 5:52.

It is best to begin with the call, that we may see who and what type they are called to this ministry and in what manner. Then we shall consider how faithfully they discharge their office ... they choose a lawyer who knows how to plead in a court rather than how to preach in a church.[99]

Restoration of the primitive Church's method of electing pastors according to the proper gift of preaching is, therefore, one of the foremost points of Calvin's plan of reforming church government:

> The pastoral office we have restored, both according to the apostolic rule and the practice of the primitive Church, by insisting that every one who rules in the Church shall also teach. We hold that none are to be continued in the office but those who are diligently in performing its duties. In selecting them our advice has been that this is a matter where greater and more religious care should be exercised, and we have ourselves studied so to act.[100]

The *Ordinances* prescribes that a candidate should be examined in two areas: the first being "doctrine—to ascertain whether the candidate for ordination has a good and holy knowledge of Scripture; and whether he be a fit and proper person to communicate it edifyingly to the people." The second area concerns "life—to ascertain whether he is of good habits and conducts himself always without reproach."[101] Testing for the proper gifts in these two areas is the principle by which not only pastors but also elders and deacons should be appointed: "only those are to be chosen who are of sound doctrine and of holy life, not notorious in any fault which might both deprive them of authority and disgrace the ministry. The very same requirements apply to deacons and presbyters."[102]

In his idea of the fourfold ecclesiastical office, which he thinks is instituted in Scripture, and the appointment of the right person to each office according to his gifts, Calvin shows his ecclesiological conviction that God distributes the proper gifts for the unity and health of the Church.

---

99. *Institutes*, IV.5.1, OS 5:73.

100. *Necessity of Reforming the Church*, LCC 22:206, CO 6:490.

101. *Ordinances*, LCC 22:59, OS 2:329.

102. "The very same requirements apply to deacons and presbyters (Timothy 3: 8-13). We must always see to it that they be adequate and fit to bear the burden imposed upon them, that is, that they be instructed in those skills necessary for the discharge of their office." *Institutes*, IV.3.12, OS 5:53.

Charity and Mutual Care

The spiritual principle of mutual love within the body of Christ compels Calvin to suggest various policies of charity and ministerial care in his proposal of church government. To begin with, he emphasises the principle of mutual love as part of what he feels the office of pastor should involve. As we saw in the previous chapter, Calvin argues that God wishes to work through the imperfect human ministers in regenerating His children. One of the important purposes of this accommodating grace is to enhance mutual love within the Church: "nothing fosters mutual love more fittingly than for men to be bound together with this bond: one is appointed pastor to teach the rest, and those bidden to be pupils receive the common teaching from one mouth."[103]

Calvin's suggestion that the office of deacons be restored is evidence of his attempt to realise the principle of mutual love within church government:

> The number of procurators appointed for this hospital seems to us to be proper; but we wish that there be also a separate reception office, so that not only provisions be in time made better, but that those who wish to do some charity may be more certain that the gift will not be employed otherwise than they intend.[104]

He insists that the ecclesiastical office of deacon has been instituted by God in order that the poor might be taken care of, because this duty is "a holy thing" and "a godly order."[105] For this reason, he charges the Roman church with having downgraded the original role of deacons "as the stewards of the poor" to a purely ritual function: "Whereby it appears how licentiously the Papists mock God and men, who assign unto their deacons no other office but this, to have a charge of the paten and chalice."[106]

---

103. *Institutes*, IV.3.1, OS 5:43.

104. *Ordinances*, LCC 22:64, OS 2:342.

105. "We know what a holy thing it is to be careful for the poor. Therefore, forasmuch as the apostles prefer the preaching of the gospel before if we gather thereby that no obedience is more acceptable to God. Notwithstanding, the hardness is also declared, when as they say that they cannot discharge both these duties." *Comm. Acts* 6:3, CO 48:119. "That was, indeed, a godly order ... , whereof Luke made mention before, when the goods of all men being consecrated to God, were distributed to every man as he had need; when as the apostles, being, as it were, the stewards of God and the poor, had the chief government of the alms." *Comm. Acts* 6:1, CO 48:117.

106. *Comm. Acts* 6:3, CO 48:120. McKee argues that contrary to many Roman

PART TWO—Calvin's Ecclesiology

Calvin's focus on the principle of mutual love within the body of Christ leads him to propose a number of other practical instructions in the *Ordinances*. These include the visiting of the sick and of prisoners, the frequent celebration of the Lord's Supper, the services of marriage, funeral, and burial, and the education of children. All these prescriptions are proposed to foster the unity of the Church in mutual love. For example, the *Ordinances* recommends the frequent administration of the Lord's Supper with this purpose:

> Since the Supper was instituted for us by our Lord to be frequently used, and also was so observed in the ancient Church until the devil turned everything upside down, erecting the mass in its place, it is a fault in need of correction, to celebrate it so seldom.[107]

In the final draft of the *Ordinances*, Calvin suggests instead that the Supper should be administered in the city at least once a month. However, his original desire was to celebrate the Supper in all parishes every Sunday, although he had to compromise this due to the practical difficulty of administering the Lord's Supper so often.[108] The *Article concerning the Organisation of the Church and Worship* at Geneva (1537) makes it clear why Calvin desires to celebrate the sacraments frequently: "Finally, we are to live as Christians, being joined together in one peace and brotherly unity as members of one and the same body."[109]

The detailed prescriptions for the visiting of the sick and prisoners in the *Ordinances* also demonstrate Calvin's conviction of the importance of mutual care for the unity of the Church:

> It will be good therefore that their Lordships ordain and make public that no one is to be totally confined to bed for three days without informing the minister, and that each be advised to call the ministers when they desire it in good time, in order that they

---

Catholics and most of protestant theologians, Calvin understands Acts 6:1-6 as "prescriptive for church order" and concludes that "the office of deacon is a necessary and permanent part of proper church order." McKee, *John Calvin on the Diaconate and Liturgical Almsgiving*, 157–58.

107. *Ordinances*, LCC 22:66, OS 2:344.

108. Wallace says, "Calvin in practice was forced to adapt himself to the capacity of the people more than he could have wished." Wallace, *Calvin's Doctrine of the Word and Sacrament*, 252–53. See Gerrish, *Grace and Gratitude*, 151, 159.

109. *Articles*, LCC 22:49, OS 1:370.

be not diverted from the office which they publicly discharge in the Church.[110]

These practical instructions are proposed not to promote social welfares but to reform church government according to Calvin's ecclesiological principle of "mutual love."

Conclusion: Spiritual Principles for Reforming the Visible Church

To sum up, for Calvin, the spiritual identity of the Church as the body of Christ is the corporative dimension of the individual Christian's identity, which is established and sustained in their union with Christ. Thus Calvin presents his idea of the spiritual identity of the body of Christ from the trinitarian perspective and with the same concern of providing Christians with a secure foundation of their salvation in God's grace just as he does in his anthropological discussion of the Christian identity.

However, Calvin's idea of the spiritual identity of the Church does not remain merely either an expansion of his anthropology or a subsidiary doctrine of his soteriology. The spiritual identity of the Church as the body of Christ provides the principles by which Calvin proposes the concrete reformation plan of the government of the visible Church: Christ's headship, the communication of diverse gifts, and mutual love. In Calvin's theology, in a sense, ecclesiology is the theological process by which the principles of the invisible Church or the spiritual community of the Christians as the body of Christ can be applied to the concrete and practical aspects of the visible Church. It can be seen here that Calvin's ecclesiology has close relationships with the other doctrines within the entire system of his theology in general, and anthropology in particular.

---

110. *Ordinances*, LCC 22:68, OS 2:380. "It will be good that their Lordships ordain a certain day each week on which admonition be given to prisoners, to reprove and exhort them."

6

The Church and the Kingdom of Christ

Introduction: The Invisible and the Visible Church

AS WE SAW IN CHAPTERS 4 AND 5, IN CALVIN'S ECCLESIOLOGY, THE Church has a twofold identity: its spiritual identity as the fellowship of the elect, which is defined as the invisible Church; and its functional identity as the means of grace, which is defined as the visible Church. In his discussion of the Church, Calvin concentrates on both the inseparability and the distinctiveness of these two identities from an eschatological perspective.

The purpose of this chapter is to argue that Calvin holds the two identities of the Church together from an eschatological perspective: he tries to understand the present situation of the visible Church in terms of the eschatological progress of the invisible Church within this world toward the final perfection on the last day. The first section will examine Calvin's focus on the inseparability between the two identities of the Church in his description of the present situation of the visible Church by analogy with the eschatological nature of the invisible Church. This examination aims to show through this analogy, how he tries to provide Christians with consolation over the miserable condition of their visible Church. The next section will examine Calvin's idea of the distinct characteristics of the Church's two identities in their relationship with the Kingdom of Christ. Calvin thinks that each identity of the Church can be called Christ's Kingdom for different reasons: whilst the visible Church can be called Christ's Kingdom in the sense that God entrusts the Word into this Church, the invisible Church is called Christ's Kingdom because this Church refers to the fellowship of the elect who are governed by Christ. Moreover, he thinks that each identity will reach different states of perfection on the last day: the perfection of the visible Church will be the completion and cessation of its functions of teaching and proclaiming the Word; that of the invisible Church will be the attainment and perfect enjoyment of spiritual blessings with God. Finally, Calvin's idea about church discipline will be examined to show that his eschatological understanding of the Church as the Kingdom of Christ directs his practical proposals for discipline as a means of maintaining order in the visible Church.

Calvin's Eschatological Understanding of the Church

Calvin's ecclesiology is notable for its distinct eschatological perspective: both the invisible Church and visible Church experience an eschatological tension between present imperfection, pertaining to the "not yet" aspect, and progress toward future perfection, part of the "already" aspect.[1] This eschatological perspective can be seen in his expositions of Christ's parables in Matthew 13: "Christ will put the last hand to the cleansing of the Church by means of angels, but he now begins to do the work by means of pious teachers."[2] Calvin identifies the present situation of the visible Church with the progress of the invisible Church towards the final perfection in order to provide consolation for Christians, who can only be taught and nourished by the ministries of the visible Church in this world. To understand this properly, we need to examine three points of Calvin's eschatological understanding of the Church in turn: the present situation of the Church, its progress toward future perfection and Calvin's concern to provide Christians with consolation. Examination of these three points will shed light on the fact that there is a parallel between Calvin's anthropological and his ecclesiological discussions in the sense that he presents both discussions from the common eschatological perspective.

The Present Imperfection of the Church

Calvin speaks of the present imperfection of the visible Church by analogy with the imperfection of Christians in this world. As we saw in chapter 3, he frequently uses metaphors of "warfare" and "pilgrimage" to describe the present condition of the Christian. He uses the same metaphors to explain the present condition of the Church: "So long as the Church shall continue

---

1. For the meanings of these two terms, see chapter 3, introduction.

2. *Comm. Matt.* 13:39; *Caeterum quanquam tunc extremam manum purgandae ecclesiae apponet per angelos, idem tamen nunc facere incipit per pios doctores.* CO 45:370.

PART TWO—Calvin's Ecclesiology

to be a pilgrim on the earth, she will never enjoy rest, but will be exposed to many attacks; for when it is declared that Satan will not conquer, it is implied that he will be her constant enemy."[3] In Calvin's ecclesiology, there are three reasons for the present imperfection of the Church: firstly, the imperfection of its members and the presence of hypocrites among the faithful prevent the Church from attaining perfect holiness as a whole; secondly, the Church is dispersed and suffered in this world, and thirdly, the attacks of the devil continuously disturb the peace of the Church. Both of these will be explained in turn.

Firstly and inwardly, Calvin counts the imperfection of Christians in the visible Church as the reason for the present imperfection of the Church:

> But to consider the church already completely and in every respect holy and spotless when all its members are spotted and somewhat impure—how absurd and foolish this is! It is true, therefore, that the church has been sanctified by Christ, but only the beginning of its sanctification is visible here; the end and perfect completion will appear when Christ, the holy of holies, truly and perfectly fills the church with his holiness.[4]

In addition, the Church cannot reach perfection in this world due to the presence of hypocrites within it:

> So long as the pilgrimage of the Church in this world continues, bad men and hypocrites will mingle in it with those who are good and upright, that the children of God may be armed with patience, and in the midst of offences which are fitted to disturb them, may preserve unbroken steadfastness of faith.[5]

Interpreting the parable of the wheat and tares in Matthew 13:24, Calvin argues that the reasons for the imperfection of the Church are distinct from the reasons for the infirmities of individual believers:

---

3. *Comm. Matt.* 16:18, CO 45:474. "But let us remember that the Church, so long as she is a pilgrim in this world, is subjected to the cross, that she may be humble and may be conformed to her Head." *Comm. Isa.* 49:23, CO 37:219.

4. *Institutes*, IV.8.12, OS 5:144–45.

5. *Comm. Matt.* 13:24; *Quamdiu in hoc mundo peregrinator ecclesia, bonis et sinceris in ea permixtos fore malos et hypocrites, ut se patientia arment filii Dei, et inter offendicula, quibus turbari possent, retineant infractam fidei constantiam.* CO 45:368. "Christ informs us, that a mixture of the good and the bad must be patiently endured till the end of the world; because, till that time, a true and perfect restoration of the Church will not take place." *Comm. Matt.* 3:47, CO 45:376.

The Church and the Kingdom of Christ

Although Christ has cleansed the Church with his own blood, that it may be without spot or blemish, yet hitherto he suffers it to be polluted by many stains. I speak not of the remaining infirmities of the flesh, to which every believer is liable, even after that he has been renewed by the Holy Spirit.[6]

Since, according to Calvin's definition of the invisible Church, hypocrites are not members of the body of Christ, it is the visible and institutional Church that is imperfect due to their presence.[7]

Secondly, the Church is dispersed in this world. Calvin explains the dispersion of the Church by means of an analogy between the persecution of the Christian and that of the visible Church. In his commentary on Daniel 12:7, he identifies the prophecy about the "dispersion" of the Church of God, that is, the spiritual Church, with the present suffering of the visible Church:

> The angel again proclaims how the Church of God should be oppressed by many calamities . . . The Church should be a stranger in the world, and be dispersed throughout it. This was continually fulfilled from that day to the present. How sad is the dispersion of the Church in these days! . . . how does the body of the Church now appear to us? How has it appeared throughout all ages? Surely it has ever been torn in pieces and dispersed.[8]

Calvin regards the scriptural description of the affliction and dispersion of the invisible Church to be a prediction of the suffering and persecution of the visible Church. From this idea, he tries to explain the present situation of the Reformed Church and the expectations of its prosperity in the life to come: "Hence the angel's prediction is not in vain, if we adopt the interpretation—the hand of the holy people should be dispersed—but yet the end

---

6. *Comm. Matt.* 13:24; *Etsi enim sanguine suo ecclesiam mundavit Christus, ut sit absque ruga et macula, adhuc tamen multis vitiis laborare patitur. Nec de residuis infirmitatibus carnis loquor, quibus obnoxii sunt singuli fideles, postquam regeniti sunt Dei spiritu.* CO 45:367. Fulop argues that Calvin follows Bucer and Capito's interpretations of Christ's parables in Matthew 13, which sharply contrast with the interpretation of Balthasar Hubmaier, a representative of the early sixteenth-century Anabaptists. According to Fulop, Hubmaier interprets this parable as a description of society at large rather than the Church, because for Hubmaier the purity of the Church should be "insured by the use of discipline and the ban." Fulop, "The Third Mark of the Church?" 27–29. Also see Davis, "No Discipline, No Church," 43–58.

7. "In this [visible] church are mingled many hypocrites who have nothing of Christ but the name and outward appearance." *Institutes*, IV.1.7, OS 5:12.

8. *Comm. Dan.* 12:7, CO 40:605.

PART TWO—Calvin's Ecclesiology

should be prosperous, as he has previously announced, when treating of its resurrection and final salvation."[9]

Thirdly and spiritually, the Church cannot enjoy perfect peace in this world because it is under the continuous attacks of Satan: "Satan, by innumerable arts, invades and assails the Church, and is in no want of servants and attendants, who direct their whole energy to destroy, or spoil, or hinder the Lord's building."[10] Calvin applies the idea of suffering as a result of Satan's unceasing attacks not only to the spiritual Church, but also to the visible Church. In his commentary on Daniel, Calvin first speaks of Satan's attacks against the invisible Church and its members: "What prevents Satan from daily absorbing a hundred times over the whole Church both collectively and individually? It clearly becomes necessary for God to oppose his fury, and this he does by angels."[11] Later in the same commentary, Calvin continues to speak of Satan's attacks against the visible Church:

> We observe in these days how many fall off from the Church. Persecution sifts all those who profess to belong to Christ, and thus many are winnowed like chaff, and but a small portion remain steadfast. Their backsliding ought not to overthrow our faithfulness when they so carelessly forsake all piety, either through being enticed by the allurements of Satan.[12]

By using the metaphors of "pilgrimage" and "warfare," Calvin tries to describe the present imperfection of the visible Church by analogy with the imperfections and tribulations of the individual Christians in this world: just as the members of the invisible Church suffer from imperfection and tribulation, so the visible Church also suffers from the presence of hypocrites, its miserable condition and Satan's attacks in this world.

The Progress of the Church toward Perfection

As in his idea of the gradual regeneration of the individual Christians,[13] Calvin repeatedly emphasises that God gradually progresses the Church's holiness until the end of its inevitable imperfection on the last day:

9. *Comm. Dan.* 12:7, CO 40:605.

10. *Comm. Isa.* 49:17, CO 37:211. In this commentary, Calvin interprets the "wall" of the "new Jerusalem" to mean the "prosperity" and "peace" of the Church.

11. *Comm. Dan.* 10:13, CO 40:205.

12. *Comm. Dan.* 11:32, CO 40:223.

13. "This restoration does not take place in one moment or one day or one year; but

The Church and the Kingdom of Christ

> Yet it also is no less true that the Lord is daily at work in smoothing out wrinkles and cleansing spots. From this it follows that the church's holiness is not yet complete. The church is holy, then, in the sense that it is daily advancing and is not yet perfect: it makes progress from day to day but has not yet reached its goal of holiness.[14]

It is noteworthy that Calvin uses this statement to defend the legitimacy and the unity of the visible Church against the "perfectionists" who are "imbued with a false conviction of their own perfect sanctity, spurned association with all men in whom they discern any remnant of human nature."[15] Calvin argues, "if we are not willing to admit a church unless it be perfect in every respect, we leave no church at all."[16]

Since Calvin defines the invisible Church as being the fellowship of the elect who, in this world, are progressing in the course of regeneration by grace, in his ecclesiology it is the invisible Church which is experiencing a gradual progress in holiness: the members of the invisible Church are already holy in this world because they are justified by grace, but they are not perfectly holy yet in their course of regeneration until the end of their present life. Calvin applies this eschatological idea, of the holiness of members of the invisible Church, to his explanation of the present condition of the visible Church in order to defend the legitimacy and the unity of the visible Church against the perfectionists' idea of the Church:

> First, he who voluntarily deserts the outward communion of the church (where the Word of God is preached and the sacraments are administered) is without excuse. Secondly, neither the vices of the few nor the vices of the many in any way prevent us from duly professing our faith there in ceremonies ordained by God.[17]

Calvin's argument against the insistence of the Anabaptists that perfect holiness be a requirement of the lawful Church also shows that, in his ecclesiology, the eschatological progress of the invisible Church is identified

---

through continual and sometimes even slow advances God wipes out in his elect the corruptions of the flesh, cleanses them of guilt, consecrates them to himself as temples renewing all their minds to true purity that they may practice repentance throughout their lives and know that this warfare will end only at death." *Institutes*, III.3.9, OS 4:63–64.

14. *Institutes*, IV.1.17, OS 5:21.
15. *Institutes*, IV.1.13, OS 5:17.
16. *Institutes*, IV.1.17, OS 5:21.
17. *Institutes*, IV.1.19, OS 5:23.

PART TWO—Calvin's Ecclesiology

with the present situation of the visible Church. In his discussion of the regeneration of the individual Christian in the *Institutes* III, Calvin argues that the Anabaptists have an "illusory" idea of the perfection of individual believers:

> Certain Anabaptists of our day conjure up some sort of frenzied excess instead of spiritual regeneration... For Christians the Spirit of the Lord is not a disturbing apparition, which they have either brought forth in a dream or have received as fashioned by others.[18]

He makes a similar statement in his ecclesiological discussion in the *Institutes* IV, namely, that the Anabaptists' assertion of the perfect purity of the Church is "ill-advised zeal for righteousness":

> But though this temptation sometimes springs up even among good men from ill-advised zeal for righteousness, we shall perceive that this overscrupulousness is born rather of pride and arrogance and false opinion of holiness than of true holiness and true zeal for it. Therefore, those who more boldly than others incite defection from the church, and are like standard-bearers, have for the most part no other reason than by their contempt of all to show they are better than the others.[19]

Thus the visible Church is holy not because it is thoroughly perfect, but because its holiness is that of the invisible Church concealed within it:

> Indeed, because they [the Anabaptists] think no church exists where there are not perfect purity and integrity of life, they depart out of hatred of wickedness from the lawful church, while they fancy themselves turning aside from the faction of the wicked... But in order that they may know that the church is at the same time mingled of good men and bad, let them hear the parable from Christ's lips that compares the church to a net in which all kinds of fish are gathered and are not sorted until laid out on the shore.[20]

In his interpretation of Christ's parable of the tares and wheat in Matthew 13, Calvin speaks of the future perfection of the individual believers: "But as the life of the godly is now hidden, and as their salvation is invisible,

---

18. *Institutes*, III.3.14, OS 4:70.

19. *Institutes*, IV.1.16, OS 5:20. In his exposition of the parable of the wheat and tares in Matthew 13, Calvin does not forget to refute the Anabaptists' view of the Church: "This passage has been most improperly abused by the Anabaptists and by other like them, to take from the Church the power of the sword." *Comm. Matt.* 13:40, CO 45:370.

20. *Institutes*, IV.1.13, OS 5:17.

because it consists in hope, Christ properly directs the attention of believers to heaven, where they will find the glory that is promised to them."[21] In the same commentary, he also points towards the future perfection of the Church: "though many wicked men now hold a high rank in the Church, yet that blessed day is assuredly to be expected, when the Son of God shall raise his followers on high and remove every thing that now tends to dim or conceal their brightness." From these two statements, we can observe that for Calvin the future perfect holiness of the invisible Church will be accomplished when the impurity of the visible Church has been stripped away in the eschaton.

Consolation in the Promise of the Triune God

Just as in his anthropology, Calvin highlights the promise of the triune God in his eschatological discussion of the Church in order to provide Christians with consolation and hope for their future perfection. To explain why Calvin identifies the eschatological nature of the life of the invisible Church with that of the visible Church, we need first to examine his discussion of the future perfection of the Church in his commentary on Christ's eschatological discourse in Matthew 24–25.[22] Calvin indicates here three characteristics of the perfection to be attained by the Church in the eschaton: purity, unity and victory. First, Christ will perfectly purify the Church by driving out the hypocrites: "He [Christ] will then order the wicked to depart from him, because many hypocrites are now mixed with the righteous, as if they were closely allied to Christ."[23] Secondly, Christ will complete the unity of the Church by gathering together the elect who have been scattered all around the world:

> The elect, even though they were carried away from the earth and scattered in the air, will again be gathered, so to be united in the enjoyment of eternal life under Him as their Head, and enjoy the expected inheritance; for Christ intended to console his disciples,

---

21. *Comm. Matt.* 13:43, CO 45:371.

22. Quistorp argues that Calvin fails to do "justice to the idea of the perfection of the new humanity as a whole, or the church in the coming kingdom of God and of the new creation in a new heaven and earth." Quistorp, *Calvin's Doctrine of the Last Things*, 12–13. However, we can find that Calvin discusses the ecclesiological dimension of the eschaton in his commentary on Christ's discourse in Matthew 23–25.

23. *Comm. Matt.* 25:41, CO 45:690.

PART TWO—Calvin's Ecclesiology

that they might not be altogether discouraged by the lamentable dispersion of the Church.[24]

Thirdly, the victory of Christ over the enemy of the Church will be accomplished:

> So then Christ now sits on his heavenly throne, as far as it is necessary that he shall reign for restraining his enemies and protecting the Church; but then he will appear openly, to establish perfect order in heaven and earth, to crush his enemies under his feet.[25]

In Calvin's ecclesiology, as we have seen, impurity, dispersion and conflict are the three significant characteristics of the present imperfection, not only of the invisible Church but also of the visible Church. In explaining the future perfection of the Church, he uses such expressions as: "be allied with Christ," "partaker of the blessed life," and "the relationship between the head and members," which are related to his idea of the Church as the body of Christ. This shows that what the visible Church lacks in purity, unity, and peace will be fully and finally restored when the spiritual identity of the invisible Church, as the body of Christ, is perfectly manifested at the end of the world.

As in his eschatological discussion of the Christian life, Calvin underlines God's promise of the future perfection of the Church to provide Christians with consolation in this world. This practical concern is clearly stated in his commentary on Matthew 24:32: "The general instruction conveyed is that the weak and frail condition of the Church ought not to lead us to conclude that it is dying, but rather to expect the immortal glory for which the Lord prepares his people by the cross and by afflictions."[26] Calvin is well aware that the present condition of the Church is so desperate that the Church seems on the verge of defeat: "When we see the Church distressed by such heavy calamities, that we think that it cannot be far from destruction, we are in danger of giving way to despondency, and of entertaining doubts about the mercy of God."[27] In this desperate condition of the Church, according to Calvin, Christians should take consolation from God's promise of future perfection for the Church: "Whenever, therefore, we perceive the Church scattered by the wiles of Satan, or torn in pieces

24. *Comm. Matt.* 24:31, CO 45:668.
25. *Comm. Matt.* 25:31, CO 45:685.
26. *Comm. Matt.* 24:32, CO 45:670.
27. *Comm. Isa.* 10:22, CO 36:102.

The Church and the Kingdom of Christ

by the cruelty of the ungodly, or disturbed by false doctrines, or tossed by storms, let us learn to turn our eyes to this gathering of the elect [on the last day]."[28] This concern, of course, presupposes the identification of the invisible Church with the visible Church from an eschatological perspective.

In his ecclesiology, Calvin explains the certainty of God's protection of the visible Church from a trinitarian perspective, similar to that by which he highlights God's promise in order to provide the assurance of the individual Christians' future perfection.[29] In his commentary on Matthew 24:22, Calvin quotes Isaiah 10:22 and argues that God the Father promises to preserve the Church amid severe tribulation in this world:

> This [Isaiah 10:22] affords us a striking proof of the judgment of God, when he afflicts his visible Church to such a degree, that we would be ready to conclude that it had altogether perished; and yet, in order to preserve some seed, he miraculously rescues from destruction his elect, though few in number, that, contrary to expectation, they may escape from the jaws of death.[30]

It is the Son who protects the Church in this world: "Therefore, whenever we hear of Christ as armed with eternal power, let us remember that the perpetuity of the church is secure in this protection."[31] During their pilgrimage in this world, therefore, all members of the Church are united with each other under Christ's protection while Satan attempts unceasingly to scatter them: "by whatever methods Satan endeavours to scatter the children of God in various directions, still in Christ himself is the sacred bond of union, by which they must be kept united."[32] For Calvin, belief in Christ's judgment of the hypocrites on the last day should encourage Christians to continue their efforts at progress in this world:

> The Son of God, who commands his followers to walk in the midst of stumbling-blocks, will unquestionably give us strength to overcome them all. He pronounces likewise an awful punishment

---

28. *Comm. Matt.* 24:31, CO 45:668. "Against all the power of Satan the firmness of the Church will prove to be invincible, because the truth of God, on which the faith of the Church rests, will ever remain unshaken." *Comm. Matt.* 16:18, CO 45:474.

29. The trinitarian perspective in Calvin's eschatology and his concern to provide Christians with consolation and hope in the present life were discussed in chapter 3.

30. *Comm. Matt.* 24:22, CO 45:662.

31. *Institutes*, II.15.3, OS 3:474.

32. *Comm. Matt.* 24:28, CO 45:665.

PART TWO—Calvin's Ecclesiology

against any hypocrites and reprobate persons, who now appear to be the most distinguished citizens of the Church.[33]

Thirdly, Calvin argues in his commentary on Matthew 24 that the Holy Spirit enables Christians to endure their tribulations through their trust in God's promise of the Church's perfect victory over Satan on the last day:

> The Spirit therefore exhorts believers to prepare themselves for the exercise of patience, not only for a single year, that is, for a long period, but to lay their account with enduring tribulations through an uninterrupted succession of many ages. There is no small consolation also in the phrase, *half a time,* (Daniel 12:7) for though the *tribulations* be of long continuance, yet the Spirit shows that they will not be perpetual.[34]

In his discussion of the future perfection of he the Church, as he does in his anthropological discussion, Calvin tires to console and encourage Christians in the miserable condition of the visible Church by highlighting the certainty of the grace of the triune God who promises the protection and perfection of the invisible Church.

Calvin's Idea of the Church as the Kingdom of Christ

While the inseparability between the invisible and the visible Church is, in Calvin's ecclesiology, supposed to provide Christians with consolation from an eschatological perspective, his idea of the distinctiveness of these two identities appears in his identification of the Church with the Kingdom of Christ. In his ecclesiology, Calvin frequently uses the biblical concept of 'the Kingdom of Christ' to explain his idea of the eschatological nature of both the invisible and the visible Church.[35] However, he gives different

---

33. *Comm. Matt.* 13:41, CO 45:370.

34. *Comm. Matt.* 24:15, CO 45:658. Also see, Comm. Matt. 24:9, CO 45:653.

35. Calvin uses the term "Kingdom of Christ" interchangeably with the concepts of "the Kingdom of God" and "the Kingdom of Heaven." However, Torrance argues that Calvin uses the term *Regnum Dei* to speak of God's eternal majesty and reign, and the term *Regnum Christi* to refer to Christ's reign over the world until the manifestation of the new heaven and the new earth. Torrance, *Kingdom and Church*, 95. Palmer also argues that "When this reign of God occurs in the lives of individuals it is frequently referred to as the *regnum Dei*. When this reign takes an institutional or social form it is frequently called the regnum Christi." But Palmer admits that "these distinctions are not always sharply drawn. Thus the terms *regnum Dei* and *regnum Christi* are often

reasons for the identifications of these two identities of the Church with the Kingdom of Christ: the visible Church is called Christ's Kingdom because it is the agent of the Word; the invisible Church is called Christ's Kingdom because it shares the spiritual blessings under Christ's rule in an eschatological way.

The Identification of the Church with the Kingdom of Christ

In Calvin's theology, a man enters into Christ's Kingdom when he becomes a member of the Church by the grace of forgiveness: "Forgiveness of sins, then, is for us the first entry into the Church and the Kingdom of God. Without it, there is for us no covenant or bond with God."[36] As we shall see, Calvin considers both the invisible and the visible Church when he speaks of the relationship between the Church and the Kingdom of Christ, even though each Church has a relationship with the Kingdom for different reasons.

In his study of Calvin's commentaries on the Prophets, Wilcox offers a useful investigation of the relationship between the visible Church and the Kingdom of Christ. Wilcox argues that Calvin identifies the Kingdom of Christ not with "the elect" or "the invisible" Church but with "the institutional or visible church without any qualification." He further claims, "When Calvin speaks of the Church as Christ's Kingdom in this way, he means that it is not only the realm over which Christ reigns which exists by hearing the Word, but the agency through which he exercises his reign which exists to proclaim the Word."[37]

Wilcox is correct in observing Calvin's emphasis on the Word as being the reason for the identification of the institutional Church with Christ's Kingdom. Nevertheless, he does not sufficiently take into account that Calvin's identification of the visible Church with the Kingdom of Christ is based on his eschatological idea of the relationship between the invisible Church and the Kingdom of Christ. In order to have a precise understanding of

---

interchangeable and in accordance with biblical usage." Palmer, "Kingdom and Church in Calvin," 8–22. For Calvin's interchangeable use of these two terms, see *Comm. Matt.* 11:11; CO 45:303, 10:21; CO 45:383, 28:18; CO 45:821.

36. *Institutes*, IV.1.20, OS 5:24.

37. Wilcox, "'Progress of the Kingdom of Christ' in Calvin's Exposition of the Prophets," 320.

PART TWO—Calvin's Ecclesiology

Calvin's identification of the visible Church with the Kingdom of Christ, we first need to examine Calvin's definition of the Kingdom of God:

> God reigns where men, both by denial of themselves and by contempt of the world and of earthly life, pledge themselves to his righteousness in order to aspire to a heavenly life. Thus there are two parts to this Kingdom: first, that God by the power of his Spirit corrects all the desires of the flesh which by squadrons war against him; second, that he shape all our thoughts in obedience to his rule.[38]

This definition is added in the 1559 edition as an explication of the second petition of the Lord's Prayer, and it is an expansion of the exposition of the same part of the Lord's Prayer from the *Institutes* of 1536, "The Kingdom of God is this: by his Holy Spirit, to act to rule over his own people, in order to make the riches of his goodness and mercy conspicuous in all their works."[39] These definitions show that in his ecclesiology Calvin consistently speaks of the invisible, rather than the visible, Church as the Kingdom of Christ because in his definitions of the Kingdom he concentrates on God's grace within the life of the individual Christians, whose spiritual fellowship with Christ is regarded as the invisible Church.

Calvin probably offers such anthropocentric definitions because the chief concern of the *Institutes* III is not the Christian community but God's grace in human salvation. However, it should be noted that such an anthropocentric understanding of the Kingdom consistently appears in much of his writing. In his commentary on Matthew 13, which discusses the eschatological nature of the Church, Calvin defines the Kingdom of God thus:

> The Kingdom of the Father, as the inheritance of the godly, is contrasted with the earth, to remind them that here they are pilgrims, and therefore ought to look upwards toward heaven. In another passage, the Kingdom of God is said to be within us [Luke 17:21], but we shall not obtain the full enjoyment of it till God be all in all [1 Cor. 15:28].[40]

---

38. *Institutes*, III.20.42, OS 4:352.

39. *Institutes* (1536), II, CO 1: 94. Calvin offers a similar definition in his commentary on the Lord's Prayer in *Matthew* 6:10. "We must first attend to the definition of the Kingdom of God. He is said to reign among men, when they voluntarily devote and submit themselves to be governed by him, placing their flesh under the yoke, and renouncing their desire." *Comm. Matt.* 6:10, CO 45:197.

40. *Comm. Matt.* 13:43, CO 45:371. Also see *Comm. Luke* 17:21, CO 45:424; *Comm. 1 Cor.* 15:28, CO 49:549.

168

It is certain that Calvin thinks the Church belongs to the domain of the Kingdom of Christ, whether it is institutional or spiritual. In his definition of the Church in the *Institutes* I, Calvin speaks of the invisible Church with regard to the Kingdom. "When he [Christ] assembles the souls of believers and the holy angels at the same time in the Kingdom of God ... they marvel at the manifold grace of God in the church, and that they are under Christ the Head."[41]

In his definition of Kingdom of Christ, however, Calvin holds a comprehensive idea of the Kingdom, which includes not only the visible Church but also everything under the grace of God. For Calvin, Christ's rule is not restricted to the boundaries of the visible Church but reaches the whole world.[42] While Wilcox concentrates mainly on Calvin's identification of the institutional Church with the Kingdom of Christ, for Calvin the Kingdom of Christ actually embraces not only the visible Church, but also everything that is ruled by Christ's word. Thus Wurth's account of Calvin's idea of the boundaries of Christ's Kingdom is more accurate than Wilcox's. Wurth argues, "the church is not at all identical with the kingdom" because the boundaries of the visible Church "are much narrower than those of the kingdom."[43]

The Word as the Sceptre of the Kingdom of Christ

Although Calvin thinks of the Kingdom of Christ as encompassing not only the institutional Church but also every aspect of Christian life, individual or collective, he speaks of the special relationship between the visible Church and Christ's Kingdom: "For his [Christ's] rule is not first to be found in the assembly of the elect in heaven but already in his church on earth."[44] Calvin cites two reasons for this special relationship: Firstly, Christ entrusts his Word to the ministry of the Church. Secondly, the Church already shares the spiritual blessings of Christ's Kingdom, which will be fully manifested at the end of the world. These points will be considered in turn by means

---

41. *Institutes*, I.14.9, OS 3:161.

42. "[T]he world was made through the Son," and "he upholds all things by his powerful Word." *Institutes*, I.13.7, OS 3:117. Edmondson argues that Calvin thinks that Christ's kingship embraces a cosmic dimension: "Christ as king exercises, perhaps, his primary function as Mediator, the function of uniting humanity and the angels to the Father while serving as a conduit of God's grace." Edmondson, *Calvin's Christology*, 143–47.

43. Wurth, "Calvin and the Kingdom of God," 115.

44. *Comm. Eph.* 1:14, CO 51:154.

PART TWO—Calvin's Ecclesiology

of an examination of the two proof texts of Wilcox's argument in favour of Calvin's identification of the Kingdom with the institutional Church: Calvin's statements on the Kingdom of Christ with regard to the Church in the *Institutes* IV.2.4 and in his commentary on Amos 9:13.

Calvin's identification of the Church with the Kingdom of Christ is consistently accompanied by an emphasis on the Word as the means by which Christ rules over Christians. In the *Institutes* IV.2.4, Calvin states, "since the church is Christ's Kingdom, and he reigns by his Word alone, will it not be clear to any man that those are lying words by which the Kingdom of Christ is imagined to exist apart from his sceptre (that is, his most holy Word)?"[45] This statement is directed against the Roman Catholic claim that their Church alone is the Church of God. Calvin seeks to refute this claim by interpreting "apostles and prophets" in Ephesians 2:20 not as the ecclesiastical structure of the priesthood but as the objective of their offices: "the church was founded not upon men's judgment, not upon priesthood, but upon the teaching of apostles and prophets [Eph. 2:20]." He then speaks of the authority of the Word as the sole standard by which we can discern the true from the false Church: "He who is of God hears the words of God. The reason why you do not hear them is that you are not of God."[46] Thus when Calvin identifies the Church with the Kingdom of Christ, he tries to argue the authority of the true (visible) Church as the agent of the Word. His argument in the *Institutes* IV.24 shows this point:

> Why do we wilfully act like madmen in searching out the church when Christ has marked it with an unmistakable sign [the Word], which wherever it is seen, cannot fail to show the church there; while where it is absent, nothing remains that can give the true meaning of the church?[47]

Calvin frequently compares the Word to a "sceptre" to point out the legitimate power of the Word over the Kingdom of Christ:

> Now, because the word of God is like a royal sceptre, we are bidden here to entreat him to bring all men's minds and hearts into voluntary obedience to it. This happens when he manifests the working

---

45. *Institutes*, IV.2.4; *In summa, quum Ecclesia regnum sit Christi, regnet autem ille nonnisi per verbum suum: an ullis iam obscurum erit quin illa mendacii verba sint, quibus Christi regnum absque eius sceptro (id est sacrosancto ipsius verbo) esse fingitur?* OS 5:36.

46. *Institutes*, IV.2.4, OS 5:35–36.

47. *Institutes*, IV.2.4, OS 5:35.

of his word through the secret inspiration of his Spirit in order that it may stand forth in the degree of honour that it deserves.[48]

Throughout salvation history, the Word has been the means of divine rule over God's Kingdom. It was by the Word that the patriarchs of Israel were able to enter God's Kingdom: "Adam, Abel, Noah, Abraham, and the other patriarchs cleaved to God by such illumination of the Word. Therefore I say that without any doubt they entered into God's immortal Kingdom."[49] It was, however, Christ's first coming that disclosed the Kingdom of God: "They [the Law and the Prophets] gave a foretaste of that wisdom which was one day to be clearly disclosed, and pointed to it twinkling afar off. But when Christ could be pointed out with the finger, the Kingdom of God was opened."[50] Before his ascension, Christ instituted the office of apostles in order to expand his Kingdom by means of their preaching:

> Apostles, then, were sent out to lead the world back from rebellion to true obedience to God, and to establish his Kingdom everywhere by the preaching of the gospel, or if you prefer, as the first builders of the church, to lay its foundations in all the world.[51]

Since then, the preaching of the visible Church has continued these apostolic functions. Calvin argues from this idea that "the power of the keys" in Matthew 16:19 refers to the authority of the preaching ministry of the Church:

> This command concerning forgiving and retaining sins and that promise made to Peter concerning binding and loosing ought to be referred solely to the ministry of the Word, because when the

---

48. *Institutes*, III.20.42, OS 4:353.

49. *Institutes*, II.10.7, OS 3:408.

50. *Institutes*, II.11.5, OS 3:428. "So far as relates to the beginning of Christ's Kingdom, I have already said that it should not be referred to the time of his birth but to the preaching of the gospel." *Comm. Dan.* 2:45, CO 40:606. However, Calvin does not clearly point out exactly when the Kingdom of Christ began in the salvation history. He indicates several possible events as the starting point of the Kingdom, such as the end of the Babylonian exile (*Comm. Jer.* 3:17-18, CO 37:566), Christ's proclaiming of repentance (*Institutes*, II.9.4, OS 3:401; *Comm. Dan.* 2:44, CO 40:606) and his ascension to heaven (*Institutes*, II.16.14, OS 3:502; *Comm. Dan.* 7:8, CO 41:50). Wilcox, "The Progress of the Kingdom of Christ," 318. Edmondson argues, "Christ's kingdom, then, appeared to be circumscribed at its beginning by God's initiation of the covenant as a response to Adam's fall, though its duration is everlasting, through to God's final judgment of the world." Edmondson, *Calvin's Christology*, 143.

51. *Institutes*, IV.3.4, OS 5:46.

Lord committed his ministry to the Apostles, he also equipped them for the office of binding and loosing.[52]

In his commentary on Matthew 16:19, Calvin compares ministers to the "porters" who open or close the gate of the heavenly Kingdom on earth by the authority of the Word that they should preach:

> First, he [Christ] says that the ministers of the Gospel are porters, so to speak, of the kingdom of heaven, because they carry its keys ... We know that there is no other way in which the gate of life is opened to us than by the word of God; and hence it follows that the key is placed, as it were, in the hand of the ministers of the word.[53]

With regard to the importance of the ministry of the visible Church, Calvin argues that the ministry of education is the mark of the Kingdom of Christ:

> We see how God, who could in a moment perfect his own, nevertheless desires them to grow up into manhood solely under the education of the church ... Isaiah had long before distinguished Christ's Kingdom by this mark: "My spirit which is upon you, and my words which I have put in your mouth, shall never depart out of your mouth, or out of the mouth of your children, or ... of your children's children" (Isa. 59:21).[54]

The visible Church, therefore, has a special relationship with Christ's Kingdom because Christ's rule, by means of the Word, is manifested and expanded by the preaching ministry of the Church in this world.

The Eschatological Manifestation of the Kingdom of Christ

In Calvin's ecclesiology, the special relationship between the Church and the Kingdom of Christ is manifested in eschatological terms.[55] The second

---

52. *Institutes*, IV.11.1, OS 5:196.

53. *Comm. Matt.* 16:19, CO 45:475.

54. *Institutes*, IV.1.5, OS 5:8.

55. Quistorp has noted an eschatological perspective in Calvin's idea of the relationship between the Church and the Kingdom: "The church stands indeed in a peculiar relation to the kingdom of God, but may not be identified with the latter, or only in so far as it bears the embryonic spiritual kingdom of Christ." Quistorp, *Calvin's Doctrine of the Last Things*, 165. Likewise, Torrance notes that the correlativity between Church and Kingdom "is to be understood in terms of the eschatological tension and reserve involved in the overlap of the two ages, for here and now the Church is not so correlative

proof text for Wilcox's argument appears in Calvin's commentary on Amos 9:13:

> At the same time, the Spirit under these figurative expressions declares, that the Kingdom of Christ shall be happy and blessed, or that the Church of God, which means the same thing, shall be blessed, when Christ shall begin to reign.[56]

In the first place, although the English translation seems to suggest that the Church of God is here identified unequivocally with the Kingdom of Christ, we can see from the Latin text that Calvin identifies the happiness of the Kingdom with the blessedness of the Church "when Christ shall begin to reign." Thus the focal point of this statement is not the identification of the visible Church with Christ's Kingdom, but the beginning of Christ's reign in the Christian or the invisible Church. According to his commentary on Amos, the Church shares the same blessings with the Kingdom of Christ and these blessings are spiritual: "Further, what is here said of the abundance of corn and wine, must be explained with reference to the nature of Christ's Kingdom. As then the Kingdom of Christ is spiritual, it is enough for us, that it abounds in spiritual blessings."[57]

Calvin argues that Christians enjoy these spiritual blessings in an eschatological way. In the *Institutes*, he identifies these spiritual blessings with the new life of salvation bestowed upon Christians by grace: "By proclaiming the Kingdom of God, he [John the Baptist] was calling them to faith, for by the Kingdom of God, which he taught was at hand, he meant that forgiveness of sins, salvation, life, and utterly everything that we obtain

---

to the Kingdom that it transcribes the perfect form of the Kingdom in the earthly existence." Torrance, *Kingdom and Church*, 95–96.

56. *Comm. Amos* 9:13; *Interea sub istis figuris spiritus pronuntiat, modis omnibus regnum Christi felix et beatum fore, vel ubi regnare Christus coeperit, beatam fore ecclesiam Dei, quod idem valet.* CO 43:172.

57. *Comm. Amos* 9:15; *Caeterum quod hic dicitur de tritici et vini abundantia, debet exponi pro natura regni Christi. Ergo quia spirituale est Christi regnum, sufficiat nobis etiam affluere spiritualibus bonis,* CO 43:175. Muller argues that Calvin's exegesis of "the Lord's day" and "the Kingdom" in the Old Testament prophecies is presented in "the hermeneutics of promise and multiple fulfilment" which include an eschatological perspective: "The promises of the Old Testament find their fulfillment in the New Testament and in the establishment of Christ's Kingdom. Yet it is precisely in this establishment of the kingdom that an indirect or mediate reference to the eschaton occurs." Muller, "The Hermeneutic of Promise and Fulfilment in Calvin's Exegesis of the Old Testament Prophecies of the Kingdom," 70–71.

PART TWO—Calvin's Ecclesiology

in Christ."[58] Calvin argues that the "new people" or the (invisible) Church already enjoys these spiritual blessings of the Kingdom in this world:

> Thus the new people is distinguished from the ancient people; for, as the Kingdom of Christ is spiritual, since he has risen from the dead, believing souls must be raised up along with him. But now he promises that the Church will never be deprived of his invaluable blessings, but will be guided by the Holy Spirit and sustained by heavenly doctrine.[59]

The spiritual blessings of the Kingdom, however, will not be fully manifested until the last day:

> For though we very truly hear that the Kingdom of God will be filled with splendour, joy, happiness, and glory, yet when these things are spoken of, they remain utterly remote from our perception, and, as it were, wrapped in obscurities, until that day comes when he will reveal to us his glory, that we may behold it face to face.[60]

When considering the eschatological tension between the "already" and the "not yet" aspects of the spiritual blessings of Christ's Kingdom, Calvin compares the present situation of the Church with the warfare of Christ's Kingdom against Satan's Kingdom in this world:

> But the frequent mention of Satan or the devil in the singular denotes the empire of wickedness opposed to the Kingdom of Righteousness. For as the church and the fellowship of saints has Christ as Head, so the faction of the impious and impiety itself are depicted for us together with their prince who holds supreme sway over them.[61]

In this spiritual warfare, the spiritual Church makes progress by means of God's grace as the Kingdom of Christ expands in this world:

> Whenever the prophets speak of fulfilment under the Kingdom of Christ, we should not restrict what they say to one day or a short time. Instead, we ought to include its whole course from

---

58. *Institutes*, III.3.19, OS 4:76.
59. *Comm. Isa.* 59:21, CO 37:395.
60. *Institutes*, III.25.10, OS 4:452–53.
61. *Institutes*, I.14.14, OS 3:165.

The Church and the Kingdom of Christ

beginning to end. For Lord will carry through to the end what is now making constant progress, until it is completed.[62]

Torrance offers one of the best analyses of Calvin's idea of this progressive feature of the Church: "Calvin does not, however, think primarily in terms of individual but in terms of the Church as the Body of Christ growing up into Him, and therefore in terms of His reign or Kingdom as it is manifested in the growth and extension of the Church."[63]

Yet, there is a difference between the final perfection of the invisible Church and that of the visible Church. While the perfection of the invisible Church at the end of this progress will be found in enjoyment of the spiritual blessings of the Kingdom of Christ, the perfection of the visible Church is reached with the accomplishment of its functions. Regarding this difference, Calvin pays special attention to Paul's statement in 1 Corinthians 15:24 that "Christ will deliver up the kingdom to the Father":

> He [Paul] proves that the time is not yet come when Christ will deliver up the kingdom to the Father, with the view of showing at the same time that the end has not yet come, when all things will be put into a right and tranquil state, because Christ has not yet subdued all his enemies.[64]

According to Calvin, Paul is here declaring the termination of the mediating role of Christ's humanity between God and Christians:

> But Christ will then restore the kingdom which he has received, that we may cleave wholly to God. Nor will he in this way reign the kingdom, but will transfer it in a manner from his humanity to his glorious divinity, because a way of approach will then be opened up, from which our infirmity now keeps us back.[65]

In his idea of the eschaton, Calvin shares with Luther the idea that all ecclesiastical authorities and the external means of grace will also be terminated when the mediating role of Christ's humanity terminates:

> Nay more, there will be then an end put to angelic principalities in heaven, and to ministries and superiorities in the Church, that God may exercise his power and dominion by himself alone,

---

62. *Comm. Zech.* 14:21, CO 44:390-91.
63. Torrance, *Kingdom and Church*, 95.
64. *Comm. 1 Cor.* 15:25, CO 49:547. For Calvin's idea of the termination of the ministry of the Church in the end, see Quistorp, *Calvin's Doctrine of the Last Things*, 162-71.
65. *Comm. 1 Cor.* 15:27, CO 49:549.

PART TWO—Calvin's Ecclesiology

and not by the hands of men or angels . . . Bishops, teachers, and Prophets will cease to hold these distinctions, and will resign the office which they now discharge.[66]

In an anthropological sense, the human ministry of the Word will be irrelevant to regeneration after death because all believers, both in their soul and body, will see God face to face. In an ecclesiological sense, the purpose of the ministry of the visible Church will be accomplished and then terminated because "God may exercise his power and dominion by himself alone, and not by the hands of men or angels."[67]

Calvin thus finds a close relationship between the invisible Church and the Kingdom of Christ in the eschatological pattern of their progress toward the perfect manifestation of Christ's rule on the last day. Until Christ's Kingdom is perfectly manifested and delivered to the Father, the invisible Church is imperfect because its members are imperfect, even though this Church can be called the Kingdom of Christ because its members as God's children already taste and enjoy spiritual blessings in union with Christ. Until the last day, God entrusts the external means of His grace of salvation into the visible Church, the agent of the Word Kingdom, that it might teach and nourish His children and expand Christ's Kingdom in this world.

Unless the identity of the visible Church as Christ's Kingdom is clearly distinguished from the identity of the invisible Church in Calvin's ecclesiology, Calvin's idea of the progress of the Kingdom of Christ can be misunderstood as an insistence on the growth and expansion of the visible Church in this world. For example, Wilcox argues thus: "Calvin considered the pastors despatched from Geneva to France (as well as ministers and magistrates committed to the reformed cause elsewhere) to be engaged in the establishment of 'true' churches, by the preaching of the Gospel, and thus to be contributing to the propagation of Christ's Kingdom."[68] When Calvin refers

---

66. *Comm. 1 Cor.* 15:24, CO 49:547. In his commentary on *1 Corinthians* 15:24, Luther compares the present state of the Kingdom as "the Kingdom of faith" or "the Kingdom of the Lord Christ" and the future perfection of the Kingdom as the "Kingdom of clarity and manifest being" or "God's Kingdom." He then argues that, in the Kingdom of clarity "Christ will put an end to all, both to the spiritual rule which He now administers in the world, consisting of Baptism, preaching, Sacrament, office of the Keys, or Absolution, etc., and to the secular government with its estates and offices, such as father, mother, child, manservant, maidservant, lords, princes, peasant, burgher etc." Luther, *Comm. 1 Cor.* 15:24; *LW* 28:125–26, WA 36:571–72.

67. *Comm. 1 Cor.* 15:24, CO 49:547.

68. Wilcox, "Progress of the Kingdom," 321.

The Church and the Kingdom of Christ

to the progress of Christ's Kingdom, however, he fundamentally means the eschatological progress of the invisible Church, that is, the new spiritual birth and growth of Christians, rather than the quantitative growth or the territorial expansion of the visible Church in this world. In his commentary on Psalms 45: 16, another proof text of Wilcox's argument, Calvin talks about the increase of the spiritual gifts of the invisible Church rather than the expansion of the visible Church:

> In the estimation of the world, the ignominy of the cross obscures the glory of the Church; but when we consider how wonderfully it has increased, and how much it has been distinguished by spiritual gifts, we must confess that it is not without cause that her glory is in this passage celebrated in such sublime language.[69]

With regard to the eschatological dimension of the Church as the body of Christ in this world, Calvin speaks of the Kingdom as "the new condition of the Church" in salvation history: "The Kingdom of heaven and the Kingdom of God denote the new condition of the Church ... for it was promised that at the coming of Christ all things would be restored."[70] The new condition of the Church in the eschaton includes the completion of the regeneration of all members of the body of Christ, and the accomplishment or the termination of the maternal functions of the visible Church. In his commentary on "the Kingdom of God" in Matthew 5, Calvin defines the Kingdom of heaven as "the renovation of the Church," which includes both the prosperity of the invisible Church and the completion of the ministry of the visible Church:

> The Kingdom of heaven means the renovation of the Church, or the prosperous condition of the Church, such as was then beginning to appear by the preaching of the Gospel ... God, restoring the world by the hand of his Son, has completely established his kingdom. Christ declares that, when his Church shall have been renewed, no teachers must be admitted to it, but those who are faithful expounders of the law, and who labour to maintain its doctrine entire.[71]

---

69. *Comm. Ps.* 45:16, CO 31:453.

70. *Comm. Matt.* 11:11; *Regnum coelorum Dei pro novo ecclesiae statu capitur, ut aliis superioribus locis, quod Christi adventu promissa esset rerum omnium instauratio.* CO 45:303.

71. *Comm. Matt.* 5:19, CO 45:172. For the meaning of "the restoration of the Church" to Calvin, see Wilcox, "'Restoration of the Church' in Calvin's Commentaries of Isaiah the Prophet," 68–95.

PART TWO—Calvin's Ecclesiology

Church Discipline in Calvin's Eschatological Ecclesiology

In Calvin's idea of church discipline, there are three significant points which reflect his idea of the eschatological relationship between the Church and the Kingdom of Christ: the force of excommunication; the necessity of discipline for the effective ministry of the Church; and the authority of ecclesiastical jurisdiction to administer discipline.

Church Discipline and the Kingdom of Christ

In his explanation of the legitimacy, necessity and exercise of excommunication, Calvin's idea of the close relationship between the visible Church and the Kingdom plays a key role. Firstly, when he argues for the necessity of mutual correction among believers in the Church, Calvin refers to the Church as the Kingdom of heaven:

> Let all godly men strive to equip themselves with this armour [mutual correction], lest, while they seem strenuous and courageous vindicators of righteousness, they depart from the Kingdom of Heaven, which is the only kingdom of righteousness. For because God willed that the communion of his church be maintained in this outward society, he who out of hatred of the wicked breaks the token of that society treads a path that slopes to a fall from the communion of saints.[72]

For Calvin, this mutual correction implies church discipline, the "sinews" of the Church: "Accordingly, as the saving doctrine of Christ is the soul of the church, so does discipline serve as its sinews, through which the members of the body hold together, each in its own place."[73] Of the many punishments available within church discipline, excommunication is the severest.[74] Excommunication is established in the Church not by human invention, but by God's ordinance in order to correct or remove "whatever fault there is."[75]

---

72. *Institutes*, IV.1.16, OS 5:20.

73. *Institutes*, IV.12.1, OS 5:212.

74. "For the severest punishment of the church, the final thunderbolt, so to speak, is excommunication, which is used only in necessity." *Institutes*, IV.11.5, OS 5:200–201.

75. *Comm.* 1 *Cor.* 5:5, CO 49:381. "Excommunication is an ordinance of God, and not of men; on any occasion, therefore, on which we are to make use of it, where shall we begin, if not with God. For it is certain that the power of Christ is not tied to the inclination or opinion of mankind, but is associated with his eternal truth." *Comm.* 1 *Cor.* 5:4, CO 49:380.

The Church and the Kingdom of Christ

Calvin explains that the expression "delivery to Satan" in 1 Corinthians 5:5 and 1 Timothy 1:20 indicates the severity of excommunication:

> As, then, we are received into the communion of the Church, and remain in it on this condition, that we are under the protection and guardianship of Christ, I say, that he who is cast out of the Church is in a manner delivered over to the power of Satan, for he becomes an alien, and is cast out of Christ's kingdom.[76]

To stress the force of excommunication, Calvin even claims thus: "Since in the Church Christ holds the seat of his kingdom, out of the Church there is nothing but the dominion of Satan."[77]

Secondly, church discipline is necessary to maintain the effectiveness of the two external means of grace in the Church. The exercise of excommunication, of course, aims to safeguard the proper administration of the sacraments: "And here also we must preserve the order of the Lord's Supper, that it may not be profaned by being administered indiscriminately."[78] As we saw above, the visible Church can be called Christ's Kingdom because it discharges the ministry of the Word. According to Calvin, the ministry of preaching alone cannot maintain the Church without proper discipline:

> Therefore, all who desire to remove discipline or to hinder its restoration—whether they do this deliberately or out of ignorance—are surely contributing to the ultimate dissolution of the church . . . Yet that would happen, if to the preaching of doctrine there were not added private admonitions, corrections, and other aids of the sort that sustain doctrine and do not let it remain idle.[79]

As mentioned above, Calvin argues that the power of the keys, of "binding and loosing," means that it is a privilege for the Church to discharge a preaching ministry.[80] But he claims that this power also means the authority the Church has to correct its members by means of discipline:

---

76. *Comm. 1 Cor.* 5:5, CO 49:381.

77. *Comm. 1 Tim.* 1:20, CO 52:264.

78. *Institutes*, IV.12.5, OS 5:215; "For this reason, our Savior set up in his church the correction and discipline of excommunication." *Article* (1537), LCC 22:50, CO 10:7-9.

79. *Institutes*, IV.12.1, OS 5:212.

80. "But when it is a question of keys, we must always beware lest we dream up some power separate from the preaching of the gospel; any right of binding or loosing which Christ conferred upon His church is bound to the Word." *Institutes*, IV.11.4, OS 5:200.

> He [Christ] now repeats the same words which he had formerly used, (Matt. 16:19) but in a different sense; for there he intended to maintain their authority in doctrine, but here he appoints discipline, which is an appendage to doctrine... We must attend to this distinction, that there our Lord's discourse relates to the preached word, but here to public censures and discipline.[81]

Thirdly, contrary to Zwingli and Bullinger who insist that Christian magistrates have the ultimate authority in decisions about excommunication, Calvin maintains that this authority lies in the "spiritual" jurisdiction of the Church rather than in the "civil" jurisdiction. In his discussion of the necessity of excommunication in the *Institutes*, Calvin argues thus:

> This is the aim of ecclesiastical jurisdiction: that offenses be resisted, and any scandal that has arisen be wiped out. In its use two things ought to be taken into account: that this spiritual power be completely separated from the right of the sword; secondly, that it be administered not by the decision of one man but by a lawful assembly.[82]

Calvin's insistence on the separation of ecclesiastical jurisdiction from civil jurisdiction is based on his idea that the visible Church is Christ's Kingdom: "But whoever knows how to distinguish between body and soul, between this present fleeting life and that future eternal life, will without difficulty know that Christ's spiritual Kingdom and the civil jurisdiction are things completely distinct."[83]

In consequence, these three points show that the identification of the visible Church with the Kingdom of Christ is the theological basis for Calvin's idea of church discipline: church discipline is indispensable in the maintenance of the characteristics of the Kingdom of Christ in the visible Church, including purity, Christ's spiritual authority and faithfulness to the Word.

---

81. *Comm. Matt.* 18:18, CO 45:517.

82. *Institutes*, IV.11.5, OS 5:200. For the comparison and interaction between Calvin's idea of the church discipline and Bullinger's idea, see Baker, "Christian Discipline and the Early Reformed," 107–19. For the difference of interpretations of Matt. 18:15–18 between Zwingli and Calvin, see McKee, *Elders and the Plural Ministry*, 34–37.

83. *Institutes*, IV.20.1; *At vero qui inter corpus et animam, inter praesentem hanc fluxamque vitam et futuram illam aeternamque discernere noverit, neque difficile intelliget, spirituale Christi regnum et civilem ordinationem res esse plurimum sepositas.* CO 5:472.

Church Discipline and the Marks of the Church

Although he emphasised the necessity of church discipline and he himself made a great effort to set it up in the church of Geneva, Calvin does not include church discipline in the marks of the true Church in his *Institutes*.[84] It is certain that Bucer greatly influenced Calvin's idea of church discipline.[85] Yet Calvin did not follow Bucer's idea that church discipline was one of the marks of the true Church.[86] There are two reasons for Calvin's exclusion of discipline from the marks: the idea of church discipline as a human response to God's grace of regeneration; and the eschatological understanding of the holiness of the Church.

Regarding the first reason, Calvin argues that one should not try to discern the true Church from the false Church by any other thing than the two marks: sincere preaching and hearing of the Word; and the right administration of the sacraments according to Scripture. As we saw in chapter 4, in Calvin's view, these two ministries of the Church are the divinely appointed means of God's grace of salvation: "We have laid down as distinguishing marks of the church the preaching of the Word and the observance of the sacraments. These can never exist without bringing forth fruit and prospering by God's blessing."[87] Contrary to these two marks, discipline is not a means of grace like the ministry and the sacraments, but it is a human response to God's grace: "every member of the church is charged

---

84. The Geneva Consistory is the most significant result of Calvin's effort to establish discipline in the visible Church. For a general introduction to Calvin's idea of the Consistory and its application in the Church of Geneva, see Kingdon, *Registers of the Consistory of Geneva in the Time of Calvin*, xvii–xxxv. Kingdon has produced a plenty of useful studies of Calvin's idea of the consistory. Kingdon, "Geneva Consistory as Established by John Calvin," 30–44; "Calvin and the Establishment of Consistory Discipline in Geneva," 158–72.

85. Augustijn, "Calvin in Strasbourg," 166–77. Spijker, "Bucer's Influence on Calvin," 32–44.

86. Bucer's idea of the necessity of church discipline for the Kingdom of Christ appears in his *De Regno Christi* [1550] thus: "The Kingdom of our Saviour Jesus Christ is that administration and care of the eternal life of God's elect, by which this very Lord and King of Heaven by his doctrine and discipline, administered by suitable ministers chosen for this very purpose, gathers to himself his elect, those dispersed throughout the world who are his but whom he nonetheless wills to be subject to the power of the Word." Bucer, *De Regno Christi*; *LCC* 19:225, BO 15:55. About Bucer's idea that church discipline is one fo the marks of the true church, see Wendel, *Calvin*, 301; Hamman, *Entre la secte et la cite*, 231–49; Burnett, *Yoke of Christ*, 9–24, 207–16.

87. *Institutes*, IV.1.10, OS 5:14.

with the responsibility of public edification according to the measure of his grace, provided he performs it decently and in order. That is, we are neither to renounce the communion of the church nor, remaining in it, to disturb its peace and duly ordered discipline."[88]

With regard to the second reason, as Balke contends, Calvin does not think that church discipline can establish perfect holiness in the visible Church enough for Christians to call it a true Church.[89] For, as we have seen, the establishment of holiness of the Church is an eschatological process that will be completed on the last day in the same way as the individual Christians' regeneration toward perfect holiness.

Scholars have noted that Calvin's exclusion of church discipline from the marks of the true Church is distinctive, and have sought historical and theological reasons for this. But most of them ignore Calvin's eschatological idea of the Church as a reason for this exclusion. On the one hand, some have identified a historical reason in Calvin's preference for the views of Luther and Oecolampadius about church discipline over Bucer's.[90] However, there is little textual evidence in Calvin's writings that he was influenced by Luther and Oecolampadius rather than Bucer in his ideas of church discipline.[91] It has also been suggested that Calvin's encounter with the Anabaptists in Strasbourg led him to reject church discipline as a mark.[92] As White demonstrates, however, Calvin had maintained his exclusion of church discipline from the marks of the Church from his *Institutes* of 1536, almost three years before he first encountered the Anabaptists in Strasbourg.[93] When considering theological reasons for the exclusion of discipline from Calvin's marks of the true Church, Wendel argues that for Calvin, church

---

88. *Institutes*, IV.1.12, OS 5:16.

89. Balke argues that "Calvin's primary concern was not for the purity of the church in itself." Balke, *Calvin and the Anabaptist Radicals*, 223.

90. For Oecolampadius's influence on Calvin's concept of church discipline, see Rupp, *Patterns of Reformation*, 37–46.

91. Kuhr has dealt with the possible influence of Oecolampadius on Calvin's idea of church discipline, especially. But Kuhr does not provide any evidence of Oecolampadius' influence for Calvin's exclusion of discipline from the marks. Kuhr, "Calvin and Basel," 19–33.

92. White, "Oil and Vinegar," 31–32. Also see, Johnson, "'The Sinews of the Body of Christ,'" 90–91. For the comparative studies of Calvin's concept of church discipline with that of the Anabaptists, see Balke, *Calvin and the Anabaptist Radicals*, 223–28; Davis, "No Discipline, No Church," 43–58; Fulop, "The Third Mark of the Church?," 35; Girolimon, "John Calvin and Menno Simmons on Religious Discipline," 5–29.

93. White, "Oil and Vinegar," 27–29.

discipline "was simply a measure of defence and a means of sanctification, and as such it belonged to the organisation and not to the definition of the Church."[94] Likewise, Caswell argues that Calvin's idea of the close and subordinate relationship of discipline with and to the Word leads him repeatedly to discount discipline as a mark of the Church.[95] But their accounts are descriptions, not explanations of the theological reason for this exclusion. It is correct that Calvin describes church discipline as an "appendix" of the Word in his commentary on Matthew 18:18. However, this does not yet answer the question of why Calvin does not think of discipline as one the marks of the Church whilst he does include the sacraments, which he also refers to as "a sort of appendix" to the Word.[96] Avis compares Calvin's ideas of the marks of the Church with those of Luther and Melanchthon and argues that "Calvin's overriding concern here is for the objectivity of the Church; like Luther, he is not prepared to make its existence dependent on the subjectivity and fluctuating criteria of human states of the soul."[97] But Avis does not explain why Calvin categorises discipline as so-called "subjectivity," while the preaching of the Word and the administration of the sacraments as so-called "objectivity" of the Church.

For Niesel, it is the "Christo-centric direction" of Calvin's theology that leads him to exclude church discipline from the marks of the Church. According to Niesel, Calvin maintains that "the reality of the church depends not upon our standards, even though they may have been commanded us, but solely upon the work of Christ accomplished towards us and within us through Word and Sacrament."[98] As Niesel notes, Calvin is nonetheless aware that human elements are involved in the preaching ministry and the administration of sacraments, and believes that the grace of Christ should be involved in the exercise of church discipline in order to achieve its purposes.

According to Calvin, the purpose of the marks of the Church is to enable believers to recognise the true Church in this world:

---

94. Wendel, *Calvin*, 301.

95. Caswell, "Calvin's View of Ecclesiastical Discipline," 211.

96. "Now, from the definition that I have set forth we understand that a sacrament is never without a preceding promise but is joined to it as a sort of appendix, with the purpose of confirming and sealing the promise itself, and of making it more evident to us and in a sense ratifying it." *Institutes*, IV.14.3, OS 5:260.

97. Avis, *Church in the Theology of the Reformers*, 30–31.

98. Niesel, *Theology of Calvin*, 199.

PART TWO—Calvin's Ecclesiology

> From this the face of the church comes forth and becomes visible to our eyes. Wherever we see the Word of God purely preached and heard, and the sacraments administered according to Christ's institution, there, it is not to be doubted, a church of God exists.[99]

Unlike Bucer, Calvin does not think that the Kingdom of Christ, that is, the Church, can be recognised in this world by its holiness. His reason is that the Church can never attain perfect holiness in this world. In Calvin's view, if Christians have to take holiness of the Church into account in discerning the true from the false Church, it becomes impossible for them to see the true Church in this world because there is no Church holy enough for everyone to agree to call it the true Church. He then insists that Christians should not reject the Church simply because it is not holy:

> The pure ministry of the Word and pure mode of celebrating the sacraments are, as we say, sufficient pledge and guarantee that we may safely embrace as church any society in which both these marks exist. The principle extends to the point that we must not reject it so long as it retains them, even if it otherwise swarms with many faults.[100]

After this statement in the *Institutes*, Calvin suggests the eschatological characteristics of the Church as the reason for his rejection of the perfectionists' view of holiness as the mark of the true Church: "But if the Lord declares that the church is to labor under this evil—to be weighed down with the mixture of the wicked—until the Day of Judgment, they are vainly seeking a church besmirched with no blemish."[101]

For Calvin, the purpose of church discipline is to preserve order in the visible Church as much as possible in this world: "if no society, indeed, no house which has even a small family, can be kept in proper condition without discipline, it is much more necessary in the church, whose condition should be as ordered as possible."[102] Calvin appeals to Paul's assessment of the church at Corinth concerning the marks of the Church and its holiness:

> Among the Corinthians no slight number had gone astray; in fact, almost the whole body was infected. There was not one kind of sin only, but very many; and they were no light errors but

99. *Institutes*, IV.1.9, OS 5:13.
100. *Institutes*, IV.1.12, OS 5:15–16.
101. *Institutes*, IV.1.13, OS 5:18.
102. *Institutes*, IV.12.1, OS 5:212.

frightful misdeeds. What does the holy apostle—the instrument of the Heavenly Spirit, by whose testimony the church stands or falls—do about this? Does he seek to separate himself from such? Does he cast them out of Christ's Kingdom? . . . Yet the church abides among them because the ministry of Word and sacraments remains unrepudiated there.[103]

Thus Calvin does not include perfect holiness in the purposes of such an order. This order aims to to preserve the honour of Christ,[104] to protect Christians from the possible corruption,[105] and to help the excommunicated person to repent.[106] In Calvin's *Institutes*, therefore, discipline is not the outward mark of the true Church because of his eschatological understanding of the holiness of the Church.

Moderation in the Exercise of Excommunication

Calvin's constant emphasis on moderation in the exercise of excommunication also results from his eschatological understanding of the Church: since the holiness of the Church will be perfectly accomplished in the invisible Church only when Christ makes the final and eternal judgement of the reprobate, ecclesiastical jurisdiction in the visible Church should punish only the wrong doing of members of the Church provisionally and temporally. Concerning Calvin's insistence on the necessity of excommunication, Graham argues that Calvin's idea of discipline was harsh.[107] However, Calvin himself was well aware of the possible danger of exercising excommunication without "a spirit of gentleness." He thus repeatedly exhorts that "the use of discipline ought to be in such a way as to consult the welfare of those on whom the Church inflicts punishment."[108] For the same

---

103. *Institutes*, IV.1.14, OS 5:18.

104. "For since the church itself is the body of Christ, it cannot be corrupted by such foul and decaying members without some disgrace falling upon its Head." *Institutes*, IV.12.5, OS 5:216.

105. *Institutes*, IV.12.5, OS 5:215. Also see *Comm. 2 Thess.* 2:14, CO 52:206.

106. "They who under gentler treatment would have become more stubborn so profit by the chastisement of their own evil as to be awakened when they feel the rod." *Institutes*, IV.12.5, OS 5:215. Also see *Comm. 2 Thess.* 2:14, CO 52:206.

107. "[S]uspicion arises that in practice Calvin's views concerning private and public admonition really amounted to something only a few steps removed from an inquisition." Graham, *The Constructive Revolutionary*, 165–70, 171–72.

108. *Comm. 2 Thess.* 2:14, CO 52:206.

PART TWO—Calvin's Ecclesiology

reason, Calvin even criticises the excessive severity of the ancient church as it "both completely departed from the Lord's injunction and was also terribly dangerous."[109]

Calvin's emphasis on moderation is based on the principle that the ultimate authority of judgment on the reprobate belongs to God: "While we follow this rule, we rather take our stand upon the divine judgment than put forward our own. Let us not claim for ourselves more license in judgment, unless we wish to limit God's power and confine his mercy by law."[110] Any exercise of church discipline beyond this principle is unlawful because this may infringe upon God's grace of regeneration:

> For God, whenever it pleases him, changes the worst men into the best, engrafts the alien, and adopts the stranger into the church. And the Lord does this to frustrate men's opinion and restrain their rashness—which, unless it is checked, ventures to assume for itself a greater right of judgment than it deserves.[111]

More concretely, Calvin presents three reasons for the moderate exercising of excommunication in the *Institutes* IV.12.9. First, excommunication does not aim "to erase from the number of the elect those who have been expelled from the church, or to despair as if they were already lost."[112] Secondly, excommunication is merely a provisional and temporal punishment compared to the final and eternal judgment of Christ in the last day:

> It is lawful to regard them as estranged from the church, and thus, from Christ—but only for such time as they remain separated. However, if they also display more stubbornness than gentleness, we should still commend them to the Lord's judgment, hoping for better things of them in the future than we see in the present.[113]

Thirdly, church discipline should not "condemn to death the very person who is in the hand and judgment of God alone" but only judge "the

---

109. *Institutes*, IV.12.8, OS 5:219.

110. *Institutes*, IV.12.9, OS 5:220.

111. *Institutes*, IV.12.9, OS 5:220. When considering his strong recommendation of moderation, White argues that Calvin's restraint is not only "a legacy of his humanistic education" but also "the fruit of a mature biblical understanding of man and of God," as the *Institutes* "lays repeated stress on man's creatureliness and fallenness." White, "Oil and Vinegar," 28.

112. *Institutes*, IV.12.9, OS 5:220.

113. *Institutes*, IV.12.9, OS 5:220.

character of each man's works by the law of the Lord."[114] For this reason, Calvin sharply distinguishes excommunication from anathema:

> Excommunication differs from anathema in that the latter, taking away all pardon, condemns and consigns a man to eternal destruction; the former, rather, avenges and chastens his moral conduct. And although excommunication also punishes the man, it does so in such a way that, by forewarning him of his future condemnation, it may call him back to salvation.[115]

All three reasons show that Calvin understands the necessity of church discipline from an eschatological perspective. In his interpretation of "the destruction of the flesh" and "the salvation of the spirit" in 1 Corinthians 5:5, Calvin argues thus: "For as the salvation equally with the condemnation of the spirit is eternal, he [Paul] takes "the condemnation of the flesh" as meaning temporal condemnation, we will condemn him [the wicked] in this world for a time, that the Lord may preserve him in his kingdom."[116] With regard to Calvin's emphasis on moderation, White correctly says that there is an eschatological dimension in Calvin's understanding of the visible Church as a *corpus mixtum*, "whose true destiny and inner purity will be revealed only at Christ's return."[117]

Conclusion: Ecclesiology for the Church in Affliction

In Calvin's ecclesiology, the spiritual identity of the invisible Church is manifested in eschatological terms as the Kingdom of Christ. Although the invisible Church "already" enjoys the spiritual blessings of Christ's Kingdom through the ministries of the visible Church, its perfection is "not yet" come. Calvin presents his idea of the invisible Church in relation to the Kingdom of Christ from an eschatological perspective with the purpose of providing suffering Christians with hope, by highlighting the certainty of the preservation of His people even though the condition of the visible Church appears miserable and hopeless:

> Heaven will not be darkened immediately, but after that the Church shall have passed through the whole course of its tribulation. Not

114. *Institutes*, IV.12.9, OS 5:221.
115. *Institutes*, IV.12.10, OS 5:221.
116. *Comm. 1 Cor.* 5:5, CO 49:381.
117. White, "Oil and Vinegar," 32.

PART TWO—Calvin's Ecclesiology

that the glory and majesty of the Kingdom of Christ will not appear till his last coming, but because till that time is delayed the accomplishment of those things which began to take place after his resurrection, and of which God gave to his people nothing more than a taste, that he might lead them farther on in the path of hope and patience.[118]

While discussing the final perfection of the Church, in its special relationship with the Kingdom, in his commentary on 1 Corinthians 15, Calvin does not forget to repeat this pastoral concern: "Let us wait patiently until Christ shall vanquish all his enemies, and shall bring us, along with himself, under the dominion of God, that the kingdom of God may in every respect be accomplished in us."[119]

Calvin maintains his eschatological understanding of the Church when he deals with church discipline in connection with the idea of Kingdom of Christ. Especially, Calvin's idea of church discipline concerning the marks of the true Church, and his emphasis of the moderate administration of excommunication reflect his eschatological understanding of the Church.

---

118. *Comm. Matt.* 24:29, CO 45:667.
119. *Comm.* 1 *Cor.* 15: 27, CO 49:549.

Conclusion

This study has shown that in his ecclesiology Calvin posits a twofold identity of the Church: a functional identity as the mother of all believers, and a spiritual identity as the body of Christ. Calvin envisages a distinct but inseparable relationship between these two identities of the Church. On the one hand, they are distinct from each other: while the functional identity of the Church concerns the existence and characteristics of the visible Church, in which there are false churches and in which hypocrites are mingled with the faithful even in the true churches, the spiritual identity of the Church concerns the invisible Church, that is, "the saints presently living on earth" and "all the elect from the beginning of the world";[1] again, while the functional identity of the Church concerns the Church's maternal role in her ministries and the external means of the grace of salvation by which God wills to regenerate His children, the spiritual identity of the Church concerns the Christians who are the object of these external means. On the other hand, these two identities are inseparable: the members of the invisible Church who are presently living on earth "cannot hope for any forgiveness of sins or any salvation" away from the bosom of the visible Church;[2] furthermore, the present imperfection and affliction of the visible Church can be explained only in the light of the eschatological dimensions—the present imperfection and the continuous progress towards future perfection—of the life of true Christians, the members of the invisible Church. While Calvin deals with the themes concerning the visible and functional Church in the *Institutes* IV, the invisible and spiritual Church is treated in his anthropological and soteriological discussions in the *Institutes* III.

---

1. *Institutes*, IV.1.7, OS 5:12.
2. *Institutes*, IV.1.4, OS 5:7. "It is not sufficient, indeed, for us to comprehend in mind and thought the multitude of elect, unless we consider the unity of the church as that into which we are convinced we have been truly engrafted. For no hope of future inheritance remains to us unless we have been united with all other members under Christ, our Head." *Institutes*, IV.1.2, OS 5:4.

The Identity and the Life of the Church

Therefore, it is necessary for us to remember his anthropological discussions in the *Institutes* III in order to have a precise understanding of his ecclesiological discussions in the *Institutes* IV.

Calvin develops his ecclesiology in three points concerned with this distinct but inseparable relation between the two identities of the Church. First, the visible Church is the mother who teaches and cares for God's children, who are also members of the invisible Church. Calvin proposes that God institutes the two ministries—preaching and the sacraments—in the visible Church in order to regenerate Christians through these maternal functions. Second, the characteristics of the spiritual identity of the Church offer theological principles for the establishment of the functional identity of the Church. Calvin grounds his ideas of the ministry, government and discipline of the visible Church in his theological understanding of the invisible Church: God's accommodating grace and the spiritual needs of Christians are the theological basis of his idea of the ministry of the Church; the characteristics of the body of Christ provide him with the principles of church government, and the eschatological features of the holiness of the invisible Church direct Calvin's idea of church discipline. Thirdly, both the functional identity and the spiritual identity of the Church share similar eschatological experiences in this world. Just as individual Christians are regenerated by the grace of the triune God in an eschatological way, so too the visible Church is sustained by grace and finally accomplishes its goal at the end of the world even though, in this world, it suffers from inner imperfection and outer affliction.

This study has argued that Calvin's ecclesiology is presented in the light of his anthropology. Although, as we have seen, the other *loci* of his theology, such as the doctrines of the Trinity, Christ, salvation and the eschaton are all interwoven in his ecclesiological discussion, I have attempted to highlight the role of his anthropology because, in his ecclesiology, the spiritual identity of the invisible Church is defined as the fellowship of individual Christians, the elect, whose identity and life are the central issues in his anthropology. As we have seen, these two *loci* of Calvin's theology are associated with each other from three theological perspectives: relational, trinitarian, and eschatological. The identities of both the Christian and the Church depend on their relationship with Christ; in this relationship the grace of the triune God secures and confirms their identity; and the grace of God promises to preserve and complete the process of the regeneration of Christians and the restoration of the Church at the end of the world.

Conclusion

Thus Calvin's ecclesiology shares the same material focus as his anthropology: the regeneration of Christians by grace in their relationship with the triune God. While his anthropology fundamentally aims to explain the being and existence of Christians who are being regenerated by the grace of the triune God, his ecclesiology seeks to explain the maternal role of the visible Church by which the triune God wills to regenerate Christians, and the identity of the invisible Church in the grace of the triune God.

This focus may not be the "central dogma" by which we can explain every aspect of Calvin's ecclesiology and anthropology.[3] Indeed, it may be that attempts to identify a "central dogma" are misguided, in that they tend toward oversimplification of a diverse body of his thought. But it is certain that the grace of the triune God is the most fundamental focal point in the presentation of Calvin's anthropological and ecclesiological discussions. In his anthropology, Calvin presents his discussions of the image of God in humanity, the Christian's divided self, and Christian progress toward perfection in the final resurrection with a clear focus on the grace of the triune God. In his ecclesiology, he deals with the imperfection of the human and earthly instruments of the ministry of the Church, the dependent nature of the Church as the body of Christ, and the eschatological identification of the Church with the Kingdom of Christ in order once again to highlight the triune God's grace.

In evaluating Calvin's ecclesiology, it can be seen that his focus on the grace of God shows his concern for the afflicted Church that undergoes exile and persecution. In the *Institutes* IV, Calvin compares the miserable condition of the Jewish religion in Elijah's time with the desolate situation of his own Church:

> Although the melancholy desolation which confronts us on every side may cry that no remnant of the church is left, let us know that Christ's death is fruitful, and that God miraculously keeps his church as in hiding places. So it was said to Elijah, "I have kept for myself seven thousand men who have not bowed the knee before Baal."[4]

---

3. After reviewing previous suggestions of the "central dogma" in Calvin's theology, Partee suggests "union with Christ" as the new central dogma that penetrates Calvin's theology. Partee, "Calvin's Central Dogma Again," 191–99.

4. *Institutes*, IV.1.2, OS 5:4. "And this doctrine may also be justly applied to our time. For we are by no means to expect that God will so restore his Church in the world, that all shall be renewed by his Spirit, and unite in true religion; but he gathers his Church on all sides, and yet in such a way, that his gratuitous mercy ever appears, because there shall be remnants only." *Comm. Jer.* 31:7, CO 38:652.

The Identity and the Life of the Church

His concern for the afflicted Church is the motif not only of his ecclesiological discussions in the *Institutes* IV, but also of the *Institutes* as a whole. In the prefatory address to King Francis I, Calvin manifests this concern thus:

> For ungodly men have so far prevailed that Christ's truth, even if it is not driven away scattered and destroyed, still lies hidden, buried and inglorious. The poor little church has either been wasted with cruel slaughter or banished into exile, or so overwhelmed by threats and fears that it dare not even open its mouth . . . Meanwhile no one comes forward to defend the church against such furies.[5]

He then highlights the grace of God in preserving the Church amid severe afflictions in this world:

> Surely, the church of Christ has lived and will live so long as Christ reigns at the right hand of his Father. It is sustained by his hand; defended by his protection; and is kept safe through his power. For he will surely accomplish what he once promised: that he will be present with his own even to the end of the world [Matt. 28:20].[6]

Calvin's ecclesiology therefore tries not only to propose concrete and practical plans for the institutional Church, but also to provide suffering Christians and their communities with consolation and hope. This pastoral concern is one of the most important points that academic studies should take into account in order to analyse precisely and evaluate properly Calvin's ideas of the practical aspects of the Church. With regard to Calvin's concern for the afflicted Church, Oberman argues thus:

> Where Calvinism became the dominant culture, it showed the ugly face of suppression for which it is widely known. However, when forced to go underground and to live "East of Eden," it could regain the original vision of John Calvin, the vision of the remnant, destined to serve as pathfinder and refugee.[7]

The concluding statement of Calvin's prefatory address of the *Institutes* clearly sets out his fundamental ecclesiological concern:

---

5. *Institutes*, Prefatory Address, OS 3:11.

6. *Institutes*, Prefatory Address, OS 3:23.

7. Oberman, "*Europa afflicta*," 102. After outlining the historical background of Calvin's concern for the minority Church, Wright argues that "the remnant motif" and "an ecclesiological *theologia crucis*" are the primary motives of Calvin's doctrine of the Church. Wright, "Sixteenth-Century Reformed Perspectives on the Minority Church," 19–20.

Conclusion

Suppose, however, the whisperings of the malevolent so fill your ears that the accused have no chance to speak for themselves, but those savage furies, while you connive at them, ever rage against us with imprisonings, scourgings, rackings, maimings, and burnings. Then we will be reduced to the last extremity even as sheep destined for the slaughter. Yet this will so happen that "in our patience we may possess our souls"; and may await the strong hand of the Lord, which will surely appear in due season, coming forth armed to deliver the poor from their affliction and also to punish their despisers, who now exult with such great assurance.[8]

Ultimately, it is this pastoral concern of Calvin for the Christian and the Church under affliction that both governs his theological understanding of the scriptural and traditional descriptions of the Church and shapes his proposals for establishing and sustaining the life of the Church in the world.

---

8. *Institutes*, Prefatory Address, OS 3:30.

Bibliography

Anderson, Luke. "The *Imago Dei* Theme in John Calvin and Bernard of Clairvaux." In *Calvinus Sacrae Scripturae Professor: Calvin as Confessor of Holy Scripture*, edited by Wilhelm H. Neuser, 178–98. Grand Rapids: Eerdmans, 1994.
Armstrong, Brian G. "*Duplex cognito Dei*, or? The Problem and Relation of Scripture, Form, and Purpose in Calvin's Theology." In *Probing the Reformed Tradition: Historical Studies in Honor of Edward A. Dowey Jr.*, edited by Brian G. Armstrong and Elsie A. McKee, 135–53. Louisville: Westminster John Knox, 1989.
Armstrong, Brian G., and Elsie Anne McKee, editors. *Probing the Reformed Tradition: Historical Studies in Honor of Edward A. Dowey Jr.* Louisville: Westminster John Knox, 1989.
Augustijn, Cornelis. "Calvin in Strasbourg." In *Calvinus Sacrae Scripturae Professor: Calvin as Confessor of Holy Scripture*, edited by Wilhelm H. Neuser, 166–77. Grand Rapids: Eerdmans, 1994.
Augustine. *The City of God against the Pagans*. Translated by R. W. Dyson. Cambridge: Cambridge University Press, 2003.
Avis, Paul D. L. *The Church in the Theology of the Reformers*. London: Morgan & Scott, 1981.
Babelotzky, Gerd. *Platonische Bilder und Gedankengänge in Calvins Lehre vom Menschen*. Wiesbaden, Austria: Steiner, 1977.
Bagchi, David, and David C. Steinmetz. *The Cambridge Companion to Reformation Theology*. Cambridge: Cambridge University Press, 2004.
Baker, J. Wayne. "Christian Discipline and the Early Reformed Tradition: Bullinger and Calvin." In *Calviniana: Ideas and Influence of Jean Calvin*, edited by Robert V. Schnucker, 107–19. Kirksville, MO: Sixteenth Century Journal, 1988.
Balke, Willem. *Calvin and the Anabaptist Radicals*. Translated by William Heynen. Grand Rapids: Eerdmans, 1981.
Balserak, Jon. *Divinity Compromised: A Study of Divine Accommodation in the Thought of John Calvin*. Dordrecht: Springer, 2006.
Barth, Karl. *The Theology of John Calvin*. Translated by Geoffrey W. Bromiley. Grand Rapids: Eerdmans, 1995.
Battenhouse, R. W. "Docrtrine of Man in Calvin and in Renaissance Platonism." *Journal of Historical Ideas* 9 (1948) 447–71.
Battles, Ford Lewis. *Analysis of the Institutes of Christian Religion of John Calvin*. Grand Rapids: Baker, 1980.
———. "God Was Accommodating Himself to Human Capacity." *Interpretation* 31 (1977) 21–26.
———. *Interpreting John Calvin*. Edited by Robert Benedetto. Grand Rapids: Baker, 1996.
Beeke, Joel R., editor. *Calvin for Today*. Grand Rapids: Reformed Heritage, 2009.

Bibliography

Benoit, Jean-Daniel. "The History and Development of the *Institutio*: How Calvin worked." In *John Calvin: Courtenay Studies in Reformation Theology I*, edited by Ford Lewis Battles et al., 102–17. Abingdon, UK: Sutton Courtenay.

Biéler, André. *Calvin's Economic and Social Thought*. Translated by James Greig. Geneva: World Council of Churches, 2005.

Billings, J. Todd. "United to God through Christ: Assessing Calvin on the Question of Deification." *Harvard Theological Journal* 98 (2005) 315–34.

Billings, J. Todd Billings, and I. John Hesselink, editors. *Calvin's Theology and Its Reception*. Louisville: Westminster John Knox, 2012.

Bohatec, Josef. *Bude und Calvin: Studien zur Gedankenwelf des französischen Fruhhunamismus*. Graz: Bohlau, 1950.

Boisset, J. "Justification et sanctification chez Calvin." In *Calvinus Theologus: Die Referate des Congrès Européen de recherches Calvinienne*, edited by Wilhelm. H. Neuser, 131–48. Neukirchen: Neukirchen, 1976.

Bouwsma, William J. "Calvin and the Crisis of Knowledge in the Renaissance." *Calvin Theological Journal* 17 (1982) 190–211.

———. *John Calvin: A Sixteenth Century Portrait*. Oxford: Oxford University Press, 1988.

Bratt, John H., editor. *The Heritage of John Calvin*. Grand Rapids: Eerdmans, 1973.

Bucer, Martin. *Common Places of Martin Bucer*. Translated and edited by David F. Wright. Courtenay Library of Reformation Classics 4 Appleford, UK: Sutton Courtenay, 1972.

———. *De Regno Christi*. In *Melanchthon and Bucer*. Translated and edited by Wilhelm Pauck. Library of Christian Classics 19. Philadelphia: Westminster, 1969.

———. *Martini Buceri Opera Latina*. Vol. 15, *De Regno Christi, Libri Duo 1550*. Edited by François Wendel. Paris: Presses Universitaires de France, 1955.

Burnett, Amy Nelson. *The Yoke of Christ: Martin Bucer and Christian Discipline*. Kirksville, MO: Sixteenth Century Journal, 1994.

Burns, J. Patout, Jr. *Cyprian the Bishop*. London: Routlege, 2002.

Busch, Eberhard. *Gotteserkenntnis und Menschlichkeit: Einsichten in die Theologie Johannes Calvins*. Zürich: TVZ, 2005.

Butin, Philip W. *Revelation, Redemption and Response*. Oxford: Oxford University Press, 1995.

Cairns, David. *The Image of God in Man*. London: Camelot, 1953.

Calvin, John. *Calvin's Commentaries*. 46 vols. Edinburgh: Calvin Translation Society, 1844–1855; reprint, 22 vols. Grand Rapids: Baker, 1979.

———. *Calvin's Ecclesiastical Advice*. Translated by Mary Beaty and Benjamin Wirt Farley. Edinburgh: T. & T. Clark, 1991.

———. *Calvin: Theological Treatises*. Translated and edited by J. K. S. Reid. Library of Christian Classics 22. Philadelphia: Westminster, 1954.

———. *Concerning the Eternal Predestination of God*. Translated by J. K. S. Reid. Cambridge: Clarke, 1961.

———. *Concerning Scandals*. Translated by John W. Fraser. Edinburgh: Saint Andrew, 1978.

———. *Institutes of the Christian Religion* [1536]. Translated and annotated by Ford Lewis Battles. Grand Rapids: Eerdmans, 1986.

———. *Institutes of the Christian Religion* [1559]. Library of Christian Classics 20–21. Edited by John T. McNeil. Translated by Ford Lewis Battles. Philadelphia: Westminster, 1960.

Bibliography

———. *Institutes of the Christian Religion* [1559]. Translated by Henry Beveridge. Edinburgh, 1845; reprint, Grand Rapids: Eerdmans, 1989.

———. *Ioannis Calvini Epistolae.* Vol. 1, *1530–Sep. 1538.* Edited by Cornelis Augustijn and Frans Pieter van Stam. Geneva: Droz, 2005.

———. *Ioannis Calvini opera quae supersunt omnia.* Edited by G. Baum, Edward Cunitz, and Edward Reuss. 59 vols. *Corpus Reformatorum* 29–87. Brunsvigae: Schwetschke, 1863–1900.

———. *Ioannis Calvini opera selecta.* Edited by Peter Barth, Wilhelm Niesel, and Dora Scheuner. 5 vols. Munich: Kaiser, 1926–1962.

———. *John Calvin: Writings on Pastoral Piety.* Edited by Elsie Anne McKee. New York: Paulist, 2001.

———. *John Calvin's Sermons on Ephesians.* Translated by Arthur Golding, 1577. Translation revised by Leslie Rawlinson and S. M. Houghton. Edinburgh: Banner of Truth, 1973.

———. *John Calvin's Sermons on Galatians.* Translated by Kathy Childress. Edinburgh: Banner of Truth, 1997.

———. *Letters of John Calvin.* Edited by Henry Beveridge and Jules Bonnet. 4 vols. Vols. 1–2 translated by David Constable. Edinburgh: Thomas Constable, 1855. Vols. 3–4 translated by M. R. Gilchrist. New York, n. p. 1858.

———. *The Mystery of Godliness and Other Sermons.* Grand Rapids: Eerdmans, 1950.

———. *Opera Exegetica veteris et novi testamenti.* Edited by Helmut Feld. Geneva: Droz, 1997–.

———. *The Piety of John Calvin.* Translated and edited by Ford Lewis Battles. Grand Rapids: Baker, 1978.

———. *Sermons on the Book of Micah.* Translated and edited by Benjamin Wirt Farley. Phillipsburg, NJ: P. & R., 2003.

———. *Sermons on Deuteronomy.* Translated by Arthur Golding. London: Middleton, 1583. Facsimile reprint, Edinburgh: Banner of Truth 1992.

———. *Sermons on Isaiah's Prophecy of the Death and Passion of Christ.* Translated and edited by T. H. L. Parker. London: Clarke, 1956.

———. *Sermons on Job.* Translated by Arthur Golding. London, 1574. Facsimile reprint, Edinburgh: Banner of Truth, 1993.

———. *Sermons on Job.* Translated by Leroy Nixon. Grand Rapids: Baker, 1979.

———. *Sermons on 2 Samuel: Chapters 1–13.* Translated by Douglas Kelly. Edinburgh: Banner of Truth, 1992.

———. *Sermons on Timothy and Titus.* Translated by Laurence Thompson. London, 1579. Facsimile reprint, Edinburgh: Banner of Truth, 1983.

———. *Supplementa Calviniana.* Edited by H. Rüchert et al. Neukirchener-Vluyn: Neukirchener, 1936–.

———. *Tracts and Treatises.* 3 vols. Translated by Henry Beveridge. London: Oliver & Boyd, 1844–1851.

———. *Treatises against the Anabaptists and against the Libertines.* Translated and edited by Benjamin Wirt Farley. Grand Rapids: Baker, 1982.

Caswell, R. N. "Calvin's View of Ecclesiastical Discipline." In *John Calvin,* edited by G. E. Duffield, 210–26. Appleford, UK: Sutton Courtenay, 1966.

Compier, Don H. *John Calvin's Rhetorical Doctrine of Sin.* Texts and Studies in Religion, 86. Lewiston, NY: Mellen, 2001.

Bibliography

Cottret, Bernard. *Calvin: A Biography.* Translated by M. Wallace McDonald. Edinburgh: T. & T. Clark, 1995.
Crawford, J. R. "Calvin and the Priesthood of All Believers." *Scottish Journal of Theology* 21 (1968) 145–56.
Cyprian. *De Unitate Ecclesiae.* Translated by E. H. Blakeney. London: Society for Promoting Christian Knowledge, 1928.
Davis, Kenneth R. "No Discipline, No Church: An Anabaptist Contribution to the Reformed Traditions." *Sixteenth Century Journal* 13 (1982) 43–58.
De Greef, W. *The Writings of John Calvin: An Introductory Guide.* Translated by Lyle D. Bierma. Grand Rapids: Baker, 1993.
Demura, Akira. "Two Commentaries on the Epistle of the Romans: Calvin and Oecolampadius." In *Calvinus Sincerioris Religionis Vindex: Calvin as the Protection of the Purer Religion,* edited by Wilhelm H. Neuser & Brian G. Armstrong, 165–87. Kirksville, MO: Sixteenth Century Journal, 1997.
DeVeries, Dawn. *Jesus Christ in the Preaching of Calvin and Schleiermacher.* Louisville: Westminster John Knox, 1996.
Douglass, Jane Dempsey. "The Image of God in Humanity: A Comparison of Calvin's Teaching in 1536 and 1559." In *In Honor of John Calvin, 1509-64: Papers from the 1986 International Calvin Symposium McGill University,* edited by E. J. Furcha, 175–203. Montreal: ARC, 1987.
Doumergue, Emile. *Jean Calvin: Les homes et les choses de son temps.* 7 vols. Lausanne: Bridel, 1897–1917.
Dowey, Edward A., Jr. "The Structure of Calvin's Thought as Influenced by the Twofold Knowledge of God." In *Calvinus Ecclesiae Genevensis Custos,* edited by Wilhelm H. Neuser, 135–48. Frankfurt: Lang, 1984.
———. *The Knowledge of God in Calvin's Theology.* New York: Columbia University Press, 1952.
Edmondson, Stephen. *Calvin's Christology.* Cambridge: Cambridge University Press, 2004.
Eire, Carlos M. N. *War Against Idols.* Cambridge: Cambridge University Press, 1986.
Elwood, Christopher. *The Body Broken: the Calvinist Doctrine of the Eucharist and the Symbolism of Power in Sixteenth-century France.* Oxford: Oxford University Press, 1999.
Engammare, Max. "Calvin: A Prophet Without a Prophecy." *Church History* 67 (1998) 643–61.
Engel, Marry Porter. *John Calvin's Perspectival Anthropology.* Atlanta: Scholars, 1988.
Engelland, H. *Gott und Mensch bei Calvin.* Munich: Kaiser, 1934.
Faber, Jelle. *Essays in Reformed Doctrine.* Neerlandia, Alberta: Inheritance, 1990.
Ferguson, Sinclair B. "The Reformed Doctrine of Sonship." In *Pulpit and People,* edited by S. Cameron and S. B. Ferguson, 81–88. Edinburgh: Rutherford House, 1986.
Fields, Paul, et al., compilers. *The Calvin Bibliographies: 1997-2007.* H. Henry Meeter Center for Calvin Studies. Online: http://www.calvin.edu/meeter/bibliography.
Foxgrover, David, editor. *Calvin and the Church: Papers Presented at the 13th Colloquium of the Calvin Studies Society May 24-26, 2001.* Grand Rapids: CRC, 2002.
Frankel, Peter, editor. *Natural Theology.* London: Centenary, 1946.
Fulop, Timothy E. "The Third Mark of the Church? Church Discipline in the Reformed and Anabaptists Reformations." *Journal of Religious History* 19 (1995) 27–29.

Bibliography

Furcha, Edward J., editor. *In Honor of John Calvin 1509-1564: Papers from the 1986 International Calvin Symposium at McGill University.* Montreal, Québec: McGill University Press, 1991.

Gamble, Richard C., editor. *Calvin's Ecclesiology: Sacraments and Deacons.* Articles on Calvin and Calvinism 10. New York: Garland, 1992.

Ganoczy, Alexandre. *Calvin: Théologien de l'église et du ministère.* Paris: Cerf, 1964.

———. "L'Église, Comunauté our institution? l'Heritage Ecclésiologique de Calvin." *Revue de Theologie et de Philosophie* 3 (1977) 223-34.

———. "Obervations on Calvin's Trinitarian Doctrine of Grace." In *Probing the Reformed Tradition: Historical Studies in Honor of Edward A. Dowey Jr*, edited by Brian G. Armstrong and Elsie A. McKee, 96-107. Louisville: Westminster John Knox, 1989.

———. *The Young Calvin.* Translated by David Foxgrover. Edinburgh: T. &. T. Clark, 1987.

George, Timothy, editor. *John Calvin and the Church: A Prism of Reform.* Louisville: Westminster John Knox, 1990.

Gerrish, Brian. A. *Grace and Gratitude: The Eucharistic Theology of John Calvin.* Minneapolis: Fortress, 1993.

———. *The Old Protestantism and the New: Essays on the Reformation Heritage.* Chicago: University of Chicago Press, 1982.

Girardin, Benoît. *Rhétorique et théologique: Calvin le commentaire de l'épître aux Romains.* Paris: Beauchesne, 1979.

Girolimon, Michael Thomas. "John Calvin and Menno Simmons on Religious Discipline: a Different in Degree and Kind." *Fides et Historia* 27 (1995) 5-29.

Graham, W. Fred. *The Constructive Revolutionary: John Calvin and His Socio-Economic Impact.* Atlanta: John Knox, 1971.

Grenz, Stanley J. *The Social God and the Relational Self: A Trinitarian Theology of the Imago Dei.* Louisville: Westminster John Knox, 2001.

Griffith, Howard. "'The First Title of the Spirit': Adoption in Calvin's Soteriology." *Evangelical Quarterly* 73 (2001) 135-53.

Hall, Charles, M. N. *With the Spirit's Sword: the Drama of Spiritual Warfare in the Theology of John Calvin.* Basel Studies of Theology 3. Zurich: EVZ, 1968.

Hammann, Gottfried. *Entre la secte et la cité: Le projet d'Eglise du Réformateur Martin Bucer (1491-1551).* Geneva: Labor et Fides, 1984.

Hancock, Ralph C. *Calvin and the Foundations of the Modern Politics.* Ithaca, NY: Cornell University Press, 1989.

Hedtke, Reinhold. *Erziehung durch die Kirche bei Calvin: Der unterweisungs-und Erziehungsauftrag der Kirche und seine anthropologischen und theologischen Grundlage.* Heidelberg: Quelle & Meyer, 1969.

Hesselink, I. John. *Calvin's First Catechism: A Commentary.* Louisville: Westminster John Knox, 1997.

Higman, Francis M. "Calvin et l'*imago Dei*." In *De l'Humanisme aux Lumières, Bayle et le protestantisme:Mélanges en l'honneur d'Elisabeth Labrousse*, edited by Michelle Magdelaine et al., 139-48. Paris: Voltaire Foundation, 1996.

———. *The Style of John Calvin in His French Polemical Treatises.* Oxford: Oxford University Press, 1967.

Hirzel, Martin Ernest, and Martin Sallmann, editors. *John Calvin's Impact on Church and Society. 1509-2009.* Grand Rapids: Eerdmans, 2009.

Bibliography

Holder, R. Ward. *John Calvin and the Grounding of Interpretation: Calvin's First Commentaries*. Leiden: Brill, 2006.
Hoogstra, Jacob T., editor. *John Calvin Contemporary Prophet*. Grand Rapids: Baker, 1959.
Hopfl, Haro. *The Christian Polity of John Calvin*. Cambridge: Cambridge University Press, 1982.
Hörcsik, Richard. "John Calvin in Geneva, 1536-38." In *Calvinus Sacrae Scripturae Professor: Calvin as Confessor of Holy Scripture*, edited by Wilhelm H. Neuser, 155-64. Grand Rapids: Eerdmans, 1994.
Hughes, Philip E., editor. *The Register of the Company of Pastors in Geneva in the Time of Calvin*. Grand Rapids: Eerdmans, 1966.
Jones, Serene. *Calvin and the Rhetoric of Piety*. Louisville: Westminster John Knox, 1995.
Johnson, Stephen M. "'The Sinews of the Body of Christ': Calvin Concept of Church Discipline." *Westminster Theological Journal* 59 (1997) 87-100.
Kayayan, Eric. "Accommodation, Incarnation et sacreament dans l'institution de la religion Chrétienne de Jean Calvin: L'utilisation de metaphores et de similitudes." *Revue d'histoire et de philosophie religieuses* 75 (1995) 273-87.
Kendall, R. T. *Calvin and English Calvinism to 1649*. Oxford: Oxford University Press, 1980.
Kingdon, Robert M. *Geneva and the Coming of the War of Religion in France, 1555-1563*. Geneva: Droz, 1956.
———. *Geneva and the Consolidation of the French Protestant Movement, 1564-1572*. Madison: University of Wisconsin Press, 1967.
———. "The Control of Morals in Calvin's Geneva." In *The Social History of the Reformation*, edited by L. P. Zuck and J. W. Zophy, 3-16. Columbus: Ohio State University Press, 1972.
———. "Calvin and the Government of Geneva." In *Calvinus Ecclesiae Genevensis Custos*, edited by Wilhelm H. Neuser, 49-67. Frankfurt: Lang, 1984.
———. "The Geneva Consistory as Established by John Calvin." *On the Way* 7 (1990) 30-44.
———. "Calvin and the Establishment of Consistory Discipline in Geneva: The Institution and the Men who direct it." *Nederlands Archief voor Kerkgeshiednis* 70 (1990) 158-72.
———. *Adultery and Divorce in Calvin's Geneva*. Cambridge: Harvard University Press, 1995.
———. "A New View of Calvin in the Light of the Registers of the Geneva Consistory." In *Calvinus Sincerioris Religionis Vindex: Calvin as the Protection of the Purer Religion*, edited by Neuser Wilhelm H. et al., 21-33. Kirksville, MO: Sixteenth Century Journal Publishers, 1997.
———. "Effort to Control Hate in Calvin's Geneva." In *Calvin Studies IX: Papers Presented at the Ninth Colloquium on Calvin Studies*, edited by John H. Leith, 113-22. Decatur, GA: Columbia Theological Seminary, 2000.
Kingdon, Robert M., et al., editors. *Registers of the Consistory of Geneva in the Time of Calvin*. Vol. 1, *1542-1544*. Grand Rapids: Eerdmans, 2000.
Kittelson, James. *Toward an Established Church: Strasbourg from 1500 to the Dawn of the Seventeenth Century*. Mainz: Zabern, 2000.
Kok, Joel E. "Heinrich Bullinger's Exegetical Method: The Model for Calvin?" In *Biblical Interpretation in the Era of the Reformation*, edited by Richard A. Muller and John L. Thompson, 241-54. Grand Rapids: Eerdmans, 1996.

Kolfhaus, Wilhelm. *Vom Christlichen Leben nach Johannes Calvin*. Neukirchen: Moers, 1949.
Kraus, Hans-Joachim. "The Contemporary Relevance of Calvin's Theology." In *Toward the Future of Reformed Theology: Tasks, Topics, Traditions*, edited by David Welker and Michael Willis, 323–38. Grand Rapids: Eerdmans, 1999.
Kroon, Marijn de. *The Honour of God and Human Salvation*. Translated by Lyle D. Bierma. Edinburgh: T. &. T. Clark, 2001.
Kuhr, Olaf. "Calvin and Basel: the Significance of Oecolampadius and the Basel Discipline Ordinance for the Institution of Ecclesiastical Discipline in Geneva." *Scottish Bulletin of Evangelical Theology* 16 (1998) 19–33.
Lane, Anthony N. S. *John Calvin: Student of the Church Fathers*. Edinburgh: T. & T. Clark, 1999.
———. *Justification by Faith in Catholic-Protestant Dialogue: An Evangelical Assessment*. London: T. & T. Clark, 2002.
Leith, John H. "Doctrine of the Proclamation of the Word." In *Calvin Studies II: Presented at a Colloquium on Calvin Studies at Davidson College*, edited by J. H. Leith and Charles Raynal, 55–78. Davidson, NC: Davidson College and Davidson College Presbyterian Church, 1984.
———. *John Calvin's Doctrine of the Christian Life*. Louisville: Westminster John Knox, 1989.
Link, Christian. "Die Finalität des Menschen Zur Perspektive der Anthropologie Calvins." In *Calvinus Praeceptor Ecclesiae: Papers of the International Congress on Calvin Research, Princeton August 20–24, 2002*, edited by Herman J. Selderhuis, 159–78. Geneva: Droz, 2004.
Loeschen, John R. *The Divine Community: Trinity, Church, and Ethics in Reformation Theologies*. Kirksville, MO: Sixteenth Century Journal, 1981.
Luther, Martin. *Luthers Werke*. Kritische Gesamtausgabe. 65 vols. Weimar: Böhlau, 1883–1993.
———. *Luther's Works*. 56 vols. Edited by Jaroslav Pelikan and Helmut Lehmann. St. Louis: Concordia, 1955–1986.
Maag, Karin, editor. *Melanchthon in Europe: His Work and Influence beyond Wittenberg*. Grand Rapids: Baker, 1999.
MacGregor, Geddes. *Corpus Christi: The Nature of the Church according to the Reformed Tradition*. London: Macmillan. 1959.
McDonnell, K. *John Calvin, the Church and the Eucharist*. Princeton University Press: Princeton, 1967.
McGrath, Alister E. *Iustitia Dei: A History of the Christian Doctrine of Justification*. 3rd ed. Cambridge: Cambridge University Press, 2005.
———. *A Life of John Calvin*. Oxford: Blackwell, 1990.
———. *Reformation Thought: An Introduction*. 3rd ed. Oxford: Blackwell, 1999.
McKee, Elsie Anne. *Elders and the Plural Ministry: the Role of Exegetical History in Illuminating John Calvin's Theology*. Geneva: Droz, 1988.
———. "Exegesis, Theology and Development." In *Probing the Reformed Tradition: Historical Studies in Honor of Edward A. Dowey Jr*, edited by Brian G. Armstrong and Elsie A. McKee, 154–72. Louisville: Westminster John Knox, 1989.
———. *John Calvin on the Diaconate and Liturgical Almsgiving*. Geneva: Droz, 1984.
McKim, Donald K., editor. *Calvin and the Bible*. Cambridge: Cambridge University Press, 2006.

Bibliography

———. *The Cambridge Companion to John Calvin*. Cambridge: Cambridge University Press, 2004.

McNeill, John Thomas. "Calvin as an Ecumenical Churchman." *Church History* 32 (1963) 379–91.

Melanchthon, Philip. *Commentary on Romans*. Translated by Fred Kramer. St. Louis: Concordia, 1992.

———. *Corpus Reformatorum. Philippi Melanchthonis opera quae supersunt omnia*. Edited by Karl Bretschneider and Heinrich Bindseil. 28 vols. Halle: Schwetschke & Sons, 1834–1860.

———. *Loci Communes Theologici*. In *Melanchthon and Bucer*. Translated and edited by Wilhelm Pauck. Library of Christian Classics 19. Philadelphia: Westminster, 1969.

———. *Melanchthon on Christian Doctrine: Loci Communes 1555*. Translated and edited by Clyde L. Manschreck. Oxford: Oxford University Press, 1965.

———. *Melanchthon Werke in Auswahl*. Edited by Robert Stupperich. 7 vols. Gütersloh: Mohn, 1951–1975.

Mentzer, Raymond A. "Action on Calvin's Ideas: The Church in France." In *Calvin and the Church: Papers Presented at the 13th Colloquium of the Calvin Studies Society May 24–26, 2001*, edited by David Foxgrover, 46–64. Grand Rapids: CRC, 2002.

Miles, Margaret R. "Theology, Anthropology, and the Human Body in Calvin's *Institutes of the Christian Religion*." *Harvard Theological Review* 74 (1981) 303–23.

Millet, Olivier. *Calvin et la dynamique de la parole: Étude de rhétorique réformée*. Paris: Slatkine, 1992.

Milner, B. C. *Calvin's Doctrine of the Church*. Leiden: Brill, 1970.

Monter, William. *Calvin's Geneva*. New York: Wiley & Sons, 1967.

Moser, Carl. "The Greatest Possible Blessing: Calvin and Deification." *Scottish Journal of Theology* 55 (2002) 36–57.

Muller, Richard A. "The Hermeneutic of Promise and Fulfillment in Calvin's Exegesis of the Old Testament Prophecies of the Kingdom." In *The Bible in the Sixteenth Century*, edited by David C. Steinmetz, 68–82. Durham, NC: Duke University Press, 1990.

———. "'Scimus enim quod ex spiritualis est': Melanchthon and Calvin on the Interpretation of Romans 7:14–23." In *Philip Melanchthon (1497–1560) and the Commentary*, edited by Timothy J. Wengert and M. Patrick Graham, 216–37. Sheffield: Sheffield Academic, 1997.

———. *The Unaccomodated Calvin: Studies in the Foundation of a Theological Tradition*. Oxford Studies in Historical Theology. New York: Oxford University Press, 2000.

Muller, Richard A., and John L. Thompson, editors. *Biblical Interpretation in the Era of the Reformation*. Grand Rapids: Eerdmans, 1996.

Naphy, William G. *Calvin and the Consolidation of the Genevan Reformation*. Manchester: Manchester University Press, 1994.

———. "Church and State in Calvin's Geneva." In *Calvin and the Church: Papers Presented at the 13th Colloquium of the Calvin Studies Society May 24–26, 2001*, edited by David Foxgrover, 13–28. Grand Rapids: CRC, 2002.

Neuser, Wilhelm H., editor. *Calvinus Ecclesiae Doctor. Die Referate des Congres International des Recherches Calviniennes vom 25. bis 28. September 1978 in Amsterdam*. Kampen, Netherlands: Kok, 1979.

———. *Calvinus ecclesiae Genevensis custos: International Congress for Calvin Research*. Frankfurt: Lang, 1984.

———. *Calvinus Sacrae Scripturae Professor: Calvin as Confessor of Holy Scripture*. Grand Rapids: Eerdmans, 1994.

———. *Calvinus Servus Christi: Die referate des Internationals Kongresses fur Calvinfoschung, vom 25. bis 28. August 1986 in Debrecen*. Budapest: Presseabteilung des Ráday-Kollegiums, 1988.

Neuser, Wilhelm H., and Brian G. Armstrong, editors. *Calvinus Sincerioris Religionis Vindex: Calvin as the Protection of the Purer Religion*. Kirksville, MO: Sixteenth Century Journal, 1997.

Niesel, Wilhelm. "The Reformed View: the Church as the Mother of Believers and the Body of Christ." In *Reformed Symbolics: a Comparison of Catholicism, Orthodoxy, and Protestantism*, edited by Wilhelm Niesel, 247-56. Edinburgh: Oliver & Boyd, 1962.

———. *The Theology of John Calvin*. Translated by Harold Knight. Philadelphia: Westminster, 1956.

———. *Wesen und Gestalt der Kirche nach Calvin*. Münich: Evangelische Theologie, 1936.

Oberman, Heiko A. *The Dawn of the Reformation: Essays in Later Medieval and Early Reformation Thought*. Edinburgh: T. & T. Clark, 1992.

———. "*Europa afflicta*: The Reformation of the Refugees." *Archiv für Reformationsgeschichte* 83 (1992) 91-100.

———. "*Initia Calvini*: The Matrix of Calvin's Reformation." In *Calvinus Sacrae Scripturae Professor: Calvin as Confessor of Holy Scripture*, edited by Wilhelm H. Neuser, 113-54. Grand Rapids: Eerdmans, 1994.

Palmer, Thomas. "Kingdom and Church in Calvin: The Question of the Identification of Kingdom and Church in the Theology of John Calvin." PhD thesis, University of Aberdeen, 1991.

Parker, T. H. L. *Calvin's Doctrine of the Knowledge of God*. Grand Rapids: Eerdmans, 1959.

———. *Calvin's New Testament Commentaries*. Edinburgh: T. &. T. Clark, 1992.

———. *Calvin's Old Testament Commentaries*. Edinburgh: T. &. T. Clark, 1986.

———. *Calvin's Preaching*. Edinburgh: T. &. T. Clark, 1992.

———. *Commentaries on the Epistle to the Romans 1532-1542*. Edinburgh: T. & T. Clark, 1986.

———. *John Calvin: A Biography*. London: Dent, 1975.

Partee, Charles. *Calvin and Classical Philosophy*. Leiden: Brill, 1977.

———. "Calvin's Central Dogma Again." *Sixteenth Century Journal* 18, no. 2 (1987) 191-99.

Pattison, Bonnie L. *Poverty in the Theology of John Calvin*. Princeton Theological Mongraph 69. Eugene, OR: Pickwick, 2006.

Peter, Rodolphe, and Jean François Gilmont. *Bibliotheca Calviniana: les œuvres de Jean Calvin publiées au XVIe siècle*. 3 vols. Geneva: Droz, 1991-2005.

Phillips, Timothy R., and Dennis L. Okholm. "John Calvin: The Transformationist Church." In *A Family of Faith: An Introduction to Evangelical Christianity*, 209-21. Grand Rapids: Baker, 2001.

Pitkin, Barbara. "Nothing but Concupiscence: Calvin's Understanding of Sin and the *Via Augustini*." *Calvin Theological Journal* 34 (1999) 347-69.

———. *What Pure Eyes Could See: Calvin's Doctrine of Faith in Its Exegetical Context*. Oxford: Oxford University Press, 1999.

Prestwick, Menna. *International Calvinism 1541-1715*. Oxford: Clarendon, 1985.

Bibliography

Prins, R. "The Image of God in Adam and the Restoration of Man in Jesus Christ: A Study in Calvin." *Scottish Journal of Theology* 25 (1972) 32–44.
Puckett, David L. *John Calvin's Exegesis of the Old Testament*. Louisville: Westminster John Knox, 1995.
Quirinus, Breen. *John Calvin: A Study in French Humanism*. Hamden, CT: Archon, 1968.
Quistorp, Heinrich. *Calvin's Doctrine of the Last Things*. Translated by Harold Knight. London: Lutterworth, 1955.
Richard, Lucien Joseph. "John Calvin and the Role of the Church in the Spiritual Life." *Journal of Ecumenical Studies* 11 (1974) 477–500.
———. *The Spirituality of John Calvin*, Atlanta: John Knox, 1974.
Riggs, John W. *Baptism in the Reformed Tradition: An Historical and Practical Theology*. Louisville: Westminster John Knox, 2002.
Rupp, Gordon. *Patterns of Reformation*. London: Epworth, 1969.
Scholl, Hans. *Calvinus Catholicus: Die Katholische Calvinforschung im 20. Jahrhundert*. Freiburg: Herder, 1974.
———. "Karl Barth as Interpreter of Calvin's *Psychopannychia*." In *Calvinus Sincerioris Religionis Vindex: Calvin as the Protection of the Purer Religion*, edited by Wilhelm H. Neuser and Brian G. Armstrong, 291–307. Kirksville, MO: Sixteenth Century Journal, 1997.
Schreiner, Susan E. *The Theater of His Glory: Nature and the Natural Order in the Thought of John Calvin*. Grand Rapids: Baker, 1991.
Schümmer, Léopold. *L'ecclesiologie de Calvin a la lumiere de l'Eccleia Mater: Son approt aux rechereches ecclesiologiques tendant a exprimer l'unite en voie de manifestation*. Bern: Lang, 1981.
———. "L'homme, image de Dieu: Le corps, temple du Saint-Esprit dans la synthese biblique de Calvin. " *La Revue Réformée* 47 (1996) 63–82.
Schwendemann, Wilhelm. *Leib und Seele bei Calvin: Die erkenntnistheoretische und anthropologische Funktion des platonischen Leib-Seele-Dualismus in Calvins Theologie*. Stuttgart: Calwer, 1996.
Selderhuis, Herman J. *Calvin's Theology of Psalms*. Grand Rapids: Baker, 2007.
———. "Church on Stage: Calvin's Dynamic Ecclesiology." In *Calvin and the Church: Papers Presented at the 13th Colloquium of the Calvin Studies Society May 24–26, 2001*, edited by David Foxgrover, 46–64. Grand Rapids: CRC, 2002.
Selderhuis, Herman J., editor. *The Calvin Handbook*, Grand Rapids: Eerdmans, 2009.
———. *Calvinus Praeceptor Ecclesiae: Papers of the International Congress on Calvin Research, Princeton August 20–24, 2002*. Geneva: Droz, 2004.
Selinger, Suzanne. *Calvin against Himself*. Hamden, CT: Archon, 1984.
Shepherd, Victor. *The Nature and Function of Faith in the Theology of John Calvin*. Vancouver: Regent College Publishing, 1983.
Slater, Jonathan. "Salvation as Participation in the Humanity of the Mediator in Calvin's Institutes of the Christian Religion: a Reply to Carl Mosser." *Scottish Journal of Theology* 58 (2005) 39–58.
Spijker, Willem van't, editor. "Bucer's Influence on Calvin: church and community." In *Martin Bucer: Reforming Church and Society*, edited by David F. Wright, 17–31. Cambridge: Cambridge University Press, 1994.
———. *Calvin: Erbe und Auftrag: Festschrift für Wilhelm Heinrich Neuser zum 65. Geburtstag*. Kampen, Netherlands: Pharos, 1991.

———. *The Ecclesiastical Offices in the Thought of Martin Bucer.* Translated by John Vriend and Lyle D. Bierma. Leiden: Brill, 1996.

———. "The Kingdom of Christ according to Bucer and Calvin." In *Calvin and the State: Papers Presented at the Seventh and Eighth Colloquia on Calvin and Calvin Studies*, edited by Peter de Klerk, 114–25. Grand Rapids: Calvin Studies Society, 1993.

Sproul, R. C. "We Are Voluntary Slaves: John Calvin." In *Willing to Believe: The Controversy over Free Will*, 103–122, 209–10. Grand Rapids: Baker, 1997.

Stauffer, Richard. *Dieu, la création et la Providence dans la predication de Calvin.* Frankfurt: Lang, 1978.

———. *The Humaneness of John Calvin.* New York: Abingdon, 1964.

Steenkamp, Johan J. "A Review of the Concept of Progress in Calvin's Institutes." In *Calvin: Erbe und Auftrag: Festschrift für Wilhelm Heinrich Neuser zum 65. Geburtstag*, edited by Willem van't Spjiker, 69–76. Kampen, Netherlands: Pharos, 1991.

Steinmetz, David C. "Calvin as an Interpreter of Genesis." In *Calvinus Sincerioris Religionis Vindex: Calvin as the Protection of the Purer Religion*, edited by Wilhelm H. Neuser and Brian G. Armstrong, 53–65. Kirksville, MO: Sixteenth Century Journal, 1997.

———. *Calvin in Context.* Oxford: Oxford University Press, 1995.

Steinmetz, David C., editor. *The Bible in the Sixteenth Century.* Durham, NC: Duke University Press, 1990.

Stephens, Peter W. *The Holy Spirit in the Theology of Martin Bucer.* Cambridge: Cambridge University Press, 1970.

Stevenson, William R. *Sovereign Grace: The Place and Significance of Christian Freedom in John Calvin's Political Thought.* Oxford: Oxford University Press, 1999.

Tamburello, Dennis E. *Union with Christ: John Calvin and the Mysticism of St. Bernard.* Louisville: Westminster John Knox, 1994.

Tarvard, George H. *The Starting Point of Calvin's Theology.* Grand Rapids: Eerdmans, 2000.

Thompson, Mark D., editor. *Engaging with Calvin: Aspects of the Reformer's Legacy for Today.* Nottingham, UK: Apollos, 2009.

Thompson, John L. "*Creata ad Imaginem Dei, Licet secundo Gradu*: Woman as the Image of God According to John Calvin." *Harvard Theological Review* 81 (1988) 125–43.

Torrance, Thomas Forsyth. *Calvin's Doctrine of Man.* London: Lutterworth, 1949.

———. *Calvin's Doctrine of Man.* Grand Rapids: Eerdmans, 1957.

———. *The Hermeneutics of John Calvin.* Edinburgh: T. &. T. Clark, 1988.

———. *Kingdom and Church: A Study in the Theology of Reformation.* London: Oliver & Boyd, 1956.

———. *Trinitarian Perspectives: Toward Doctrinal Agreement.* Edinburgh: T. & T. Clark, 1994.

VanDrunen, David. "The Two Kingdoms: A Reassessment of the Transformationist Calvin." *Calvin Theological Journal* 40 (2005) 254–55.

Van Oort, Johannes. "John Calvin and the Church Fathers." In *The Reception of the Church Fathers in the West: From the Carolingians to the Maurists*, edited by Irena Backus, 661–700. Leiden: Brill, 1997.

Volf, Miroslav. *After Our Likeness: The Church as the Image of the Trinity.* Grand Rapids: Eerdmans, 1998.

Walker, Williston. *John Calvin, the Organizer of Reformed Protestantism.* 3rd ed. New York: Schocken, 1969.

Wallace, Ronald S. *Calvin, Geneva and Reformation: A Study of Calvin as Social Reformer, Churchman, Pastor and Theologian.* Grand Rapids: Baker, 1988.

Bibliography

———. *Calvin's Doctrine of Christian Life*. Grand Rapids: Eerdmans, 1952.
———. *Calvin's Doctrine of the Word and Sacrament*. London: Oliver & Boyd, 1953.
Wandel, Lee Palmer. *The Eucharist in the Reformation: Incarnation and Liturgy*. Cambridge: Cambridge University Press, 2006.
Wendel, François. *Calvin et l'humanisme*. Paris: Université de France, 1976.
———. *Calvin: The Origins and Development of his Religious Thought*. Translated by Philip Mairet. London: Collins, 1950.
Wengert, Timothy J. "The Biblical Commentaries of Philip Melanchthon." In *Philip Melanchthon and the Commentary*, edited by Timothy J. Wengert and M. Patrick Graham, 133-39. Sheffield: Sheffield Academic, 1997.
———. "Philip Melanchthon's 1522 Annotations on Romans and the Lutheran Origins of Rhetorical Criticism." In *Biblical Interpretation in the Era of the Reformation*, edited by Richard A. Muller and the John L. Thompson, 118-40. Grand Rapids: Eerdmans, 1996.
Westhead, Nigel. "Adoption in the Thought of John Calvin." *Scottish Bulletin of Evangelical Theology* 13 (1995) 102-15.
White, Robert. "Oil and Vinegar: Calvin on Church Discipline." *Scottish Journal of Theology* 38 (1985) 31-32.
Wilcox, Peter. "'The Progress of the Kingdom of Christ' in Calvin's Exposition of the Prophets." In *Calvinus Sincerioris Religionis Vindex: Calvin as the Protection of the Purer Religion*, edited by Wilhelm H. Neuser & Brian G. Armstrong, 315-22. Kirksville, MO: Sixteenth Century Journal, 1997.
———. "'The Restoration of the Church' in Calvin's 'Commentaries of Isaiah the Prophet.'" *Archiv für Reformationsgeschichte* 85 (1994) 68-95.
Wiley, David N. "The Church as the Elect." In *John Calvin and the Church: A Prism of Reform*, edited by Timothy George, 96-117. Louisville: Westminster John Knox, 1990.
Williams, George Huntston. *The Radical Reformation*. 3rd ed. Kirksville, MO: Sixteenth Century Journal, 2000.
Willis, E. David. "Rhetoric and Responsibility in Calvin's Theology." In *The Context of Contemporary Theology: Essays in Honor of Paul Lehmann*, edited by A. J. McKelway and E. David Willis, 43-63. Atlanta: John Knox, 1974.
Witte, John Jr. *Law and Protestantism: The Legal Teachings of the Lutheran Reformation*. Cambridge: Cambridge University Press, 2002.
Wright, David F. "Calvin's Accommodating God." In *Calvinus Sincerioris Religionis Vindex: Calvin as the Protection of the Purer Religion*, edited by Wilhelm H. Neuser & Brian G. Armstrong, 3-20. Kirksville, MO: Sixteenth Century Journal, 1997.
———. "Calvin's Pentateuchal Criticism: Equity, Hardness of Heart, and Divine Accommodation in the Mosaic Harmony Commentary." *Calvin Theological Journal* 21 (1986) 33-50.
———. *Martin Bucer: Reforming Church and Society*. Cambridge: Cambridge University Press, 1994.
———. "Sixteenth-Century Reformed Perspectives on the Minority Church." In *Calvin Studies VII: Papers Presented at the Seventh Colloquium on Calvin Studies, Davidson College, January 1994*, edited by John H. Leith, 19-29. Davidson, NC: Davidson College, 1994.
———. "Was John Calvin a 'Rhetorical Theologian'?" In *Calvin Studies IX: Papers Presented at the Ninth Colloquium on Calvin Studies, Davidson College, 1989*, edited

Bibliography

by John H. Leith and Robert A. Johnson, 46-69. Davidson, NC: Davidson College, 1989.

Wurth, G. Brillenburg. "Calvin and the Kingdom of God." In *John Calvin: Contemporary Prophet*, edited by Jacob T. Hoogstra, 113-26. Grand Rapids: Baker, 1959.

Zachman, Randall C. *The Assurance of Faith: Conscience in the Theology of Martin Luther and John Calvin*. Minneapolis: Fortress, 1993.

―――. *John Calvin as Teacher, Pastor and Theologian: The Shape of His Writings and Thought*. Grand Rapids: Baker, 2006."

―――. "What Kind of Book is Calvin's *Institutes*?" *CTJ* 35 (2000) 238-61.

Zillenbiller, Anetter. "Calvins Uminterpretation Cyprians bei der Beantwortung der Fragen: Auf wen ist die Kirche gegründet und Von wem wird der Bischof gewählt?" In *Calvinus Sincerioris Religionis Vindex: Calvin as the Protection of the Purer Religion*, edited by Wilhelm H. Neuser and Brian G. Armstrong, 323-33. Kirksville, MO: Sixteenth Century Journal, 1997.

Index

accommodation, 14, 101, 115
accommodation, grace of, 116–18
Acts, 1, 03, 114
adoption, 40, 55, 56, 69, 122, 134
adoption, grace of, 11, 131
affliction, Christian's, 73–74, 86, 91
affliction, Church's, 159, 164, 187, 189–90, 192–93
Amos, 170, 173
Anabaptists, 76, 79, 80, 161–62, 182
analogy, 156–57, 159–60
anathema, 187
ancient Church, 143–44, 154, 186
anthropology, 10–13, 16, 19–25, 30–31, 40–42, 43–44, 47, 51, 60, 67–68, 70, 76–78, 81, 87, 95, 127, 136, 155, 163, 190–91
anthropology, idea, 2, 5, 10–11, 14–15, 100–101, 117–18, 123–25
anthropology, theological, 10, 19–20, 23, 42, 60
anti-trinitarian opinions, 61
appendix, church discipline, 183
appendix, sacraments, 120, 183
Aquinas, Thomas, 24
Arianism, 61
Augustine of Hippo, 24, 32, 45, 101, 103
authenticity of the Church, 14, 105, 109
Avis, Paul D. L., 121, 183

Balke, Willem, 182
baptism, 2, 117, 121–24
bearing the cross, 90, 92
bishop, 106, 108, 149, 176

body as prison house, 49, 51, 72, 89
body, human, 1, 25, 26–29, 49–51, 58–59, 70, 76, 79–82, 84, 86–87, 89–90
Bouwsma, William J., 6–7, 22
Bucer, Martin, 46, 143, 181–82, 184
Bullinger, Heinrich, 47, 180

Cairns, David, 21–22, 34
candidates for the ministry, 142, 146, 151–52
Capito, Wolfgang, 77
Caroli, Pierre, 61
Caswell, R. N., 183
Catholic Church, 84, 130
central dogma, 191
charity, 95, 127, 141, 153
children of God, 4, 11–15, 43–44, 51–52, 55–57, 59, 62, 67–68, 69, 86, 90, 100–101, 105–05, 108–09, 111, 115, 117–25, 131, 134, 153–54, 158, 165, 172, 176, 189–90
Christ as the head, 15, 35, 53, 66, 88, 126, 128–31, 135, 137–39, 144–48, 163–64, 169, 174
Christ's Headship, 2, 5, 127, 137–38, 144–45, 148, 155
Christ's parable, 157, 158, 162
Christian identity, 1, 11, 14, 43–67, 100, 128–30, 132, 136, 150
Christian identity, assurance of, 55
Christian life, 1–2, 11–16, 39, 65, 69–96, 164, 169
Christian life, exile, 72, 191
Christian life, journey, 73, 89

209

Index

Christian life, race, 19, 55, 73, 85
Christian life, sojourn, 73, 74
Christian self, 11, 42, 46, 48, 51–52, 65
Christian self, divided, 14, 44, 48, 191
christological perspective, 3, 21, 60
Christology, 3, 60
Chrysostom, John, 24–25
Church as a school, 7, 120
Church as the body of Christ, 1–7, 14–16, 56, 102, 126–56, 159, 164, 177–79, 189–91
Church as the mother, 1–4, 6, 14–16, 99–125, 126
Church as the spouse of Christ, 102–4, 106–7, 109
church discipline, 2, 5–6, 8, 10, 14–15, 149, 157, 178–88, 190
church government, 2, 7–8, 10, 14–15, 126–27, 142–45, 148–50, 152–53, 155, 190
church ministry, 2, 5, 10, 100, 105–14, 116–20, 125, 135, 143, 145, 148, 150–52, 169, 171–72, 176–79, 181, 183–85, 190–91
Church, invisible, 6, 15, 107, 126, 131, 133–34, 136, 155, 156–57, 159,-169, 173, 175–77, 185–87, 189–91
Church, visible, 2, 15, 106–09, 117, 126, 130, 133, 137, 144, 155, 156–69, 171–73, 175–82, 184–85, 187–88, 189–90
clergy, 147, 150
comfort, 9, 92–93
common good of the Church, 139–40
communion of the Church, 161, 178, 182
communion with Christ, 9, 53, 57, 64
concupiscence, 33–34, 50
condemnation, 84, 187
consciousness, 45, 108, 124
Consistory of Geneva, 7, 181
consolation, 13–16, 70–71, 75, 77–78, 84, 87–89, 93, 95–96, 156–57, 163–64, 166, 192
consummation, 75, 78, 80, 83

Corpus Christi, 102, 127, 136–37, 139, 142, 149
corpus mixtum, 8–9, 187
creation, 5, 20, 23–24, 26, 28–32, 37–40, 42, 52, 135

Daniel, 159–60, 166
deacons, 142, 149–50, 152–53
death, Christ's, 58, 90
desolate situation of the Church, 191
dispersion of the Church, 108, 159, 164
doctors, 149
Dowey, Edward A., 114
Draft Ecclesiastical Ordinances (1541), 15, 127, 143, 146, 147, 149–55

ecclesia militans, 8–9
ecclesia ministrants, 8–9
ecclesiastical polity, 143
ecclesiology, 2–16, 44, 99–101, 103–4, 107, 109, 127, 131–32, 136, 142–43, 155, 156–57, 161, 164–66, 168, 172, 176, 178, 187, 189–92
ecclesiology, discussion, 67, 99–100, 103, 130, 132, 190–192
ecclesiology, ideas, 5, 128, 134, 176,
ecclesiology, Calvin's, 1–16, 44, 99, 103–4, 107, 109, 115–16, 127, 129, 131–32, 136, 142, 146, 155, 156–58, 161, 165–66, 172, 187, 189–92
elders, 145–47, 149–50, 152
election, God's, 4, 43, 103, 131–36
elements, earthly, 113, 116
elements, human, 183
encouragement, 92
Engel, Mary Porter, 22, 34, 60, 70
engrafting, 56–57, 90, 117, 122, 127–29, 132, 135–36, 186
episcopal Church, 107
Epistle to Colossians, 39, 52, 126, 137–38
Epistle to Galatians, 46, 94, 103, 128
Epistle to Philippians, 79
Epistle to Titus, 146

Index

Epistle to Ephesians, 2, 15, 39, 48, 52, 55, 119, 127, 128, 137, 138, 141, 144, 147, 170
Epistle to Hebrews, 58
Epistle to Romans, 41, 44–48, 50–52, 56, 83, 85, 128
eschatology, 75, 77, 83, 86–87
eschatology, idea, 2, 69, 70, 76, 89, 96, 157, 161, 167, 174, 181, 185, 188
eschatology, perspective, 6, 12–15, 72, 74, 95, 156–57, 165–66, 187, 190
eschatological progress, 69, 156, 161, 176, 177, 182
eternal life, 8, 62, 63, 119, 150, 163, 180
ethical, implication, 6, 21, 22
ethical, perspective, 6
ethical, responsibilities, 33, 37, 41
ethical, teaching, 96
excommunication, 178–80, 185, 187–88
external means of grace, 99, 121, 175–76, 179, 189

Faber, Jelle, 21–22, 31
fall, 5, 20, 30–38, 40–42, 49–50, 83, 138, 160
fall, Adam's, 36, 40
false Church, 105, 170, 181, 184, 189
Farel, Guillaume, 143
First Epistle to Corinthians, 78, 82, 83, 118, 138, 151, 175, 179, 184, 187, 188
First Epistle of John, 71
First Epistle to Timothy, 150, 179
fourfold office, 127, 143, 149, 152
Francis I, King of France, 77, 192
free will, 32

Genesis, 3–24, 27, 30–31, 33, 36–37, 39, 42
Geneva, 7–8, 10
Genevan Catechism (1542), 88, 119
Gentile, Valenti, 61
Gerrish, Brian A., 119

gifts, diverse, 15, 127, 137, 139, 140, 144, 149, 155
gifts, natural, 32, 33
gifts, supernatural, 32, 34
God's glory, 4, 9, 21, 26–30, 34–35, 38–39, 42, 64, 69, 79, 81, 85–86, 90–92, 113, 136, 163
godliness, 30, 77
Gospel of John, 29, 63, 65, 112–13, 135
Gospel of Luke, 168
Gospel of Matthew, 94, 157–58, 162–66, 168, 171–72, 177, 180, 183, 192
gospel, 1, 36, 45, 69, 104–06, 110, 118–19, 125, 135, 150, 171–72, 176–77
grace, justification, 69, 72
grace, God's adoptive, 56
grace, the triune God, 1, 11, 13–16, 43, 59, 63, 67–68, 87–88, 90, 134, 166, 190–91
grace, regeneration, 14, 38, 41, 42, 90, 104, 181, 186
Grenz, Stanley J., 20
Griffith, Howard, 56

harmony in the church, 140–42
harmony of Christian life, 40, 69, 90
harmony of the Trinity, 63
health of the Church, 137–40, 152
hierarchy, Roman Church, 145, 148
Higman, Francis M., 22
holiness, Church's, 158, 160–63, 181–82, 184–85, 190
holiness, Christian's, 39, 40, 64, 129
Holy Spirit, assistance of, 54
Holy Spirit, illumination of, 112, 114, 135
Holy Spirit, mortification of, 91–93
Holy Spirit, sanctification, 11, 71, 131, 135
Holy Spirit, teaching of, 43
Holy Spirit, the bond, 62–63, 66, 131–32
Holy Spirit, the power of, 66–67, 88, 111

Index

Holy Spirit, the work of, 5–6, 14, 66, 88–89, 101, 110, 112, 115, 166, 168, 174
hope, 13, 16, 56, 75, 77–78, 80–81, 85–87, 89, 91–95, 104, 129, 133, 163, 187–89, 192
Höpfl, Haro, 143, 150
humanity, division, 34, 44–46, 48–49
humility, 39, 40, 116, 145
hypocrite, 9, 107, 158–60, 163, 165–66, 189

identity of the Church, spiritual, 1–6, 14–16, 107, 126–34, 136, 144, 155, 156, 164, 187, 189–90
identity of the Church, mystical, 100, 102–04, 107, 120, 126
identity of the Church, functional, 1–7, 14, 99–100, 126, 156, 189–90
identity of the Church, twofold, 1–4, 9, 14–15, 156, 166, 189–90
image of God, *imago Dei*, 11–14, 19–35, 37–42, 49, 54, 55, 58, 69, 80, 191
image of God, partial survival of, 31–32, 37
image of God, restoration of, 13, 20–21, 38, 40, 42, 54, 65
image of God, total destruction of, 21, 31–32, 34, 37
image of God, two aspects of, 13, 20, 30, 38, 42
image of God, vestiges of, 35, 41
image, Christ's, 58
immortality of the soul, 13, 21–22, 25, 30, 32, 50, 65, 70, 75–79, 83, 88, 91
imperfection, human ministry, 14, 101,
imperfection, present life, 15, 40, 43, 45, 70, 71–73, 75, 89, 101
imperfection, the church, 157–58, 160, 161, 164, 189
incapacity of humanity, 37, 62, 63–65
infirmity, 72, 175
inner calling, 151
instruments, human or earthly, 14, 105, 109, 115, 191

integrity, 28–29, 39, 41, 113, 162
intermediate state, 78
Isaiah, 104, 165, 172

Joel, 104
judgment, God's, 186
jurisdiction, civil, 180
jurisdiction, ecclesiastical, 178, 180, 185
jurisdiction, spiritual, 180
justification, 46, 51, 53–57, 62–63, 66, 68
justification, doctrine of, 83

Kingdom of Christ, 5, 9, 12, 15, 146, 156–57, 166–80, 184–85, 187–88, 190
Kingdom of God, 50, 56, 82, 130, 137, 168, 171, 173, 177, 188
Kingdom of heaven, 171, 177–78
Kingdon, Robert M., 7, 142
knowledge of God, 19, 29, 30, 60, 78, 79, 82, 134
knowledge of man, 19, 20, 39, 40
Kroon, Marijn de, 3–5, 101, 142

laity, 150
last day, 75, 78–85, 156, 160, 165–66, 174, 176
law, 45, 47, 48, 100, 177, 186
law of sin, 51
law of the Lord, 187
law, natural, 23
Loeschen, John R., 3, 6, 61, 99, 142
Lord's prayer, 168
Lord's Supper, 112–13, 117, 121–24, 154, 179
love of neighbours, 14, 33, 70, 93–95
Luther, Martin, 6, 46, 55, 101, 175, 182–83

MacGregor, Geddes, 133, 146
mark, children of God, 111
mark, grace, 41
mark, kingdom of Christ, 172
mark, superiority of humankind, 23

Index

mark, true Church, 15, 109, 181–85, 188
McKee, Elsie Anne, 143
mediating role of Christ's humanity, 175
meditation on the future life, 90, 92–93, 96
Melanchthon, Philip, 47, 183
metaphors, 10, 12–14, 63, 65, 70, 72–74, 100–104, 120, 126–27, 137–38, 149, 157, 160,
Milner, B. C., 3, 5–6, 101–2, 142
ministerial care, 153
moderation of discipline, 15, 185, 188
moderation of pastors, 148
mortification of the flesh, 89–90, 92–93, 121
mutual communication, 140
mutual connection, 140–141
mutual love, 15, 127, 137, 140–42, 144, 153–55

nature, human, 30, 34, 37, 45, 48, 50, 52, 54, 63, 68, 93, 109, 115, 123, 161
Necessity of Reforming the Church (1543), 147
necessity of the Church, 101, 104–6
new man, inner man, 38–39, 48, 51–52, 67
Niesel, Wilhelm, 3, 5, 21, 60, 101, 106, 142, 183

obedience, 7, 29, 36, 40, 52, 69, 90, 103, 145, 168, 170, 171
Oberman, Heiko A., 192
Oecolampadius, Johannes, 47, 182
old man, outer man, 26, 41, 48, 50, 51, 58, 67, 90
omnipotence of God, 88
ontological change, 38, 65
order, church, 107
order, divine, 30
order, the Word, 5–6
original purpose, 25, 28, 32, 37–40, 42
Osiander, Andreas, 26–27, 66

Papists, 105, 109, 153
pastoral concern, 14–16, 188, 192–93
pastors, 1, 7, 127, 144–53, 176, 188
pastors, election of, 146–47
pastors, examination of, 127, 147
patriarchs of Israel, 171
Psalms, 8, 177
perfection, Christ's, 65
perfection, final, 70, 79–82, 156
perfection, future, 13–14, 15, 70, 75, 87–89, 92–93, 95, 163–65
perfection, the church, 106, 119, 160, 163, 175, 187–88, 190–11
perfection, the universe, 84–85
persecution of Christians, 92, 159, 160, 191
philosophers' view, 29, 70, 91, 113
philosophical speculation, 30, 42, 50, 145
piety, 19, 94, 124, 160, 174
pilgrimage, 12, 14, 70, 73–74, 86, 88, 157–58, 160, 165
Plato, 29, 49–50
Platonic dualism, 49
Platonic idea, 50, 72, 77–78
Platonic view, 51
Platonism, 70, 76
pope, primacy of, 144
pope, the kingdom of, 138
pope, the ministerial head, 138
power of the keys, 171, 179
preaching, 1, 14, 101, 105–7, 109–12, 114–21, 123, 125, 135, 151–52, 171–72, 176–77, 179, 181, 183, 190
preservation, 70, 139–40, 187
priest, selecting of, 147
primitive Church, 147, 152
Prins, R., 21
progress, church, 2, 156–57, 160–161, 174–77, 189
progress, christians, 9, 43, 44, 80, 141, 191, 165, 191
progress, eschatological, 69
promise of God, 3, 13–14, 16, 45, 60, 67–68, 70, 75, 77, 84, 86–96, 112, 114, 121, 134–35, 163–65

213

Index

protection, 9, 13, 16, 92–93, 165–66, 179, 192
Psychopannychia (1534), 75–78, 80

Quistorp, Heinrich, 70

reason, human, 20–22, 25, 27–29, 32, 35–36, 38–39, 41, 46, 85, 91
reconciliation, 54
reformation, God's work of, 38
reformation, human sin, 50
reformation, Church, 10, 147, 155
Reformed Church, 142, 159
regeneration, 1, 13–16, 20, 38–42, 43–59, 62–68, 69, 80, 86, 89–90, 101, 104–5, 109, 112, 121, 123–24, 160–62, 176–77, 181–82, 186, 190–91
Regnum Dei, 102
relationship, Christians and Christ 9, 15, 21, 43, 44, 54, 56, 59, 67, 128–30, 135, 136, 164, 190
relationship, church and state, 8
relationship, God and man, 4, 13, 19, 28, 36–38, 42, 53, 59, 78–79, 191
relationship, God and the Church, 102, 117, 124
relationship, the soul and the body, 29, 82
repentance, 39, 55, 57, 89
reprobate, 85, 113, 131, 133, 135–36, 166, 185–86
restoration, Christ's lordship, 83
restoration, Church, 2, 142, 147, 152, 179, 190
restoration, the image of God, 13, 20, 38, 40–42, 54–55, 65, 80
restoration, the universe, 83–85
resurrection, Christ, 87–88
resurrection, final, 14, 70, 75, 77–81, 84–85, 91, 160, 191
resurrection, flesh, 50, 70, 80
reward, 94–95
rhetoric, Calvin's, 22, 23, 47
rhetorical effect, 12
rhetorical style, 13

rhetorical usage, 13
Riggs, John W., 114
righteousness, 54, 59, 66, 67, 82, 87, 88, 119, 128, 150, 162, 178
righteousness, Christ's, 55, 57, 67
righteousness, essential , 66
righteousness, God's, 39, 40, 46, 52, 58, 69, 71, 90, 168
righteousness, kingdom of, 174
righteousness, law, 45
Roman Catholics, 46, 138, 144, 170
Roman Church, 105, 138, 142, 147, 148, 151, 153

sacraments, 10, 14, 101, 109, 112–17, 121, 123–24, 149, 154, 161, 183–85
sacraments, doctrine of, 8
sacraments, ministry of, 120, 179, 181, 183, 190
Sadolet, Jacob Cardinal, 108
salvation history, 42, 75, 95, 171, 177
sanctification , 4, 11, 54, 66, 71, 131, 136, 158, 183
Satan, 59, 158, 160, 164–66, 174, 179
sceptre, 169–70
Schreiner, Susan E., 20–22, 24
Schümmer, Léopold, 102, 104
Scripture, 10, 33, 40, 41, 51, 54, 58, 66, 70, 76, 84, 85, 88, 90, 112, 128–29, 137, 143, 144, 146, 148, 150, 152, 181
Second Epistle to Corinthians, 75, 110, 131
Second Epistle to Timothy, 86
Selderhuis, Herman J., 6, 8–9
self-denial, 90–92
Selinger, Suzanne, 70, 76
Sermons on Galatians, 105, 111
Servetus, Michael, 61
signs, earthly, 101, 112
signs, visible, 113, 115, 117
Simons, Menno, 6
sin, forgiveness of, 167, 171, 173, 189
sin, 2, 31–32, 37–39, 41, 45–46, 49–52, 67, 69, 71–72, 90, 103–4, 121, 132–33, 184

Index

sinews, 178
sinfulness, 22, 35, 38, 48, 50, 52, 59
sinner, 4, 38, 55, 57–59, 62, 72, 111, 123
social welfare, 155
soteriology, 44, 136, 155, 189
soteriology, idea, 12, 24, 61, 128, 134, 136
soul sleep, 76, 79, 80
soul, human, 13, 20–21, 25–30, 32–33, 36, 38–39, 41, 45, 48–51, 70, 72–82, 85, 108, 110, 114, 117, 169, 174, 176, 178, 180, 186, 193
Spijker, Willem van't, 143
spiritual exercises, 14, 70, 89–90, 92–93, 96
Steinmetz, David C., 46
Stephens, Peter, 46
Strasbourg, 77, 182
struggle, Christian's, 14, 44–46, 48, 54–55, 80, 92
struggle, church's, 134
superiority, humankind, 23–26
superiority, the soul, 28–29
symmetry, 139–41

Tamburello, Dennis E., 60, 64
teleological perspective, 11, 20, 28–31, 34, 37, 40, 42
Torrance, Thomas F., 21, 24, 175
trinitarian perspective, 44, 59–61, 63, 67, 87, 127, 130–32, 134, 136, 155, 165
Trinity, doctrine of, 61

true Church, 15, 100, 105, 109, 176, 181–86, 188–89

union with Christ, 14–15, 44, 52–54, 57, 59–60, 64–68, 117, 122–23, 127–30, 155, 176
unity of the Church, 5–6, 9, 14, 79, 100–101, 104, 106–9, 127, 129, 132, 134, 137–40, 152, 154, 161, 164
universal Church, 99, 106, 130

victory, 86–87, 89, 163–64, 166
vivification of the spirit, 89

Wallace, Ronald S., 123
warfare, 12, 14, 70–72, 79, 85–86, 157, 160
warfare, spiritual, 2, 71–72, 75, 174
weakness, Christians, 115, 121, 123
weakness, faith, 124
weakness, human, 5, 11, 55, 71, 89, 116, 124
Wendel, François, 3–5, 11, 59–60, 101, 142, 182
White, John Jr., 182, 187
Wiley, David N., 99
Word of God, 5–6, 9, 15, 39, 66, 104–6, 108–9, 111–12, 116, 118, 120–21, 135, 139, 144–46, 148–50, 156–57, 161, 167, 169–72, 176, 179–81, 183–84
Wurth, G. Billenburg, 169

Zwingli, Ulrich, 180

www.ingramcontent.com/pod-product-compliance
Lightning Source LLC
Chambersburg PA
CBHW062025220426
43662CB00010B/1483